PALGRAVE *Studies in Oral History*

Series Editors: Linda Shopes and Bruce M. Stave

Editorial Board

The Order Has Been Carried Out: History, Memory, and Meaning of a Nazi Massacre in Rome, by Alessandro Portelli (2003)

Sticking to the Union: An Oral History of the Life and Times of Julia Ruuttila, by Sandy Polishuk (2003)

To Wear the Dust of War: From Bialystok to Shanghai to the Promised Land, an Oral History, by Samuel Iwry, edited by L. J. H. Kelley (2004)

Education as My Agenda: Gertrude Williams, Race, and the Baltimore Public Schools, by Jo Ann Robinson (2005)

Remembering: Oral History Performance, edited by Della Pollock (2005)

Postmemories of Terror: A New Generation Copes with the Legacy of the "Dirty War," by Susana Kaiser (2005)

Growing Up in The People's Republic: Conversations between Two Daughters of China's Revolution, by Ye Weili and Ma Xiaodong (2005)

Life and Death in the Delta: African American Narratives of Violence, Resilience, and Social Change, by Kim Lacy Rogers (2006)

Creating Choice: A Community Responds to th̶ ̶ ̶ ̶ ̶ ̶ ̶ ̶ ̶rol, 1961–1973, by David P. Cline (2006)

D1572035

Voices from This Long Brown Land: Oral Recollections of Owens Valley Lives and Manzanar Pasts, by Jane Wehrey (2006)

Radicals, Rhetoric, and the War: The University of Nevada in the Wake of Kent State, by Brad E. Lucas (2006)

The Unquiet Nisei: An Oral History of the Life of Sue Kunitomi Embrey, by Diana Meyers Bahr (2007)

Sisters in the Brotherhoods: Working Women Organizing for Equality in New York City, by Jane LaTour (2008)

Iraq's Last Jews: Stories of Daily Life, Upheaval, and Escape from Modern Babylon, edited by Tamar Morad, Dennis Shasha, and Robert Shasha (2008)

Soldiers and Citizens: An Oral History of Operation Iraqi Freedom from the Battlefield to the Pentagon, by Carl Mirra (2008)

Overcoming Katrina: African American Voices from the Crescent City and Beyond, by D'Ann R. Penner and Keith C. Ferdinand (2009)

Bringing Desegregation Home: Memories of the Struggle toward School Integration in Rural North Carolina, by Kate Willink (2009)

I Saw It Coming: Worker Narratives of Plant Closings and Job Loss, by Tracy E. K'Meyer and Joy L. Hart (2010)

Speaking History: Oral Histories of the American Past, 1865-Present, by Sue Armitage and Laurie Mercier (2010)

Surviving Bhopal: Dancing Bodies, Written Texts, and Oral Testimonials of Women in the Wake of an Industrial Disaster, by Suroopa Mukherjee (2010)

Living with Jim Crow: African American Women and Memories of the Segregated South, by Anne Valk and Leslie Brown (2010)

Gulag Voices: Oral Histories of Soviet Incarceration and Exile, by Jehanne M. Gheith and Katherine R. Jolluck (2011)

Detained without Cause: Muslims' Stories of Detention and Deportation in America after 9/11, by Irum Shiekh (2011)

Soviet Communal Living: An Oral History of the Kommunalka, by Paola Messana (2011)

No Room of Her Own: Women's Stories of Homelessness, Life, Death, and Resistance, by Desiree Hellegers (2011)

Oral History and Photography, edited by Alexander Freund and Alistair Thomson (2011)

Place, Writing, and Voice in Oral History, edited by Shelley Trower (2011)

Oral History, Community, and Displacement: Imagining Memories in Post-Apartheid South Africa, by Sean Field (2012)

Second Wind: Oral Histories of Lung Transplant Survivors, by Mary Jo Festle (2012)

Displaced: The Human Cost of Development and Resettlement, by Olivia Bennett and Christopher McDowell (2012)

Exodus to Shanghai: Stories of Escape from the Third Reich, by Steve Hochstadt (2012)

Oral History in Southeast Asia: Memories and Fragments, edited by Kah Seng Loh, Stephen Dobbs, and Ernest Koh (2013)

Oral History Off the Record: Toward an Ethnography of Practice, edited by Anna Sheftel and Stacey Zembrzycki (2013)

Sharecropper's Troubadour: John L. Handcox, the Southern Tenant Farmers' Union, and the African American Song Tradition, by Michael K. Honey (2013)

Previous publications of Michael K. Honey

All Labor Has Dignity, by Dr. Martin Luther King, Jr., edited by Michael K. Honey (2011)

Going Down Jericho Road: The Memphis Strike, Martin Luther King's Last Campaign (2007)

Black Workers Remember: An Oral History of Segregation, Unionism, and the Freedom Struggle (1999)

Southern Labor and Black Civil Rights: Organizing Memphis Workers (1993)

Sharecropper's Troubadour

John L. Handcox, the Southern Tenant Farmers' Union, and the African American Song Tradition

Michael K. Honey

First published in 2013 by
PALGRAVE MACMILLAN®
in the United States—a division of St. Martin's Press LLC,
175 Fifth Avenue, New York, NY 10010.

Where this book is distributed in the UK, Europe and the rest of the world,
this is by Palgrave Macmillan, a division of Macmillan Publishers Limited,
registered in England, company number 785998, of Houndmills,
Basingstoke, Hampshire RG21 6XS.

Palgrave Macmillan is the global academic imprint of the above companies
and has companies and representatives throughout the world.

Palgrave® and Macmillan® are registered trademarks in the United States,
the United Kingdom, Europe and other countries.

ISBN: 978–0–230–11127–1 (hc)
ISBN: 978–0–230–11128–8 (pbk)

Library of Congress Cataloging-in-Publication Data is available from the
Library of Congress

A catalogue record of the book is available from the British Library.

Design by Newgen Knowledge Works (P) Ltd., Chennai, India.

First edition: November 2013

10 9 8 7 6 5 4 3 2 1

Be Consolated

Have you ever woke up in the morning
And your day of toil started wrong?
Nothing in this world would console you
But to start singing the good old union song.

Sometimes you go to the door or window and begin
Wondering and looking across the field,
Thinking of what wealth the farmer has added
While he has to live on such a scanty yield.

Often you go to the shelf and get your Bible,
And sit down and begin to read;
And you find therein where God will punish
The rich man for every unjust deed.

Be of good cheer; be patient; be faithful,
And help the union to grow strong.
And if at any time you become the least discouraged,
Revive yourself by singing the good old union song.

When thinking of how horrid the past has been,
And know the labor road hasn't been smooth.
Deep down in your heart you keep singing:
"We shall not, we shall not be moved!"

> John Handcox, Union Poet and Singer
> In *The Disinherited Speak, Letters from Sharecroppers*
> (New York: Workers Defense League, ca. 1937)

Contents

List of Illustrations   xi

Acknowledgments   xiii

"He Was an Inspiration to us All"   xvii
Foreword by Pete Seeger

Introduction: Music, Memory, and History   1

CHAPTER 1
"Freedom After 'While' ": Life and Labor in the Jim Crow South   11

CHAPTER 2
Raggedy, Raggedy Are We: Sharecropping and Survival   31

CHAPTER 3
The Planter and the Sharecropper: The Southern Tenant
Farmers' Union   47

CHAPTER 4
There Is Mean Things Happening in This Land: Terror in Arkansas   71

CHAPTER 5
Roll the Union On: Interracial Organizing in Missouri   95

CHAPTER 6
Getting Gone to the Promised Land: California   119

CHAPTER 7
"I'm So Glad to Be Here Again": The Return of John Handcox   141

Notes   157

Bibliography   193

Index   203

Illustrations

1 A sharecropper's dwelling in Marked Tree, Arkansas, 1935

2 Sam Nichols, a tenant farmer in the upcountry of Boone County, Arkansas

3 The predominantly white 18 founding delegates

4 Working in the cotton fields

5 Sharecroppers evicted from their homes by the owner

6 Some of the sharecroppers evicted in a cooperative farm near Hill House

7 Women played a powerful role in the STFU at the local level

8 Workers listening to speakers at an outdoor STFU meeting

9 Refugees in Charleston, Missouri who fled a massive flood in January of 1937

10 A line of tents at a food refugee camp in Forrest City

11 Thousands of laborers went across the bridge from Memphis to Arkansas

12 Pete Seeger introduces a panel of labor and civil rights singers

13 John with fellow folk musician Joe Glazer

14 John at the 1986 Great Labor Arts Exchange

15 John singing with unidentified guitarist

16 John at Evelyn Smith Munro's house in Laguna Beach

17 John with participants in a labor-themed Augusta Heritage folk festival

18 John with the author Michael Honey and Pat Krueger

19 John Handcox and the author in 1986

Acknowledgments

John Handcox's oral history, songs, and poems touch upon many facets of the African American experience and on music and social movement history. I owe a debt of gratitude to historians and song researchers who helped me to put John's story in historical context. I list major sources for this book in the bibliography. I can't give enough thanks to the scholars and friends who read parts or all of this manuscript. Here I wish to acknowledge their help without implicating them in any of the book's defects. Erik Gellman and Elizabeth Stevens offered line-by-line edits of the last version of the text, and Jeannie Whayne provided expert guidance on Arkansas history. Other readers who gave invaluable suggestions included Jessica Auer, Millie Beik, William Beik, David Black, Ron Cohen, Robert Hunt Ferguson, Mark Alan Jackson, Jason Manthorne, David Roediger, Jarod Roll, Henry Rosemont, Jr., David Smith, and Palgrave Macmillan Oral History series editors Linda Shopes and Bruce Stave. I especially thank Linda for helping me to get John's oral history narrative into chronological order. The late Susan Hollister provided great research assistance into the microfilm files of the Southern Tenant Farmers Union. Jessica Auer at the University of North Carolina-Chapel Hill did prodigious genealogical and archival research and helped me to correct and format the endnotes and bibliography. Robert Hunt Ferguson, Rebecca Schroeder, the late Donald Lance, and Joe Riggs, all provided me with transcripts and tapes of interviews, and Mark Alan Jackson has long been a great help in locating material and people for this project. Ron Cohen provided unstinting, invaluable help in locating music sources. Blues and folklore scholar William Ferris joined me in doing one last interview with John Handcox and taking marvelous photographs in 1990. Joyfully, Pete Seeger, Joe Glazer and Ralph Rinzler helped to launch this project in 1985. Jim Gregory, Joe Trotter, Jeannie Whayne, Nancy Bristow, and Cynthia Bogle all helped me to get grant support. Music professor and ethnographer Pat Krueger expertly created the transcript of my interviews with John that are the basis for this book and she has made many strategic suggestions at crucial points. Senior Editor Chris Chappell at Palgrave Macmillan offered patience and help in getting this to final production.

John Handcox himself encouraged this project, sending me hand written and typescript songs, poems, and letters and urging their publication. I owe special thanks to John's grand daughters Camelia Cook and Darlene Kasmer, who graciously gave permission for me to include John's writings and songs in this volume. Camelia has given unstinting support and offered helpful insights into family history. Saul Schniderman, long-time labor folklorist and Labor Heritage Foundation supporter, searched long and hard through the library files of the US Copyright Office to locate any copyrights on John Handcox's songs. Saul and labor heritage activist David Winters sent me clippings and photos and other important materials on John's return to the labor music circuit in the 1980s. Some of the proceeds from this book will go to the John Handcox Fund at the Labor Heritage Foundation to promote the next generation of labor singers. Special thanks to those who offered wonderful photographs for this book, without fees. These include Abigail C. Munro, Hannah M. Flom, and Rebecca Munro, daughters of Evelyn Smith Munro, the office secretary of the STFU, who turned out to be a fine photographer as well as organizer; Larry Rubin, who provided huge help in documenting John's return to the music scene late in his life; David Winters; Jimmy Kelley; and thanks to Elizabeth Payne for highlighting the beautiful images from the estate of Louise Boyle and to Ms. Boyle's nephew James Rogers for his support. Thanks also to William Ferris for access to his photos, and to Jeannie Whayne who helped me to discover public archive photos. The Library of Congress provides to the public the most accessible collection of some of the most famous pictures in American history. Other institutions that house archival collections and their archivists and librarians made primary research possible. Thanks to the Wilson Library Manuscript Collection at the University of North Carolina-Chapel Hill; to Melissa Holland and Patrizia Sione at the Kheel Center for Labor-Management Documentation and Archive in the Catherwood Library at Cornell University; and the Western Historical Manuscript Collection at the University of Missouri-Columbia. Suzanne Klinger, Theresa Mudrock, Glenda Perason, Judy Tsou, and other librarians at the University of Washington proved immensely helpful.

Other institutions and people helped to make it possible for me to write this book. The project began in 1996 at the National Humanities Center with a fellowship from the National Endowment for the Humanities, where the Center's Karen Carroll transcribed John's poems and songs. The Guggenheim Foundation in New York provided a fellowship for this work, which I combined with a fellowship at the Simpson Humanities Center at the University of Washington. The UW's Helen Riaboff Whiteley Center and its staff provided fabulous support for my periodic writing retreats. The Simpson Center's fellows and its Director Kathleen Woodward helped me to persevere when, in the midst of writing this manuscript, both of my parents passed away. I especially thank my sister Maureen Honey and my brother Charles Honey and my partner Pat Krueger, as well as Nancy Bristow, Gordon Jackson, John

Lear and Marisela-Fleites-Lear, Lyle and Bobby Mercer, John Hanson, David Smith, Mike McNeilly, Earl Wolfe, Martha Allen and Jonathan Zeitlin, Henry and JoAnn Rosemont, David Black, the Krueger family, Otto and Corrine Olsen, and other close friends and relatives who did much to lift my morale. I continue to thank my parents Betty and Keith Honey, whose humane and generous impulses and love made it possible for me to choose a path to human rights through the humanities. Special thanks to the Interdisciplinary Arts and Sciences program and the Fred and Dorothy Haley Professorship at the University of Washington Tacoma (and the Haley family), whose support enabled me to both teach and write history. Keith Ward and Paul Lovelady of our UWT staff have been stalwart supporters in all my research. All of these people and institutions helped to make it possible to know the stories of John Handcox and others like him who loved and fought before.

Tacoma, Washington

"He Was an Inspiration to us All"

Foreword by Pete Seeger

I was a teenager in college around 1937, when my father Charles Seeger wrote me about John Handcox. A delegation of white and black southern tenant farmers had come to Washington to petition Congress to get them some help in their struggle for justice. My father, a musicologist working as a minor bureaucrat down there in those New Deal days, heard them singing, and immediately asked the lead singer, a man named John Handcox, to come with him to the Library of Congress, where the Archives of Folk Song had some of the early recording equipment available at that time. Scratchy aluminum disks, turning at 78 RPM.[1]

On my next vacation home I heard those disks. "There's Mean Things Happening In This Land," "Raggedy, Raggedy Are We," "Roll the Union On," and a famous old spiritual with some new words:

> *Ohhhh, Freedom!*
> *Ohhhh, Freedom!*
> *Oh, Freedom over me!*
> *And before I'd be a slave, I'd be buried in my grave*
> *Take my place with those who loved and fought before.*

Some of the songs were poems, raps of a sort:

> *The planter lives by the sweat of the sharecropper's brow.*
> *Just how the sharecropper lives the planter cares not how.*

I was bowled over by the songs and poems, and started immediately memorizing some of them and repeating them for friends. The Southern Tenant Farmers

Union eventually got broken up, not only by the powers that be, but by factional disputes between Socialists and Communists within the union.

Three years later, I met Woody Guthrie when he hitchhiked to New York from Los Angeles. (It was February, 1940; he wrote the words *"As I was walking that ribbon of highway"* while standing there in the cold wind with his thumb stuck out and the cars whipping past him, zoom, zoom, zoom). Energetic young Alan Lomax, then in charge of the Archives of Folk Song, suggested that Woody and I work together to make a songbook out of a pile of disks and paper he handed us. We worked on it in the spring of 1940, and we put a few of John Handcox's songs in it. I tried to locate John, mailed letters to Arkansas and Oklahoma, got no answer. The book, *Hard Hitting Songs for Hard-Hit People* finally got published in 1967, but again we had no luck locating John. He'd gone to San Diego during World War II, and he stayed there.[2]

Around '72, H. L. Mitchell, who had been head of the Southern Tenant Farmers' Union, wrote his autobiography. In San Diego many years later, a friend of John's said to him one day, "John, didn't you once write a song called 'Mean Things Happening in This Land'"?

"Sure did," said John.

"Well, I seen a book in a bookstore window with that title, written by a man H. L. Mitchell."

"Mitch! Didn't know he was still alive."

They got in touch and met at a reunion of old timers from the STFU held in Memphis in 1982. Joe Glazer, who for a long lifetime had been labor's troubador, was present and few years later I found out about it from him. I got John's address and phone number at last. John was now about 80 years old.

"Why, yes, I'd be glad to come east if you just send me a plane ticket." With the help of Ralph Rinzler at the Smithsonian Institution we rustled up the money, and John appeared at the next Labor Heritage gathering in Washington, D. C., in June, 1985.

He was tall and slim and straight, walked with a light step, dark blue eyes, a shock of white hair, and a fringe of white beard. He had a subtle sense of humor. I once introduced him to another person, saying that John had been living in San Diego on his Social Security. John taps me on the shoulder, says with a smile, "Just say 'existing' on Social Security."

In the last ten years of his life, John went to dozens of gatherings east and west, singing his songs, making up new ones. He was an inspiration to us all.

How lucky some of us are who knew him. Now, this wonderful book helps us get to know him better. His story will not be forgotten, now that Michael Honey has got it down on paper. As long as human beings like to sing in the English language, I believe his songs will live on. In that sense, John will never die.

It's people like John Handcox who will save this human race from the fix we've been put in by foolish and shortsighted men.

Here's to you, John Handcox, people's poet, people's songwriter. Children not yet born will carry on your work.

Pete Seeger

Beacon, New York

Introduction: Music, Memory, and History

I was out in the river draggin' for mussels. I had nets in the river . . . My mother and wife come down to the river, and she called me so distressed. (Wails in imitation.) "Heyyyyy John!" I didn't know it was her voice, and the way she called it what I thought she said something happened to my kids. On that water, you know, that sound, it can travel. As fast as I could row the boat to where she was, I rushed on down, back down to where they was. And my mother says, "John you gotta get 'way from here, if you can! . . . John, get away from here! A white fella was saying they had the rope and the limb, all they was waitin' on is you. You get away from here!"

I had a rifle, and I said "I'm going to get upside of this hill, and one who sticks his head over that transom, I'm going to put something on his mind!" Mama said, "No, John! Don't do that! If you shoot and kill or injure one of 'em, they'll kill us all." And she was just right. There wouldn't have been no Handcox's left . . . Yeah, because I was organizing the union, they said if they could stop that John Handcox, they thought they could stop the union. Yeah, that was they purpose of wanting to get me.

I left that evening, I didn't waste no time.

—John Handcox

In the spring of 1936, John Handcox could have easily become another black man lynched in the Mississippi River Delta region of eastern Arkansas. Instead, he fled to Memphis and went on to do more organizing for the Southern Tenant Farmers Union (STFU). Sometimes publishing under the pen name of John Henry, the mythical steel-driving man portrayed in one of America's best-known "folk" ballads, he wrote a score of powerful songs and poems on the union's behalf. In the spring of 1937, John sang his songs and recited his poetry for Charles Seeger and Sydney Robertson at the Library of Congress. It is largely due to these recordings, and Pete Seeger's discovery of them, that we even know that John existed. In 1940, Pete, Woody Guthrie, and Alan Lomax gathered some of John's work into an indispensable book of depression-era songs. The manuscript got lost for nearly 30 years, but finally appeared in print in 1967 as *Hard-Hitting Songs for Hard-Hit People*. John, presumed dead, missed the "folk music" boom of that era, but nearly 50 years after the Library of Congress recordings, almost like the proverbial John Henry, he reappeared, as Pete tells us in his preface. This book is one of the results.[1]

I first encountered John's work in 1970, during my time as a civil rights and civil liberties organizer for the Southern Conference Educational Fund (SCEF). At a concert held in Louisville, KY, I heard singer Barbara Dane belt out Sarah Ogan Gunning's song, "I Hate the Capitalist System." Afterwards, she sold me a copy of *Hard-Hitting Songs*, which fired my interest in southern labor history and opened a new world of music to me. The book includes "roots" music by southern coal miners, steel and iron ore workers, textile and tobacco workers, sharecroppers, farm tenants, and laborers. Blues men Huddie Ledbetter, Big Bill Broonzy, Sonny Boy Williamson, and others sang about what it meant to be busted, disgusted, broke, and blue. Florence Reece, of a Kentucky mining family, wrote "Which Side Are you on?" on the back of a calendar after gun thugs ransacked her house looking to kill her unionist husband. Southern working people in the 1930s had little voice in government or the mass media, but this book proves that they did have a voice to sing with and they made themselves heard.[2]

Some of these hard-hit singers were labor radicals, others just mad as hell. John fell into both categories and his writings provide some of the book's greatest lyrics, evocatively describing harsh depression-era conditions and asking people, who caused your problems and how can you solve them? John created his own genre: the freedom music of the cotton fields. At the Library of Congress, he sang "Freedom After 'While," with no hint of the resignation whites thought they heard in such traditional black spirituals. He drew on a motif of "roll on" used in numerous religious songs to create a powerful vehicle for group singing, "Roll the Union On." Like the STFU favorite, "We Shall Not Be Moved," it invites rhythm, hand clapping, marching, and mass congregational singing to make a statement of solidarity. He used the Christian spiritual, "In My Heart," to venerate union leaders and Socialists rather than Jesus. "Join the Union Tonight" celebrated union organizing as a joyful act. "Mean Things Happening in This Land" incorporated haunting blues sounds of the Mississippi Delta and disaster songs of southern black street singers to tell the story of a strike. "The Man Frank Weems" profiled a union martyr's sacrifice, while "Raggedy, Raggedy Are We" employed an old religious tune to depict how racial plantation capitalism impoverished southern agricultural workers.

John's songs fit into a larger tradition of social movement music, designed to build solidarity and group action through mass singing.[3] But they also go much beyond that to represent traditions of spoken and sung "oral poetry" practiced by Africans, Europeans, and Native Americans.[4] His music and poetry most clearly represent black traditions, presented in his own distinctive way. His compositions fit into a variety of forms, mixing church and secular, political and folk, formal twentieth-century poetry, and old spirituals. John's movement music is his own form of singing poetry. And one might call his spoken poetry, laced with irony, humor, and thoughts of solidarity, "hard-hitting poems for hard-hit people." In plain language he wrote harsh descriptions of the hard times that he and his people experienced and bluntly attacked and exposed the actions of the planter class. "The Planter and the Sharecropper," "King Cotton," "Landlord What in Heaven is the Matter With You?" and "Strike in Arkansas" drew on rhythms he learned as a child from the poems of Paul Laurence Dunbar. He did not write in the black "dialect" that made Dunbar the most famous black poet of his day, but in the "new Negro" mode of militant self-assertion. Much as rap artists did in later years, John weaponized the spoken word. In secret moonlit meetings and in the sanctuary of black churches, he drew word pictures that described terrible things happening to people and his rhyming cadences moved audiences to take action:

> *The planter lives by the sweat of the sharecropper's brow*
> *Just how the sharecropper lives the planter cares not how.*

Paraphrasing Pete Seeger's comments about Woody Guthrie, many people can write something complicated but it takes a genius to write something simple that communicates profound truths to masses of people. Whether protesting repression against workers in the 1930s, or, in later years, protesting union-busting assaults in the 1980s, or reflecting on his own tribulations of love, illness, and getting old, John's writings remained beautifully direct. John's oral history, poetry and songs, are interesting in their own right. But when framed by historical research, they also help to document and explain an era otherwise lost. John's music and poetry fell within African-American traditions, but at the same time inspired both whites and blacks to build a movement together, one strong enough to challenge their shared poverty and powerlessness.

Freedom music is too often slighted from the canon of African American music, while labor protest songs have been nearly excised from popular culture.[5] This book helps to restore the freedom music of the cotton fields and a type of oral expression largely lost to our literature. It also offers the first full account of John's life and struggles as a tenant farmer and union organizer, and presents his songs and poems as a documentary and oral history of the sharecropper movement from a black perspective. Hopefully, *Sharecroppers' Troubadour* will help us to understand the sharecropper's revolt of the 1930s in a personal and emotive way.

Music and Memory

Songs and poetry gave John Handcox a way of seeing, explaining, and remembering his world. In telling a story, he would frequently break into song or recite a poem to convey an event, an idea or a feeling, as his way of documenting the past. Like other organizers of labor and freedom movements—from Joe Hill of the IWW to the Freedom Singers of the Student Non-violent Coordinating Committee—John believed that people needed songs to change the world. "I found that singing was more inspirational than talking," he said. Back in the days of sharecropping, "A lot of them, they didn't know anything about the union. But in church, they usually open the church service with singing to get the people all inspired . . . so I found that through life it was the best policy to try to get the attention of the people." He felt that music and poetry helped him to say things in a more moving way than the normal written or spoken word allowed.

Pete Seeger has described John as one of the twentieth century's most important folk musicians, a true original, who drew on and replenished black freedom movement and folk traditions. Long before John, generations of African-Americans had produced marching songs, meeting songs, songs of repentance, songs of group and personal liberation, songs of love and solidarity, songs pointing out evil, songs of labor, and songs of faith and spiritual quest. The black song tradition provided an almost inexhaustible storehouse of tunes and lyrics to fight against impossible odds to achieve something glorious and new, yet preordained and righteous. Slaves, historian Lawrence Levine observed, had "frequent recourse to their music, and they used it in almost every conceivable setting for almost every possible purpose."[6] Black song, passed down from one generation to the next, provided a rhythmic form or oral history and memory that John imbibed from an early age. He learned "shape note" sheet music (with musical notation in four to seven shapes, used for sacred singing in semi-literate communities) from his Methodist mother and congregational (all together) singing in his father's Baptist church. Often a singer called out a verse with everyone responding, and such call and response, observed Levine, "placed the individual in continual dialogue with his community." Black songs often intrigued whites and even during slavery times could sweep them up into the spirit of a camp meeting, providing tunes, thoughts, emotional structure, and a sense of hope. Shared by people harmonizing their voices and clapping their hands together in a mass meeting, such songs could promote a movement culture of loyalty to others in a common cause. Bridging the racial and class walls that divided people is exactly the function that John's music and poems would have in the STFU.[7]

*   *   *

John Handcox descended from black slaves, Native Americans, and white slave owners. Born on February 5, 1904, near the tiny town of Brinkley, Arkansas, he died at age 88 in San Diego, CA on September 18, 1992. This book begins with John's story of growing up and trying to make a living in the rural, Jim

Crow (segregated) South. John's family moved from slavery to freedom and back to servitude, in one of the hardest places and at one of the hardest times to be black in America. Despite poverty, illiteracy, disfranchisement, segregation, and white racial violence, John's family combined small land holdings with renting and sharecropping and wage labor to become self-sufficient farmers. But white supremacy and the "poverty crop" of cotton dragged them into a downward cycle in the 1920s. A family tragedy, the Mississippi River floods in 1927 and 1928, a massive drought, and the man-made disaster called the Great Depression followed. John's oral history explains how the "freedom now" promised by emancipation during the Civil War became a more dimly hoped-for, long-term project: "Freedom After 'While."

The middle part of this book, bolstered by a good deal of historical research, recounts John's experiences during the Great Depression of the 1930s, when he and other desperately poor people living in the heart of Ku Klux Klan country organized white and black tenants and day laborers into the STFU. Led by Socialists and preachers, this unique organization—part labor and part freedom movement, part publicity agent, and part civil liberties champion—defied age-old racial divisions. Following a successful cotton picker's strike in 1935, some 30,000–40,000 people belonged to the union, more than half of them African Americans. John became a volunteer union organizer, but during a failed cotton chopper's strike in the spring of 1936, vigilante threats forced him to flee to Arkansas. "I was doing pretty well," John remembered, "until a friend of mine was up at the store and said some men had a rope and the limb and all they needed was me!"

John ended up in exile in Memphis, where he wrote some of his best songs and poems, publishing them in the union newspaper. He moved on to become the union's organizer in Missouri. He also became a singing and reciting ambassador for the sharecroppers' movement in New York, Chicago, and Detroit, and at STFU conventions, earning the title of "sharecropper's poet laureate" and "sharecropper's troubadour." However, vigilante terrorism backed by the iron fist of the law devastated the STFU, which also fractured internally. The union lasted as an effective organization only for about five years, but it proved that black and white workers could organize together even in Ku Klux Klan country, and it left the hope that another generation would go much further to overcome Jim Crow. The last part of the book tells how John Handcox went to Oklahoma and then joined the great war-time migration out of the South, landing in sunny San Diego, CA, in 1942.

After contributing some of the most powerful labor protest songs and poems of his generation, John seemingly disappeared for the next forty-some years, only to re-emerge in the 1980s near the end of his life to reinvigorate African American and labor song traditions.

The Power of Remembering

Several first-hand accounts of the STFU and its era exist, most notably by white union activists H. L. Mitchell and Howard Kester. Historians, their works listed in the bibliography, also provide a substantial body of work on the union and on events in Arkansas and Mississippi delta. But a detailed and first-hand account of the STFU by an African American, until now, has been missing. The stunning oral history of Ned Cobb, *All God's Dangers*, provides a parallel story of a black rural worker who organized the Alabama Sharecropper's Union and paid a heavy price for doing so. Nell Irvin Painter's path-breaking oral history of Hosea Hudson, Robin D. G. Kelley's *Hammer and Hoe,* and my own oral histories of black and white workers in Memphis offer insights into this era from the perspectives of black workers. By combining music and poetry with memory, this account of the life and work of John Handcox adds another special layer to an enduring story of struggle.[8]

Oral history provides a powerful lens that can be extremely revealing, particularly for workers and poor people of color, whose stories are largely missing from the mass media and most history books. Finding a living person with memory of some of that neglected history opens the opportunity of a lifetime. That opportunity opened up for me when I met John Handcox in June of 1985 at the Great Labor Arts Exchange in Silver Spring, Maryland. I had organized a panel of labor and civil rights singers that included Pete Seeger. He and Joe Glazer, the pre-eminent promoter of labor music, with the help of the Smithsonian Institution's Ralph Rinzler, brought John to our gathering. After the conference, Joe and I spent a day recording John's reminiscences at the Smithsonian and I spent another day recording John's oral history at the home of Joe and his wife Mildred. Some five years later, blues scholar William Ferris and I, as research fellows at the Stanford Humanities Center, jointly interviewed John. Scholars Donald Lance and Rebecca Schroeder also interviewed John and made their notes and transcripts available to me (see the bibliography and acknowledgements). John's oral history narrative in this book comes primarily from my interviews with John in 1985, supplemented by these others.

Oral historian Linda Shopes writes that there are many valid ways to present oral history.[9] I provide John's story largely as he told it to me and transcribed by music professor and ethnographer Patti J. Krueger, minus my questions and comments. I have not paraphrased him, and any words I have added for clarification (almost none) are placed in brackets. I have reorganized his narrative in some places, so that it flows in chronological order. His oral history, as told to me or told to others, appears in italics as do various unpublished writings he sent to me. In original documents such as letters or published accounts relating to John and the sharecroppers' movement, I have not corrected spelling and punctuation. Fortunately, one can readily "hear" Handcox's way of speaking, singing, and reciting, thanks to music and literary scholar Mark Allen Jackson, who published John's 1937 Library of Congress recordings along with parts of our 1985 interviews on a compact disc. Mark's liner notes on "the rough truth" of John Handcox provide a sensitive and fitting introduction.[10]

As oral historians emphasize, memory is not the same as history. More than 50 years since his experiences in the Delta, John could remember some events with riveting detail, but he sometimes confused basic facts, such as the year in which his father died. His isolation as an organizer in Arkansas and Missouri necessarily limited what he knew about what was going on in the STFU as a whole, and, in any case, he cared little about the union's internal political conflicts. One does not take any person's memory as infallible, nor expect one individual to give a full and coherent view of what happened long ago. Despite these limitations, oral history can prove extremely valuable in helping us understand the past. Historian Alessandro Portelli explains that the *way* someone remembers a past event can tell us a great deal about people's values, and *what* he or she chooses to remember or forget provides important clues to history.[11] In doing oral history, additional research is always needed to provide a crucial context, to fill in gaps and check facts, and, in this case, to expand on one person's story to help us to understand a historic social movement.

This book comes as part of a train of oral history interviews and other research on the history of labor and civil rights in the South. I first considered placing John Handcox's story in my book, *Black Workers Remember: An Oral History of Unionism, Segregation, and the Freedom Struggle* (1999), before deciding that John's story needed its own book. However, those workers taught me lessons that made this book possible. One of them has to do with how people tell stories. John's memory for some details was not always keen, but at other times he spoke as if an event had happened yesterday, as did other black workers I interviewed. Their memories of the era of Jim Crow were often embedded with violent, force-ful encounters with whites they could not forget even if they tried. I came to feel that black worker testimony provides a particularly telling and reliable kind of documentary evidence about the era of Jim Crow and I began to incorporate the stories of black workers in my other writings.[12]

The various forms of testimony from John Handcox in this book tell the life story of an organizer, poet, and troubadour during the sharecropper revolt of the 1930s. It tells of someone whose genius and political power came in large measure from his ability to artistically narrate life and tell stories. His testimony, which is partially captured here, helps us to understand how John and others cre-ated a profound grass-roots movement for change.

"A Shared Authority"

The process of *doing* oral history presents a complicated human interaction, requiring the interviewer to show a degree of sympathy, and requiring the person being interviewed to show a degree of trust, in order to open up memories about life. I had no training in doing oral history and John had left the STFU some 50 years ago by the time we met in 1985. We had just shared our music during three days of the labor arts exchange, however, and this helped us to open channels of communication. I did know that an interviewer can inadvertently redirect, sidetrack, or misinterpret someone else's narrative. So my first rule was to try to ask broad, chronological questions, listen closely, and stay out of the way of the narrator. John had been only rarely interviewed up to this point. He sometimes gave short answers and had a dim memory on some specifics, but his music and poems came readily to mind and helped him to open up his memory of the past. The work we did together fits what historian Michael Frisch described as "shared authority," in which the historian and the narrator together search to recover important details of the past.[13] It was a joyful experience. I only regret it has taken so long to bring John's memories and sung and spoken words to the printed page.

Historian Linda Shopes calls turning an oral interview into a written narrative an act of "translation," a judicious attempt to take the spoken words of an historical actor and place them appropriately on the written page. In this translation, I have not attempted to reproduce John's vernacular. Some of the inflections of his speech appear in the text, but most of his words appear the way I think he would want them to be presented, in Standard English. I have not changed his word order, but I have edited out some extraneous comments, and the usual "um" and "ah" of oral presentation. My effort is to make the spoken word, as Shopes puts it, "accessible to the reader, more or less according to the conventions of written language," while remaining "faithful to the narrator's words and word order, speech patterns and rhythm" as well as the content of the narrator's story.[14]

The question of how to edit someone else's words remains a crucial consideration, especially in the case of someone who is a poet and a songwriter. STFU organizer H. L. Mitchell wrote to John in 1935 that his first poem would appear in *The Sharecropper's Voice* as soon as Mitchell edited it. He did so, and even changed the title of John's poem. One can readily see in John's correspondence in the union's archives, or in his letters to me, that his writing contains almost no punctuation. The practice of editors helping poets and singers to arrange their words on paper in the most effective way goes back to the earliest English publishers. Thus, one can assume that John's published songs and poems have at least been minimally edited. After we first met in 1985, John sent a number of songs to me that had no musical notation and little punctuation, and his words did not always fit into the stanzas of a poem or song. I consider myself blessed to have collaborated with him in making minor wording alterations as well as in creating a tune on the guitar for several songs that we presented together at the Great Labor Arts Exchanges in 1986 and 1987. On the other hand, I left his songs and poems published in previous eras just as I found them.

Neither John's somewhat fragmented memories in written transcripts nor his songs and poems could by themselves fully tell the story of John's experiences in the South. Thus, the "shared authority" of this book also includes my efforts to place memory in context by interweaving race and labor history and the story of the STFU with John's telling and singing of his story. Knowing of the horrific Elaine Massacre of 1919, and the violence used against union organizers in the 1930s enables us to appreciate the courage it took for people like Handcox to stand up for union rights against the planters. Knowing the context helps us to understand why John's songs and poems were so needed to give heart to frightened, almost powerless people. This history helps us to see that John accomplished a lot to even survive his perilous early life. In his skeptical way of looking at life—seeing it as a sometimes amusing, and other times terrible, adventure—John tended to understate almost everything. I hope the historical details presented in this book help the reader to see the magnitude of the crisis that people like John faced and the significance of the choices they made.

To present this history, I have relied heavily on the writings and judgements of historians, as well as the help of a number of research assistants, to whom I am deeply grateful (see the bibliography and acknowledgements). Secondary accounts, as well as research in the STFU Papers at the University of North Carolina, newspapers, and other primary sources, confirm that John's story in its outlines is true, and that it in many ways reflects the experiences of thousands of other African American agricultural workers (and many whites as well) in the Deep South. This book is an act of recovery, an attempt to represent what a black man experienced in the sharecropping world of the 1930s. I have done my best to verify John's recollections and follow his leads and clues, with documentation listed in the endnotes. I have tried not to bury John's story by adding too many details or by debating what various historians have said. Pete Seeger says that simpler is better when it comes to music with a message, and sometimes that is true of history as well.

*   *   *

The story of John Handcox adds a special dimension to the "power of remembering." We are fortunate to be able to learn about the past through his oral documents that consist of speaking, singing, and reciting poems, combined here with rigorous historical research. I hope this account will not only bring the neglected story and artistry of this rural proletarian to a broader audience, but also open a new vantage point on the history of the sharecropper's movement and the STFU, and on the history of labor and freedom music. At another level, this story may also prove surprisingly relevant to our own times.

John had modest expectations. He told me, *"All of my songs and poems point directly to the conditions in which people was livin' . . . and what was causin' 'em to live that way . . . pointing out to people when they're working hard, and they ain't gettin' anything out of it."* With that purpose in mind, John did not copyright his songs and poems, although Pete Seeger copyrighted several of them on John's behalf. *"I didn't put no restriction on 'em,"* he told researcher Rebecca Schroeder. *"They have 'em in the books and things, so it's alright. Anything that I can do, anything I can say that'll help make this a better world a little bit, I don't need no pay. I get my pay from that. ... If it don't help me, maybe it'll help somebody else."* John asked me to get his writings published, and I only wish I had been able to do so sooner. John also said, *"to get the credit is alright too."* He felt that if his story and his songs and poems lived on, "I Live On."[15]

I hope this book fulfills his wishes and puts him in his rightful place as a seminal figure in the history of African-American, labor, and protest music.

*   *   *

In 1970, I joined a car caravan of civil rights supporters crossing the Hanrahan Bridge from Memphis into eastern Arkansas. As we drove through fields white with cotton, we came around a curve. There, several truckloads of white sheriffs and townspeople lounged with shotguns hoisted visibly in their truck racks. We drove into Earle, where police had viciously attacked black students and their parents for trying to hold a demonstration against segregation. A chill passed through us as the militarized band of law enforcers and their supporters closed in behind us.

Little did I know then of the interracial sharecroppers' movement that had happened in this storm center of vigilante violence thirty-five years earlier, or that I would be writing a book about that movement forty years later. What goes around comes 'round.

Michael Honey, Tacoma, Washington

CHAPTER 1

"Freedom After 'While' ": Life and Labor in the Jim Crow South

My father used to tell me that things actually got worse after we was freed. During slavery, the master wanted to protect his investment. So he would give the slaves a place to sleep, a house, and food. When we was freed, they just let us loose, and didn't care what happened to us. Whites started hangin' and shootin' blacks. They didn't care anymore. The way I see it, under slavery we used to be the master's slave, but after slavery we became everybody's slave . . . [T]here has always been open and closed seasons on hunting and game, but there has never been a closed season for killing Negroes . . .

    Everybody talkin' 'bout He'ben ain't goin' to He'ben. They sang that in church quite a bit back in my childhood days. We had a grace too: Lord, keep our neighbors back, until we eat this snack. If they come among us, they'll eat it all up from us. (laughs)

—John Handcox

Did Sanctioned Slavery bow its conquered head
That this unsanctioned crime might rise instead?

—Paul Laurence Dunbar [1]

On February 5, 1904, John Handcox entered into the world a supposedly free man. He was born on a farm two miles southwest of Brinkley, on the road to another little town called Clarendon, in the hill country of Monroe County, Arkansas.[2] More than a generation before, his people's struggles and a deadly Civil War had ended the long nightmare of America's racial slavery, one of the worst forms of labor exploitation in human history. However, in John's lifetime,

African Americans in the South still faced a regime of shocking white brutality and labor exploitation. John grew up in one of the hardest places and at one of the hardest times to be black in America.

Like his enslaved ancestors, John drew upon a musical culture of resistance and struggle for survival. Since the first ships brought them from Africa, slaves had created religious songs with haunting and beautiful melodies. Abolitionist and former slave Frederick Douglass wrote of these songs that "every tone was a testimony against slavery." In *The Souls of Black Folk,* published the year before John Handcox was born, scholar W. E. B. DuBois, himself a descendant of slaves, called them "the sorrow songs," in which "the slave spoke to the world" with "a faith in the ultimate justice of things." Whites often regarded these as songs of resignation or of happiness that focused solely on the hereafter, but Douglass wrote that "it is impossible to conceive of a greater mistake. Slaves sing most when they are unhappy." Scholar and theologian James C. Cone wrote, "So far from being songs of passive resignation, the spirituals are black freedom songs which emphasize black liberation as consistent with divine revelation." The black song tradition more often affirmed deliverance, transcendence, and redemption rather than despair. African Americans gave to the nation "a gift of story and song," creating a "stirring melody in an ill-harmonized and unmelodious land," according to DuBois. [3]

John Handcox followed the black song tradition, adapting inherited melodies and words that migrated from one tune to the next. Slave songs offered gifts of the heart to provide comfort, but sorrow songs also clearly called for freedom. Songs such as "Steal Away," "No More Auction Bloc for Me," "Didn't My Lord Deliver Daniel?" and others may have had their origins as slaves fought for their emancipation during the Civil War.[4] At the Library of Congress in March of 1937, Handcox recorded one such song, a traditional spiritual commonly titled, "Oh Freedom!" John flattened out the melody line and sang it in a plaintive voice, always repeating the first line twice:

> *No more mourning,*
> *no more mourning,*
> *no more mourning after 'while . . .*

John created each new verse by changing one word, and each one signified the travails experienced daily by generations of people who had lived through slavery and its aftermath, the racial apartheid system of Jim Crow:

> *No more cryin' . . .*
> *No more weeping . . .*
> *No more sorrows, Lordy . . .*
> *I know you're gonna miss me . . .*

No more sickness . . .
No more trouble [5]

In the 1960s, civil rights movement singers popularized this song as "Oh Freedom!" and ended each verse with the traditional wording, "And before I'd be a slave, I'll be buried in my grave, and go home to my lord and be free." John, however, sang the chorus of the song this way:

Oh freedom, oh freedom, oh freedom after 'while,
And before I'll be a slave I'll be buried in my grave
Take my place with those who loved and fought before.

When asked where he got this version of the song, John said simply, "I always sang it that way." The radical white preacher Claude Williams pinpointed the origins of John's version of the chorus as he reminisced about a conversation he and John had in a car when they worked together organizing the Southern Tenant Farmers Union (STFU) in the 1930s. "As we talked . . . we decided that people who first had sung that song could not really have lived unless they fought." Instantaneously, John interjected his new closing lyric, "take my place with those who loved and fought before."[6]

John wrote many original songs and poems, expressing in vivid language the miseries of poor people and his hope that they could change their lives through organizing. He also adapted older, traditional songs such as this one, well aware that his own life was embedded in a train of events and experiences handed down by those who came before. "Freedom after 'while" provided a subtle comment on the uncertain future and unfinished character of the freedom struggle that he and his family endured in hopes of making freedom real, someday.

Slavery and Its Aftermath

A lively man with a quick laugh and many jokes, John Handcox also had a serious story to tell. Recalling the oft-stated maxim, "kill a mule, buy another, kill a nigger, hire another," John commented, *They had laws against killin' squirrels—there'd be certain seasons you coud kill squirrels—there'd be certain seasons you could kill squirrels, but it was always open season on black people."* While blacks lived in fear for their lives, whites often claimed to exercise a sense of paternalism toward slaves. But John knew from his maternal grandfather that the legend of white paternalism was false. John's grandfather spoke of slavery's exploitation and violence and the bitter divisions that most masters inculcated among the slaves. *"I remember him telling me how the slaves they all stucked together if one or some of the slave would try to get away,"* but at other times *"they would capture them and return them to their owners."*[7] To understand his life, John insisted, one must start from the beginning:

The first thing we want to talk about is . . . the way the Negroes, or the black people you might say, was, how they come to the United States. They was brought here from Africa. The whites went out and captured them from Africa and brought them over here and used them as slaves for years. My grandfather, that is, my mother's father, used to sit down and talk, and I'd listen and ask him questions about slavery and everything. He'd point out about how the slaves had to work. The old master had 'em workin' and cay'in' [carrying] big logs. Sometimes they'd be cay'in' logs [and] they couldn't see each other over them, they'd be so big. They'd pile 'em up and burn 'em, or make a bit of lumber out of 'em. Anyhow, I'd ask him different questions about being a slave, and he would look like he'd get pleasure out of talking with me about it.

He would tell me how the old bosses used to have the big healthy slave men for breedin' with the young slave girls, somewhere around 15 or 16 years old. They'd do that just like breedin' horses or anything else that you want to try to breed the best for the market, like horses and stallions at a racing stable. I don't know if they were interested in the color of a slave so much. I don't know if color made a difference. Most who were bred were dark, I think. I never heard him saying anything about cross-breeding white and black. My grandfather was a slave in Alabama, born in Alabama. He was a big, husky, stout guy. He said they had women during that time, that's what they used him for. They had the big stout men breed these young girls to grow these big men.

John's ancestors had been part of a stream of African Americans dragged as slaves into Mississippi and Alabama from points further north and east, as the expansion of cotton production built the nation's wealth and created an affluent and increasingly aggressive slaveholder class in the Deep South.[8] His family's genealogy is sketchy. The spelling of the last name on the paternal side of John's family changed repeatedly: from Hancock, to Handcock, and, in John's generation, to Handcox. However, first names such as Vina, Willis, Lizzett, George, Liza, and Ben showed up repeatedly, linking one generation to the next among John's siblings and offspring.[9] Census records indicate that John's paternal grandfather, who he never met, was born in Mississippi in 1852. His maternal grandfather told John about his own travails in slavery, and uncles and aunts told him of their migration into Arkansas from the Deep South.[10] Clearly, his own life was rooted in the slavery and post-slavery experience.

His grandparents' generation began their lives during what DuBois, in his book *Black Reconstruction*, called the "general strike" of slaves that helped to destroy the Confederacy, [11] and also experienced the turmoil that followed the war. They had hopes for landed independenc, as federal troops seized plantations and let former slaves divide them up or farm them cooperatively, but Andrew Johnson took Abraham Lincoln's place as president after his assassination and returned confiscated lands to slave owners. Former slaves had freedom but no land or money, while plantation capitalists had land but needed black labor—yet no longer felt any obligation to feed or house their former slaves. John wrote, "The way I see it when we were slaves we were valuable but when we became free we lost our value. We were not freed we were taken out of a pen and put in a pasture and they said to us root, hog, or die a poor pig."[12]

Ex-slaves went on the move, seeking literacy, family reunification, civil and political rights, and above all, land and a degree of economic independence. John's elders fled the Deep South hoping for a better life in Arkansas.[13] John recalled his family's migration through the stories told to him by his maternal grandfather:

> He was on a big plantation farm, and when freedom came, he moved the family to Arkansas in a covered wagon. They used to have lots of covered wagons. He just wanted to get out on his own, the way I understand it, to get out from that part of the country. He had married, and he had three children, and he had some mules or horses, I don't know which one. He fixed him up a covered wagon and drove it from Alabama to a little place in Arkansas named Brinkley. He raised a little cotton and corn, and he farmed. He learned how to make cross ties and made those, and he sold wood to provide for his family, plus his little farmin'. He bought 60 acres of his own that he worked. That's where he stayed until his death. I never heard my grandfather say anything about his parents. He brought a first cousin along with him. He had a sister older than him, in Hot Springs, and a nephew he sent back for later in Alabama after he got out here and settled down. My dad's father I never seen.

John did not know much about his father's side of the family, but he knew it had something to do with his high cheekbones and a light brown complexion. He elaborated on his mixed racial heritage:

> My father's mother was half white. Her mother's master was her daddy, and her grandfather was white. I've seen her half brothers and sisters, they was his. They lived in a little place called Cotton Plant, Arkansas. My grandmother, though, she hated them. She knew they knowed that she was their sister, and they would call her "Aunt Lizard." Her name was Lisabeth, and they wanted her to come and work something for 'em. She went once to my knowledge, and after that, she didn't go no more. Her daddy didn't make no allowance or nothing for her. She had sisters and brothers as rich as cream but they never did give her nothing. Treated her like their maid, and she resented. I don't know nothin' about her brothers and sisters except her white brothers and sisters.
>
> My mother's mother was full Indian. She was a beautiful lady. She was Blackhawk or something, but don't hold me to it, I don't want to tell the wrong thing. She was from Alabama. That's where her and my grandfather married. They had as many as three or four kids when they come to Arkansas, but they [eventually]

had 14 in all. I was six or seven years old when she died. I can remember her well. My [maternal] grandfather lived with us and he passed in '33. He was 80 some years old when he passed.[14]

The Census Bureau in Arkansas in 1900 listed Lisabeth as black, but in 1910 it listed her as "mulatto"; in 1920, it also listed John, his father, and his mother as "mulatto."[15] Some of John's descendants described his eyes as green, which most people thought represented a Native American heritage, while others described his eyes as blue or hazel, representing a Euro-American strain.[16] John summed up the situation in a letter: "My father's mother were half white, and her mother was a slave. This is the reason you see in the so-called Negro race so many different colors."[17]

"Kill a Mule . . . "

John's elders succeeded in escaping the Deep South of Alabama and Mississippi for the frontier of Arkansas, but no one could escape the white racial violence that engulfed the postwar South. Arkansas began as a federal territory in 1819 and adopted slavery into its constitution when it became a state. Nearly 70 percent of the slave population concentrated in the eastern Arkansas Delta, where the sharecropper's movement would emerge in the 1930s and where white violence against blacks became endemic. Confederate soldiers slaughtered black soldiers during the war, and then took their weapons home to murder black civilians after the war. Across the Mississippi River in nearby Memphis, whites murdered scores of African Americans and burned down their schools and churches in 1866. Former slaveholder and Confederate General Nathan Bedford Forrest, a pillar of the Memphis cotton business and political elite, led a massacre of black soldiers at Fort Pillow, Tennessee, during the war, and afterward founded the Ku Klux Klan, which soon became a terror in Arkansas.[18] This is the unfortunate social terrain the Handcox family would inhabit.

White racial violence in response to black political and economic power wracked Arkansas during the Reconstruction era (1868–76), when Congress required former secessionist states to accept black male citizenship (the Fourteenth Amendment) and voting rights (the Fifteenth Amendment) in order to rejoin the union. In response, the Klan murdered African Americans and their white allies and burned their homes, and made every effort to lock them out of political power and citizenship rights. The Arkansas governor suppressed the Klan in order to make his black-white voting coalition effective, and by 1873 four black senators and sixteen black representatives served in the legislature. Blacks also served on juries and exercised civil rights, as bi-racial reform governments increased taxes on rich landowners, paved roads, and built public schools for the common people.

In 1877, Republicans in Congress withdrew federal troops and largely stopped civil rights and liberties enforcement and, in return, Democrats allowed Republican Rutherford B. Hayes to take the presidency, as a deal to resolve a stalemated national election. Nonetheless, bi-racial, Populist, and farmer-labor coalitions with reform programs persisted: the Greenback Party, the Agricultural Wheel, and the Knights of Labor formed the Union Labor Party in Arkansas, which nearly won the 1888 gubernatorial election. These progressive traditions would find expression again with the rise of the Socialist Party in Arkansas and the Southwest in the early twentieth century.

Blacks and whites continued to view Arkansas as a promising frontier, but it was hardly the Promised Land. In the 1880s, hundreds of blacks left for Oklahoma, and some even went to Africa, to get away from pervasive racial violence.[19] In the 1890s, so-called "white supremacy" campaigns of lynching and race-baiting swept the South, including in majority-black eastern Arkansas, around Forest City and St. Francis County, where John Handcox would later organize the STFU. The Arkansas legislature imposed a tax on voting (the poll tax), and in 1891 a "white primary" law turned the Democratic Party into a private club for whites and made it the only party that mattered.[20] Democrats proceeded to crush bi-racial reform.

White Democrats in control of Arkansas and other southern states passed Jim Crow laws segregating all facilities, public and private, from schools to restaurants to bathrooms to workplaces and cemeteries. The federal government caved in to Jim Crow, repealing or refusing to enforce federal civil and voting rights laws. In *Plessy V. Ferguson* (1896), the Supreme Court adopted the fiction that segregation was "separate but equal." When blacks in eastern Arkansas sought federal relief from white racial violence, the Court in 1906 overruled their efforts, concluding that blacks were no longer "wards of the nation." Federal abandonment of the Fourteenth Amendment's equal citizenship rights and the Fifteenth Amendment's right to vote now gave whites a virtual license to kill, all under the color of law.[21]

Even as the black population in Arkansas tripled in the last 30 years of the nineteenth century, white violence and disfranchisement ripped away black rights,. When black cotton pickers went on strike in Lee County in 1891, whites killed 15 of them. Lynching and frame-ups spread. Jeff Davis, a three-term governor and US senator in Arkansas elected around the turn of the century, warned, "We may have a lot of dead niggers in Arkansas, but we shall never have negro equality."[22] All of this served as a grim background to the popular saying John Handcox spoke of: "kill a mule, buy another, kill a nigger, hire another." White landowners enforced a regime of cheap labor through sharecropping and peonage that would entrap both blacks and whites for the next half of a century. Emancipation had freed some members of John's family to become small farmers, but under constantly worsening conditions.

Black Homesteaders in the Jim Crow Era

When John's grandparents migrated to Arkansas in the 1880s, the black population was growing faster there than in any other state. African Americans pushed for political power and built schools, churches, and fraternal organizations. They used kinship networks, religion, and music to enhance their sense of community and solidarity with one another.[23] John's ancestors saw hope for the future in Arkansas, since plantation owners and the cotton economy did not yet fully dominate a raw frontier awaiting settlement. Folklorist Alan Lomax's description of Mississippi likewise described the delta of eastern Arkansas: "Most of the land was a subtropical jungle of forests, swamps, and snake infested bayous, home to brown bears, seven-foot water moccasins, and hundred-pound catfish." Black and white homesteaders flooded eastern Arkansas to get land, while making cash by also working as wage laborers. Of black workers, Lomax wrote, "Their herculean labors brought daylight into the swamps, tamed the big muddy rivers, and built the roads along which wealth and change came to the Delta."[24] Some of them succeeded in gaining a degree of economic independence: at the turn of the century, one in five southern black "farm operators" listed in the US Census owned all or some of the land they tilled.[25]

After moving by covered wagon from Alabama, John's maternal grandparents settled about two miles from the tiny town of Brinkley, buying cheap, sandy hillside lands already denuded of forests by big timber companies. "You couldn't raise a fuss" on such land, John quipped. Still, the extended family made a living by cutting, hauling, and selling scrubwood used to make fence posts while raising farm animals and foodstuff for their own subsistence. In just this way, wrote Alan Lomax, "blacks were acquiring land, establishing their own communities, and rising in the world," accepting low wages as better than the "no-wages" of slavery.[26] Extended black households grew rapidly, with everyone working to produce crops or earn wages to contribute to the family economy. Said John:

> My grandmother and my father and uncles lived on the old Frank Hill farm. They farmed that land, and when my daddy [George] married my mother [Vina, sometimes spelled as Vinia], he lived on it a year or two, and then he bought a place about 15 miles from there, near Brinkley. He built house on that, and that was where we lived. My grandmother lived with us there until she died. She had five or six children, three sons—John, Nathan, and George. My daddy was the oldest one. My mother, she was born in 1877. She had a sister and brother who were older than her, at least four years older. She was 92 when she passed, and she was in good health and all, and walkin' and doin' chores and knittin' lots of shawls and bedspreads and stuff like that.[27]

John's parents, George and Vina, married on June 11, 1899[28] and emulated their parents by accumulating small parcels of land on self-sufficient farms while also working for wages. But the vision of such small farmers was at odds with that of capitalist investors, who "envisioned vast and profitable plantations of cash crops, not small homesteads," according to historian Jarod Roll.[29] Lumber companies hired workers to deforest the region, making Arkansas into the "hardwood capital of the world." Lee Wilson and other investors converted the denuded land into fertile territory for the mass production of cotton. These white landowners created what historian Jeannie Whayne termed a "Delta empire," shipping cotton and wood through Memphis as part of an international system of trade and finance.[30] Cotton capitalists created "a labor system underwritten by segregation and disfranchisement that kept black people poor and stripped of basic civil and human rights accorded to other Americans," wrote historian Nan Woodruff. Jim Crow segregation meanwhile served to keep working-class and small farming blacks and whites divided and unable to bid up the price of their labor by organizing together.[31]

By the time John came into the world in 1904, racism had spread like a contagion. When a white man or woman, rich or poor, walked down the street, they expected black pedestrians to get off the sidewalk; when whites drove automobiles, they expected black drivers to get off the road. John recalled his father telling him a story of a white woman who accused a black man of rape. *"My daddy went to the hanging . . . This girl claimed the Negro tried to rape her was about 15 miles from where they picked him up at. And my daddy said the last thing he had to say, where the law picked him up at was as far north as he'd ever been. But they hung him."* John's father brought home newspapers that gave other chilling accounts of racial atrocities. In a written account of his early life John recalled, *"I say that in every paper that I read there were one or two lynching and tar feathering of some black man."* Sometimes *"white folks would . . . burn some black person or hang sometimes [or] two or three would get shot just for fun."* In this way, plantation owners used "savage exemplary violence to keep these vigorous and ambitious people in line," in the words of Lomax.[32]

During John's youth, discrimination, exclusion, and inequality remained the law of the land. Poll taxes, white primaries, and white terror prevented blacks from voting, while segregation laws made it illegal for blacks and whites to inhabit the same space on buses, trains, or streetcars, in cafes, theaters, or hotels; African Americans could not sit on juries, serve as judges, jailers, or police, and only rarely did they serve as lawyers, and then only for black clients. Segregation confined black youngsters to separate, inadequate, underfunded primary schools, usually with no access to high school. Poor whites did not do well either as cheap wages, sharecropping and peonage blocked both African Americans and whites from achieving economic independence.[33]

Sharecropping had emerged after the Civil War when former slaves, like John's grandparents, resisted working on gangs, as under slavery, and fought to own land and control their own farm production. White landowners advanced seeds, fertilizer, and other goods on credit while allowing both former slaves and poor whites to live and work on small plots of land and sharing the crop at the end of the year. Agricultural workers hoped to save their earnings and to buy their own land, but white planters, merchants, and cotton gin owners took advantage of them. Bosses inflated what sharecroppers owed and underreported what they produced; many farm workers could not read or write and feared to question the bosses' figures, as landowners and merchants cheated them out of their share of earnings. Sharecroppers and renters had hoped to buy their own farm, but land-lords gave them unfavorable terms that mired them in debt.[34]

John's grandparents and parents did better than most. They stayed outside of the cotton-dominated Delta by purchasing marginal lands in the upcountry; they accumulated their own tools and livestock; and they stayed out of debt. John's grandfather owned his own land, and although John's father sharecropped at times, more often he rented land as a tenant farmer,. The extended Handcox family lived at subsistence, but no one went hungry. John and his older brother, George Jr., began working between the ages of six and eight, cutting and hauling timber and working in the fields. John's grandmother Lizzett (or 'Lisabeth) hung a switch on her belt and used it "to keep us moving," John recalled. John's sisters and his mother Vina ran the household and also did much of the other work associated with farming. Such black women in the rural South played a powerful role in the family economy during and after slavery and most often worked harder than the men. Not surprisingly, women would come to play a crucial role in the STFU.[35]

By owning cheap and not very productive lands, renting or sharecropping other lands, controlling the crops and goods they produced, and not getting in debt John's family achieved some independence and a viable means of living. [36] The price of cotton careened up and down, sometimes enriching and at other times destroying farmers, but John's family avoided planting cotton as their main cash crop, and thereby stayed out of debt. They raised hundreds of chickens, had mules and other farm animals, owned their own tools, and could even take in needy people, white and black. John's father George could add and subtract in his head and thus avoid unfair transactions with whites; he belonged to the Masons, a fraternal order that many whites also belonged to, and John said he never heard his Baptist father curse. John's grandfather and his father apparenty established cordial relations with some whites to shelter the family from intimidation. John's family lived at perhaps the highest level of tenancy, doing better than the great majority of African Americans and many whites. They had the independence and income that many former slaves and poor whites hoped to achieve. [37]

John thus recalled a childhood largely free from the exploitation and vio-lence that plagued blacks working on plantations. He had time to go to school, which plantation children did not and fondly remembered his childhood as a time when books and school helped him to develop his own sense of freedom based on the written and spoken word

Education of a Poet

Education proved key to John's evolution, and he was lucky to get it. Typhoid, cholera, and diphtheria, created by poor or nonexistent sanitation and plumbing facilities, stalked young people in the Delta. Bad tonsils kept John out of school for the better part of a year. "*I was a very sickly child from the time I was about one year old until I was about 11,*" he wrote. "*My mother told me many times that she never thought that I would ever live to get grown let alone to be an old man.*" John was fortunate to become literate at all. In Arkansas, the great majority of black children went no further than fourth grade. The amount of money spent for the schooling of white children, who did not fare so well either, ran to three or four times the money spent for schooling black children. Plantation owners did not want their workers to become literate, because education would "unsuit" them for labor in the fields.

John's mother taught him how to read and write at home, and this gave him a leg up on most students. Salaries for black teachers were pitiful, and so were the facilities.[38] Nonetheless, John recalled learning a great deal:

> I started writing my songs and poems and things about different ones at school, to have something funny to laugh about. Songs, that was the life of the school! We had two days of programs on the Easter Sunday, and in June there was a children's day program. We'd all have pieces, duets quartets, or recite poems. Usually around 35 or 40 children would come from about two miles square out on the little farms in our school. There weren't any big farms there like I worked on later. The school that I did manage to go to had three months in the winter and then 'bout a month and a half or two months in the summer, which made it around five months a year.
>
> But on the big plantations, they just had 'bout two months all year, and that would be between the time they finish cultivating the cotton until it's time to pick, say mid-July to maybe the first of October, or something like that. The first or second week in July, the crops was supposed to be big enough to shade the oncoming vegetation, which wouldn't grow where it's shaded out. So that would be the time, you know, they would be eligible to have a little school, between the time that they stop cultivatin' it to keep the vegetation down, and the time it was ripe and they was ready to pick, to harvest.
>
> That's all the schooling they'd have on those big plantations for sharecropper chil'ren, just 'bout two months a year. Even after Christmas, when it got cold, the wives and kids on those plantations would pick the cotton in the rough, with the

burrs and all. They would carry it to the house in these big sacks, and the family, the kids and mothers would separate them, burrs from the lint of the cotton, and they'd burn the burrs up in the fireplace while they were sittin' there. So those sharecropping chil'ren didn't go to school all winter long.

Back then, a teacher could buy a job teaching school. The last teacher I had out in the country, I'd help him with classes. He didn't know as much as I did! You just had to tip to get a teaching job. There was one man over the two schools in the county, black and white, and if you'd grease his hand, you could get a job. That hand greasin's been goin' on for a long time!

The country school had the primer to the sixth grade . . . We had to furnish our own books. You'd carry the book for the grade you were in. The last two or three years the school I attended burned down, and that's why I started going in to town.

John's father invested in a little book of poetry when John was around age 12, through which John discovered Paul Laurence Dunbar, one of the most famous poets of his time. Born during Reconstruction to parents who had been slaves in Kentucky, Dunbar crossed the Ohio River to freedom to become the only black student at Dayton High School in Ohio. He also became class president, class poet, editor of the school paper, and president of the literary society. Dunbar graduated in 1891, but discrimination blocked his intended path to journalism or law school, and he ended up working as an elevator operator. He wrote poems and stories on the side and became a "cross-over literary sensation in 1896" after literary dean William Dean Howells praised his work. Dunbar gained fame for his "dialect" poetry, which drew on minstrel shows that mimicked the language of slavery, but he wrote in a Romantic style that also criticized slavery and racism. Although Dunbar's poetry became well known, he developed tuberculosis, became dependent on alcohol and painkillers, and died at age 34.[39]

Despite Dunbar's tragic death, his poetry lived on in the John Handcox. In "When Malindy Sings," Dunbar celebrated former slaves as the salt of the earth. They would persist until Moses led them to liberty, "an' we'll shout ouah halleluyahs/On dat mighty rec'nin' day" when slaves would become citizens. In "Sympathy," he wrote, "I know why the caged bird beats his win/Till its blood is red on the cruel bars . . . I know why the caged bird sings!" Dunbar also wrote, "We wear the mask that grins and lies,/It hides our cheeks and shades our eyes," explaining how people in the generation after slavery had to grin and bear white racial oppression in order to survive, while striving for a better day. John Handcox imbibed both the spirit and the romantic language of Dunbar's call to celebrate life and resist oppression.[40]

John considered his ability to write poetry a "God given talent," and fortunately, his poetic inclinations did not die. Instead of constantly toiling in the cotton fields like so many others, he attended a country school and then moved to the equivalent of a middle school in the little town of Brinkley, where facilities and teachers were a bit better. Here, John would become more literate and imagine a better world. He had his grandparents and parents to thank for this opportunity, for most poor plantation children had their school years "split" around the production cycle of cotton, with several months of school allowed before chopping and planting, and several months more after harvest in the fall. George Stith (who later helped organize the STFU) remembered bitterly how he got pulled out of the eighth grade at the age of 14 by an overseer to take his father's place in the cotton fields when he fell ill. George never returned to school, a typical experience for many children who grew up in the cotton country.[41] Fortunately, John did not live on a plantation, and by the time he went to Brinkley, he was a precocious child. He had already developed his rhythmic and rhyming sense and recalled that he wrote poems about everyone and everything:

> *My father sent me [walking] about three miles to school in town, in Brinkley. That's where I graduated in the ninth grade. Just two years in that school, I think. That was the first time I'd ever seen a school with more than one teacher. I used to write poems when I was a kid in school. We had school programs where I started poems about kids in school, and the teacher, or whatever subject I would choose. I had read quite a few of Paul Laurence Dunbar's poems in school. He was my idol, because he wrote poignant ones. He was sincere and I love fun, clean fun. My dad bought me a book of his speeches. After I got the rhythm of Dunbar, I started writin' my own songs and poems.*
>
> *When I was going to school, I would try to write poems about different kids or teachers just for a laugh. I wrote poems for graduation or a Friday evening program. At one time, I think I could write a poem about just about anything or any person. I went to school through the ninth grade, through grade school. When I graduated into the ninth grade, my subject was "perseverance." "The man that persevered must scale the walls of paradise to gain eternal life and glory." I think I made that up. That was in my graduation speech.*

Through his imagination, John came to believe he had the capacity to create a better life of his own choosing. When the school superintendent asked students who they would like to emulate, John answered, George Washington. John recalled, he *"thought that I didn't know what I was saying so he told me that I meant Booker T. Washington not George 'cause that was the President, and I said that just what I want to be."*[42]

Music in the Baptist Church

Cotton pickers who became musicians—black Delta bluesmen like Big Bill Broonzy, Muddy Waters, B. B. King and many others—benefitted from the spread of "race records" and the recording industry in the 1920s and radio in the 1930s, all of which helped people to learn new styles that would popularize their own playing and singing. But the Arkansas hill country of John's youth in the 1910s and 1920s remained mostly isolated from centers of commercial and popular music. John did not have a record player or a radio. He encapsulated the fearful isolation of the countryside in his memory of meeting a mad dog on the road:

> *I never thought about trying to write blues, or anything. I lived out in the country, and there weren't any real musicians around there. When you live way out from town that way, unless there's a bunch goin' to town, you're halfway scared to tackle it by yourself. This time of year, you'd be afraid to walk the road anyway, on account of dogs going mad in the meadows. I remember one night we were playing, and the moon was shinin' bright, and a big dog come down the road and my brother and my cousin was down below me, and this dog passed them and they hollered up, "Look out, here come a dog!" I reached down and got me a hard clot of dirt, and I hit that dog and knocked him over. And he got up and just run on down the road. They had rabies, that was the trouble, that's how come they called 'em "mad dogs." I was fortunate not to be bit by him. I know one or two people who were bit. They treated them. They had a stone called a mad stone. Somehow they'd draw that venom out of wherever you were bit, your hand or leg. We had stock that was bit by mad dogs sometimes, also snakes. My dad's remedy was to put kerosene on it to kill that poison. I seen a cow that a mad dog had bit. That cow would just holler and run. That was a dreadful thing to see a mad cow or a mad dog. Those dogs were slobbering and foaming and running.*

Despite lack of access to recorded popular music or juke joints where country people got together to sing and dance, John was able to marry his poetry to the music embedded in the institutions of his rural world. He and other students often put on musical productions in his school. His mother, raised as a Methodist, taught him shape note singing by using sheet music out of a hymnal, with written words and four to seven shapes to represent different notes on a musical scale. John's father sang in the Baptist church choir, as John did at times in Sunday school. He learned traditional black spirituals and standard Christian music well known to blacks and whites alike, and this wellspring of music would serve him well. Even so, John did not fit easily into the South's consuming religious conservatism: he relates that he attended church as little as possible, took up domestic chores at home, and kept a jaded eye on some church practices and black ministers:

> *I grew up in the Baptist church, like my father. My mother was Methodist but changed over when she married him. We didn't much like the kids that would pass as church-goers. My parents never did force us to go to church. We went at our own*

will. I didn't go to church often, only when I felt like it, and I don't feel like it too often! Even now, I think it's better to go when you want to go, and not force yourself. (Sings):

> *Swing low, sweet chariot, comin' for to carry me home,*
> *swing low, sweet chariot, comin' for the carry me home.*
> *I'm not sure I've sung that since I was a child!*

I used to be glad when they'd go to church, and I'd have the dinner done when they'd get back. We always had two or three hundred head of chicken fryers. I'd kill four or five chicken and pick 'em and when they'd come back I'd have dinner down for 'em. I learned how to cook like that. I used to make bread, biscuits, fried fish and chicken. I've been lazy though, since I've had a wife. I used to love to cook, any kind of meats, pie, cake; they taught a little cookin' at school, maybe on Friday. Our teacher, she taught boys how to cook pretty good. She thought she was helping the kids, and thought it was necessary.

John did not adhere to church rituals and hierarchy, and instead developed his own "lived religion," drawing on basic tenets of Christianity but in his own practical way. He recalled *"We been told there's a heaven and a hell. You do good and you go to heaven, and if you do bad you go to hell."* He held to the Golden Rule of doing onto others as they should do onto you, but he also held a skeptical view of organized religion.[43] He delighted in singing, "Everybody talkin' heb'n ain't goin' to heb'n." As sung by slaves, the song reflected black criticism of white slave owners, who talked about going to heaven but would never get there because of their sins on earth. After emancipation, the song could just as easily be turned on hypocrites in the black community. John adopted the song with a sense of ironic understatement that would mark much of his own writing. As he sang it, he seemed to be reviewing some of the hypocrites, both white and black, in and out of the church, he encountered in his early life:

> *Everybody talkin' 'bout He'ben ain't going to Heaven.*
> *When I get to Heaven, goin' to jump and shout,*
> *nobody there's a-goin' to turn me out.*
> *Everybody talkin' 'bout He'ben ain't going to He'ben, He'ben,*
> *Everybody talkin' 'bout He'ben ain't going to He'ben.*
> *Well, the preacher's preachin' 'bout He'ben,*
> *some ain't goin' to He'ben, He'ben*
> *Everybody talkin' 'bout He'ben ain't goin' to He'ben He'ben*
> *Everybody talkin' 'bout He'ben ain't goin' to He'ben.*

The church didn't play a big part in my life. It didn't then, and it don't now. I think Christianity is the best thing in the world if it is carried out right. Anytime a preacher will get up in the pulpit and tell the members that he love 'em and all of that, and then be livin' better off of them than they be livin' themselves, there's a line a truth that ain't in it. Some of these preachers [today] are makin' a thousand dollars a month, when maybe the people is out here makin' pennies. If it's perfect and pure, it's great. But I think the preachers are makin' a racket out of it.

The Color Line and the Class Line

John lived in a largely black world in the hill country and was not under the thumb of a white plantation landlord, merchant or riding boss. Although his family was better off than some whites, at puberty white kids suddenly wanted him to call them "Mr." or "Miss." In a note, he wrote about how his relationship changed with a white landowner's daughter:

Yeah, I knew her. I knew her from a baby. I maybe been a year or so older, but I knew her because my dad, you know we were kids there together, we would play together and everything until she got to be about 10 or 12 years old and she come telling me to call her 'Miss Flora.' She got to be 'Miss' to me. That's what her parents wanted me to call her, 'Miss Flora.' I don't think I called her "Miss Flora" too many times because I didn't understand that—why I should call her 'Miss Flora?'

Racism rankled him, and he increasingly noticed it as he grew older. He recalled that whites, *"They always say, they'd call the white man by his name and he'd call the Negro, 'Boy, hey, boy,' somethin' like that. Whenever you passed the age of about 60, then all blacks was 'uncles' and 'aunties.'*

He hated the disrespectful way his half-white grandmother's white sisters and brothers treated her. Although most African Americans had to "wear the mask" when they related to whites, John himself never conformed to the white man's stereotype of the subservient Negro. *"I remembered when I was 18 a white man was talking about kicking me for drinking water at an ice plant; he was working there and I was hauling wood, I told him if he kick me he would never walk on that foot again."*[44]

John didn't seem to have much fear of whites, despite the ubiquitous Jim Crow system in Arkansas. He knew a few whites living nearby but found them mostly irrelevant to his day to day living. He saw his parents feeding complete strangers, white as well as black, and he did not hesitate to cross the color line when the occasion arose to do so. He related that in the hill country of his youth the color lines were not so tightly drawn as in the plantation districts:

I don't recall anything that's really worth mentioning that happened between me and young whites. We didn't have too much contact with whites, really. There was a German family that lived about a quarter of a mile from us right on the road to town. He was a nice guy, and he had two sons. We didn't exactly play together, but we'd see each other once or twice a week without any conflict. This Jones fella was a good friend of my Daddy, and he had a contract of loading cars for the railroad down below Forest City in Crow Creek. My Daddy had a good team of mules, and this man would contract him for loading rocks and gravel for roads and railroads. Every year he'd get my Daddy and go work in the gravel pit with him.

One thing is, the way some people approach other people, some people look like they're looking for trouble. He had two boys, named Joe and Ulis. Just about anytime they went to town, a bunch of town boys would get behind 'em and throw rocks at 'em and run 'em near-about home. My brother, four years older than I, we went to town, and there . . . weren't rocks [thrown] at us. My brother went to a school called the Brinkley Academy, and I went to grade school. I had my first time to be chased by a [white] southerner, town boys, then.

I think it all depends on the kids and the parents. You can take a kid from the redskins, white, Negroes, Japanese, all age five or six, and they'll all play together and be friends until some grown person tells 'em different. "I don't want my kids playing with no peckerwood," or something. I had a [black] lady who didn't want me to walk with her daughter, who was a good lookin' girl. They attended church in town, and there were one or two boys who called her high society. She wanted her daughter to associate with that high society. She [the mother] jumped on me one night, because we had gone to church and I'd gone outside [with her daughter]. Her girl was named Jesse.

John did not view all whites as bad, anymore than he saw all blacks as good. He viewed color divisions among blacks as ridiculous, as when darker-skinned relatives of his Native American grandmother, who he considered quite beautiful, shunned her light-skinned daughter. *"There are so many ways you can change things from pure to impure,"* John later wrote in a letter. *"You can plant a watermelon near a cucumber and it will not be sweet. The thing we should try to remember is everyone is a human being regardless of what nationality they are. I hold no hate for anyone because of their nationality or their ignorance."* [45]

However, John had a special contempt for blacks who, he thought, exploited other blacks, such as the rich landlord Scott Bond. After emancipation, Bond rented land from the white man who had formerly owned him as a slave. He then made a small fortune during the real estate boom years by buying and selling land and hiring other African Americans at cheap wages to cut and haul timber and clear the swamps. Bond made windfall profits when he shifted his cleared lands in St. Francis County into cotton production in 1914, just as prices shot up due to a high demand for cotton caused by the European war. He also owned and operated a store. Bond reportedly turned down an offer of two million dollars for his land in 1917. From all appearances, he was "white," as was his wife, and though he quietly supported the NAACP he did not openly fight the white power structure.[46] Although others celebrated Bond as a successful capitalist, John did not regard his exploitation of other people's labor as admirable.[47]

> There was a black landlord named Scott Bond, who someone wrote a book about. Those big rich white people were afraid of him. He said he'd beat you if you live. He owned maybe two thousand acres or so. There's a history behind him. He was real light skinned. He got his money started by having a fellow dig post oak for him. He hit something, like a pot. He told Bond about it, and Bond came out and found a pot of gold. When they had the Civil War, people hid their gold, and that's what it was. My wife's brother worked for him, did chores around the house for him. He said he had one of those big trunks, and it was filled with gold. One day he said he was down in the basement, and Bond asked him to move it for him. It was too heavy to move. Bond was so crooked that the white people didn't mess with him. If you're honest, don't mess with Bond. He was rippin' off the tenants worse than the whites.

Given his repulsion at the ways of capitalism, when John later met Socialists in the 1930s he would be a natural convert.

"Our House Was Open to Strangers"

John's early upbringing shaped his optimistic perspective on life. Because his family mixed farming with working for wages, selling and buying things came natural. Because his father could add and subtract figures in his head h always knew what he was owed and what he owed to someone else. John benefited enormously from that example and from his family's small degree of economic independence, developing entrepreneurial skills that would serve him well. His family lived better than many whites, and some people in such households looked down on poorer whites. Instead, his parents instilled a spirit of generosity that would prove invaluable to him in the STFU. Rather than disparaging poor whites, John felt empathy, mixed with some amusement at white attitudes:

> There wouldn't be a day in the year hardly that a covered wagon wouldn't pass our house goin' somewhere. They had gypsies and fortune tellers who'd come through, trying to beat people out of their money. We met them at the door, but they didn't come into the house. Our house was open to strangers. I don't know how many strangers we'd feed. Nowadays you wouldn't just take a stranger in your house and tell your wife to fix 'em somethin' to eat, and you get up and go on about your business.
>
> That's the way my daddy did. I seen him with many a person, white and black. More whites was travellin' and hoboin' around the country than there was colored. They's ask for somethin' to eat, and my father'd go in and tell my mother, "Tab, fix

these men something." Sometimes there'd be five, six of em, and she'd go in and fix 'em something and she'd put it in a bag and tell them to take it with 'em.

They could tell the country people from the city people easy; didn't make no difference whether you colored or white when it come down to being poor or being a sharecropper or livin' on those plantation. The country people was all patched up, had them raggedy clothes on 'em, and the city people were better dressed.

Only difference, you could tell ole massa—uh, ole boss's wife—she was all dressed up in a big car.

I've seen a man, he was a white fellow, I made a deal to trade rows of corn with. He come into plantin' later than I did, so I was gettin' in front of him. I just trade him so many ears of corn now, for his so many ears of corn later. But he come in and started workin' right beside me, and I knew he was gonna eat up my corn if I didn't do something. You'd see people come down the road and they were so hungry they'd eat that raw corn.

A lot of people were worse off than we were. One time I had 'bout half dozen hogs, and this white kid what lived around there said some friends come to see him. And one of those friends say, 'ooh, those are sho some beautiful hogs,' and this kid what lived there say, 'damn poor nigger got 'em though.' It tickled me.

*   *   *

American slavery marryied racism and the exploitation of cheap labor to a form of racial plantation capitalism that impoverished most of the South's people. Emerging from slavery into an ill-fated freedom, John's parents and grandparents created strong models of striving and success that helped him to form a positive attitude and gain a sense of independence. His modest schooling, education at home by his mother, and his discovery of Paul Lawrence Dunbar helped him develop a skill with words. Despite his lack of access to blues and commercial music, he absorbed traditional African-American songs and Christian church melodies. He could read and write and, like his father, calculate math in his head. His ninth-grade declaration that *"the man that perseveres must scale the walls of paradise to gain eternal life and glory,"* reflected a youthful determination and optimism that stayed with him for the rest of his life.

Other African Americans born in Arkansas during the same era as John, such as Sister Rosetta Tharpe, born in Cotton Plant, Louis Jordan, born in Brinkley, and Big Bill Broonzy, would take their artistic talents elsewhere to become famous musicians. John stayed put and continued to slog his way through farming. His sense of humor, observant eye, and rhyming genius, and his sense of self-respect, would prove invaluable as events in the 1920s shattered his world.

CHAPTER 2

Raggedy, Raggedy Are We: Sharecropping and Survival

Raggedy, raggedy are we
Just as raggedy as raggedy can be.
We don't get nothin' for our labor
So raggedy, raggedy are we.

In 1982, John Handcox attended a 48-year reunion of about 150 surviving members of the Southern Tenant Farmers Union (STFU) held at the historic First Baptist Church on Beale Street in Memphis. A reporter pictured Handcox at 78 years of age as "a lean, white-bearded black man." Asked to describe the conditions of 1934, John recalled that on the big plantations, *"The highest-paid hand was 75 cents. He worked from can to can't. That's from the time you can see till the time you can't. They used to ring the bell at 5 a.m., and you had to get down to the barn and harness the mule by lantern light."* Asked about his song, "Raggedy, Raggedy Are We," John recalled, *"It was written for rough, tough, raggedy times"* when one could tell country folk from city dwellers because they *"was all patched up, had them raggedy clothes on 'em."* He also volunteered:

> *If I wrote a song today it would be about hard times. I could write one about mod-*
> *ern conditions if I wanted to. They don't exactly compare to the '30s, but they're*
> *still hard. A lot of folks are out of work. If it wasn't for social security, it would*
> *be pitiful. The social security it not enough to live on, but it's enough to exist. I'm one*
> *of the fortunate poor because I've always had enough to eat. My stomach was never*
> *in danger of collapsing. It will do that, you know, if you don't get something between*
> *your front and your back.*[1]

In my first interview with John, he sang "Raggedy, Raggedy" and told me an arresting story about how he came to write it and what it meant to be truly raggedy. The song resulted from his encounter with a white sharecropper who lived nearby, and it suggests the ways both white and black suffered under sharecropping:

> *Those sharecroppers had to patch up their clothes til they get so many patches it wouldn't hold another patch. Patch it up, and keep wearin' it . . . I lived say about a half a mile, about a quarter of a mile from a white fellow. He had nine kids. He went and asked the [merchant] man for some clothes. And the man told him, say, "Well, you done overrun, your, what you were supposed to get, your account." Anyway, "Say, man, I got to have some clothes on my back." "Well, we can't let you have none till you pick your cotton." And he was walking sideways when he passed women. He'd have to walk sideways . . . to hide his nakedness . . . he had holes all over him, so much so that his privates was hangin' out. He had to walk out of that store sideways so the ladies wouldn't see 'em. He had patches on patches until the patches wouldn't hold patches*
>
> *That caused me to write this song: (Sings)*

> *Raggedy, raggedy are we, just as raggedy as raggedy can be,*
> *We don't get nothin' for our labor,*
>> *so raggedy, raggedy are we.*
> *Hungry, hungry are we, just as hungry as hungry can be,*
> *We don't get nothin' for our labor,*
>> *so hungry, hungry are we.*
> *Landless, landless are we, just as landless as landless*
>> *can be,*
> *We don't get nothin' for our labor,*
>> *so landless, landless are we.*
> *Cowless, cowless are we, just as cowless as cowless can be,*
> *The planters don't allow us to have 'em,*
>> *so cowless, cowless are we.*

The tune of "Raggedy" resembled a church song, "How Beautiful Heaven Would Be." Singer Johnny Cash grew up in Arkansas hearing this as a comforting song that focused strictly on a glorious hereafter, but the picture John drew in his song was not comforting or beautiful. It was a classic "zipper" song, a musical format he learned in the black church in which singers insert one new word to create a new verse: "Hungry"—"homeless"—"landless"—"cowless"—"hogless"—"cornless." Each new phrase represented a world of hurt. Planters furnished goods at exorbitant rates of interest, controlled distribution in the market, and insisted that workers devote all their resources to producing one cash crop, namely "King

Cotton." Many sharecroppers planted cotton right up to their doorstep, and the landlords did not allow them credit or space to raise farm animals.[2] John's last verse, "pitiful, pitiful are we," evoked the discouragement many experienced under the planter's rule. Singer Lee Hays would later add "union, union are we," to give the song an uplifting ending. But John's main point was to help people to see that this way of life was not right:

> *"Raggedy, Raggedy" was describin' the conditions that the people was livin'—they was workin' but yet and still they wouldn't getting' paid enough for the work or wouldn't gettin' paid anything for the work—so they was raggedy.*

John himself did not grow up "raggedy." But as the following chapter explains, the Handcox family of self-sufficient farmers in the 1920s became increasingly raggedy rural proletarians.

The "Shadow of Slavery"

The US Census of 1920 provides a picture of the Handcox family prior to its precipitous fall down the agricultural ladder. It listed his mother and his father, and John as well, as "mulatto," and depicted a large family residing in Brinkley Township, in Monroe County. George (age 46) and Vinia (or Vina) Handcock (age 42) headed the family and their children consisted of four boys: George Jr., (20), John (18 according to the census, although if born in 1904, as he believed, would make him 16), Willis (9, nicknamed Bill), and Ben (5); and five girls, Lizzitt (13), Lizzie (aka Eliza, 11), Ruth (7), Vinia (3), and Martha (less than a year old). The mother of John's father, listed in the census as Liznett (63), also lived with them. John's parents later gave birth to two more boys (Nathan and Leo), for a total of 11 children.[3] Farming families depended on large numbers of children to do the work. John's grandmother, who he called Lisabeth, had given birth to 14 children. The 1920 Census spelled the family name as Handcock; the State of Arkansas would later list the family name as Handcox on his father's death certificate. Various spellings of the name persisted, and no one in the extended family in later generations knew exactly why the named changed, nor what the middle initial L. in John's name stood for.[4]

The Census Report shows that John's family had plenty of hands to work the land, but too many mouths to feed. That made a family vulnerable when a downward economic cycle hit. Between 1914 and 1919, no one thought it would: the price of cotton had shot up while the population tripled, and early investors rejoiced in unprecedented profits. They had bought fertile "bottom-lands" near the Mississippi and St. Francis rivers at low prices and then hired people at a pittance to strip away old-growth forests, drain swamps, and expose rich lands fertilized by thousands of years of river overflows. The Lee Wilson Company organized itself like a modern corporation yet also based on familiar patterns from slavery. It employed 29 riding bosses to supervise the work of over 2,000 laborers, along with 500 tenants and sharecroppers who lived on a cotton plantation of some 65,000 acres. Wilson owned banks, lumber mills, and even a small town named after him. Although a little black bug called the boll weevil devastated cotton in parts of the Southwest, it barely touched eastern Arkansas. As planter capitalists like Wilson took control of the best lands, the state's lien laws gave landlords, merchants, and bankers first claim on the crops of people who owed them money at exorbitant rates of interest. The racial system was now firmly in place and buttressed a "plantation mentality" that drove the politics and economics of the delta.[5]

As agriculture boomed, farming became less about producing food and cash for a family's subsistence, as John's family did, and more about exploiting labor to produce huge profits, as the Wilson family did. Military demand for clothing during World War I jumped the price of cotton from 7 cents a pound in 1914 to 14 and then to 33 cents, and finally to 43 cents by the summer of 1919.[6] The rising price of cotton fueled the fortunes of the rich, but also spurred virulent, racial violence among the poor. Hundreds of thousands of African Americans, responding to a voracious demand for labor in northern factories and cities, fled the southern states to get better wages, housing, and education during the "Great Migration." Some joined steel, meatpacking, and other industries ast strikes for higher wages and unions surged forward. Employers responded with fierce repression and played whites against blacks to destroy unions during the "red summer" of 1919, when blood flowed in the streets across America. White soldiers, civilians, and police, and often white workers as well, attacked blacks, blocked their employment, and burned their neighborhoods. Many black soldiers, just returning from service overseas, fought back.[7]

The chaotic racial violence that occurred at the end of World War I in places like Chicago and Washington, D.C., however, could almost be considered as a different category of "riot" when compared to what happened in the racial tinderbox of eastern Arkansas. White employers there had long preferred to hire blacks, who had little choice but to work harder at less pay than whites, who often tried to drive them away from land and work. All-white juries readily absolved vigilantes who shot, beat, and lynched blacks.[8] Joining in interracial class alliances—as some had done in the South during the Reconstruction and Populist eras—no longer seemed an option. As black novelist Richard Wright later summarized, "poor whites are warned by the Lords of the Land that they must cast their destiny with their own color, that to make common cause with us is to threaten the foundations of civilization. Fear breeds in our hearts until each poor white face begins to look like the face of an enemy soldier."[9]

This exploding dynamic of labor competition, racial fear, and high cotton prices came to a head in June 1919, in Elaine, the county seat of Phillips County, about 50 miles south of where John's family lived. Blacks there had organized a cooperative for selling their cotton to the highest bidder called the Progressive Farmers and Household Union of America. They identified themselves with secret handshakes and passwords, much as members of fraternal orders did everywhere. Union members wrote a constitution that ended with the pledge, "WE BATTLE FOR THE RIGHTS OF OUR RACE; IN UNION IS STRENGTH." This group of African Americans sued white landlords to assert their legal right to combine to sell their goods in order to obtain "their fair share of the largest cotton crop in southern history," in the words of historian Nan Woodruff. Their union threatened the profits of cotton merchants, who claimed that state law required sharecroppers and tenants to sell their cotton crop only to them. Blacks had a vision of a future of equal opportunity that threatened the hegemony of planters, including rich northern migrants like Gerald Lambert, who owned Listerine mouthwash as well as 4000 acres of land in Arkansas. Conflict over who would benefit from the rising price of the white gold of cotton quickly led to murder and mayhem.[10]

The labor and race scares of the "red summer" resounded through the white imagination in Phillips County, where blacks outnumbered whites ten to one. Some media accounts portrayed the black union in Elaine as part of a world-wide Communist conspiracy; others called it an effort by the Industrial Workers of the World (IWW) to organize whites and blacks together (the IWW had done so among Louisiana timber workers in a previous effort crushed by bloody violence). US Military Intelligence agents likewise portrayed the movement for fair cotton prices in Elaine as the beginnings of a black insurrection. Provoked by such wild rhetoric, when whites heard that black union members were holding an organizational meeting in a church in Hoop Spur, they got a mob together, surrounded the building, and opened fire. Blacks guarding the church shot back, killing a special agent of the Missouri Pacific Railroad.[11]

The railroad company and nearly every corporate interest in the region had already sent in their armed agents. The sheriff quickly deputized them and, led by World War I veterans, a mob of 300 white men burned down the church and then spread out into the surrounding area, hunting and killing black people. On October 2, the Governor of Arkansas personally led federal and state troops armed with machine guns used in the world war, while authorities cut phone lines to Elaine and imprisoned an emissary from the union's attorney in Little Rock. Burning, arrest, torture, and murder directed at African Americans spread across a 200 mile radius.

Some eye witnesses claimed whites killed 200 while another first-hand account tallied 856 black deaths; others said 4 to 25 whites may have also died.[12] Some claimed that trains hauled black bodies out of Elaine stacked up like cord wood in boxcars. The reliable investigator Walter White, of the National Association for the Advancement of Colored People (NAACP), estimated that authorities arrested over 1,000 blacks between October 1 and 6. No whites were indicted for any crimes, but an all-white grand jury indicted 122 black women and men on October 31, 1919, charging 73 of them with murder. In eight minutes, a white jury convicted them all. The court sentenced 12 of the men to death and 67 others received sentences of up to 21 years in prison apiece.[13] The State of Arkansas claimed the black farmers' union was "banding negroes together for the killing of white people." Only a national publicity campaign by anti-lynching crusader Ida B. Wells-Barnett and court actions by a valiant Little Rock black attorney named Scipio Jones saved the convicted men from execution. No one in the white community ever paid for the deliberate instigation of mass murder in the Elaine race riot.[14]

John said nothing about Elaine, but he did not have to. Among African Americans, the memory of the Elaine Massacre, as it became known, warned succeeding generations of the devastating violence that could be inflicted on blacks who organized unions. Since most whites believed in black inferiority as an article of faith, it was easy to pit them against blacks. White racial terrorism centered in counties where poorer whites had lost their farms and wanted to seize control of land from blacks. Under these circumstances, lynching spread like a plague after the Elaine massacre. In one especially grisly incident on January 25, 1921, 600 whites slowly burned African American Henry Lowry to death in Nodena, Arkansas. Lowry had killed a landlord and fled to Texas, where police captured him and shipped him back to Arkansas, and local police let vigilantes murder him. By 1923, one source estimated that 50,000 whites belonged to the KKK in Arkansas; some 10,000 attended a Klan rally in Helena, not far from where John and his family lived that year. At least 28 reported lynchings occurred in Arkansas in the 1920s.[15]

Intensifying this charged racial context, the cotton economy went into free-fall after 1919. The price of cotton dropped in half from its war-time high, to 16 cents a pound in 1920; it kept on dropping, as cheaper cotton produced in European colonies hit world markets. Tenancy and sharecropping, once thought to be possible steps toward land ownership and economic independence, instead became deadly traps leading to peonage and extreme poverty. Tenancy was bad, but sharecropping was worse. Writer Erskine Caldwell described it this way:

> It continues in operation year after year, wringing dry the bodies and souls of men, women, and children; dragging them down to its own level . . . to take the places of those crushed and thrown aside; breeding families of eight, ten, twelve, fourteen, sixteen, and more, in order to furnish an ever-increasing number of persons necessary to supply the rent-cotton for the landlord.[16]

The nearly feudal arrangements that made cotton "King" also made the South a cash poor, technologically backward region marked by illiteracy, monoculture, hunger, disease and poverty, living, as historian Pete Daniel put it, in "the shadow of slavery."[17] Although living in that shadow, John's family had obtained small amounts of land and a degree of independence until a shattering event knocked the foundations out from under them. John's description of what ensued for his family provides one example of the terrible and worsening conditions that finally led to the sharecropper revolt.

Sucked Into the Downward Cycle

"My father got killed back in [1923], when a team of mules run away and killed him," John recalled in a matter-of-fact way.[18] When a bolting team of mules threw his father George from a buckboard wagon, he dashed head-first into a tree and broke his neck. George lay on the ground for about an hour, tended to by his son but unable to move. Living in the country, the family had nowhere to turn for medical help. As John looked on at his father, he saw that *"death was upon him."* He did not elaborate on how he felt at that moment, but what his father's death meant to John's life became quickly apparent: he had to drop out of high school after his father died to help care for and support a large family. The eldest son, George Jr., had started his own family on his own land, but was now expected to take over the family leadership. John clearly did not feel that his brother was up to the task, later saying he had no "get up," and, more caustically, that George was *"as helpless as a baby was"* when it came to running the family.[19] Upset and probably angry about his brother taking charge, at age 19 John took off for nearby Forest City. It was an all-white KKK breeding ground with signs that read, in John's words, *"nigger, don't let the sundown catch you here."*

> I went to Little Rock to visit my uncle after my daddy got killed and stayed for a few months, working. Me and my mother had an understanding [when] I was about 17. I used to be high or quick tempered. If things would go wrong with me, I'd move on. I looked for work in Forest City. I bought some army pants and shirt, and I went struttin' down Markham Street, and one of the police officers walked up and asked me, "Hey, what are you doin' with these soldier clothes?" And I said, "I'm wearin' 'em! I bought 'em, and I'm wearin' 'em." He said, "well, you go home and pull them things off, because those are army clothes, and civilians ain't supposed to wear 'em. I could put you in jail, but I'll give you a chance."
>
> So I went home and pulled them army clothes off, and I didn't wear them no more until I got back to the country! I had some friends who went to Memphis quite often. I think I went to Memphis about three times, or four. Wasn't many times. I went to Memphis in fall of '24, I think it was, and bought everything you could buy cheaper in the city, like cloth, and shoes. I was livin' in Forrest City at the time.

John's "high or quick tempered" spirit could have made him into one more lynching statistic. Southern whites after the war lynched numerous black men for signifying their manhood by wearing a military uniform. In nearby Pine Bluff, whites kidnapped a black veteran, tied him in chains, and filled him with bullets for having asserted "this is a free man's country" when a white man forced him off the sidewalk.[20] When threatened by a police officer for wearing a surplus military uniform, John had the good sense to get rid of it. But his independent spirit still put him on the list of endangered black men. So did his production of moonshine in an age of Prohibition. At this point in his narrative (not reproduced here), John described the intricacies of making and selling illegal "moonshine." He was apparently good at it:

> I've never been arrested. I was lucky; I don't say that I didn't do things that was illegal. First time I got drunk I had two quarts of whiskey to deliver in town, and I got on this horse and rode. It was sprinklin' and the guy wasn't there, so I had this outfit to carry whiskey with a cooler. The guy who sold me the outfit [to make whiskey] came back and stole it. I looked in the catalog and bought some copper cord and made my own. Anyway, when the guy wasn't home, I went up to Slim's and he was cookin' and he gave me some to drink. Then I lit over to some lady's house, and I could feel that whiskey! They tried to get me to come up, but I knew I was too loaded and they'd take my whiskey. This [white] guy named Gunter felt one of those quarts of whiskey [on me], and he paid me. I made a lot of whiskey and sold it. That was my way of livin' for awhile after my dad died.

Before he could travel further down the path of illegal bootlegging, however, John's family called on him to return to help them scratch out a living. Ten siblings plus a grandmother lived in two small houses, on infertile land that could not support them. His grandfather's 60 acres of "post oak" land apparently provided no financial help to John. He decided to move the family out of the hill country into the more fertile lands of the St. Francis River delta. John explained the circumstances as follows:

> I took over after my daddy's death as kind of the leading person in the family to make the decisions. After my father got killed, we made a crop and it didn't do no good. It was post oak land. You couldn't raise a fuss on it. Post oak is poor land, some of it wouldn't grow even grass. Post oak timber is the only thing that would grow on it. We left it, and I haven't been back but twice, and that's since I been in California. After we left our home where I was born at, we stayed one place first year and then the next we moved and I stayed one year at another place with my mother. She and my younger brother, older brother too, they stayed in another place another year, so then I wasn't connected with them. I started farmin'. I went to the farms on the Delta in 1924, made a crop in '25.

But when we moved to the delta, about 40 miles away, we moved onto a plantation in the bottoms, where the land is much richer. Somewhere around two or three hundred families lived on that big farm, and it was much different from what we knew. The big farms out there had their own cotton gins, and we had to take their prices for whatever. 'Cause they didn't buy much but cotton, and they didn't have no need for corn.

The landlords bought all the cotton was raised on the place. You have to sell it directly to the landlord, because they had the gin and everything. You sold it to them and they didn't allow you to sell it to nobody else. The land we worked on was owned by a big company, the Gennis company, and the name of the place was Lakeside. It's out from Forest City 'bout 14 miles, somethin' like that, down on the Saint Francis River. The main office was somewhere up in the northern part of Arkansas. Aside from ginning cotton bolls, they took the outer hull off and used the inner part of the cotton to make oil. They put that oil in to make lard, Crisco and all that stuff. They had some cottonseed mills in Memphis and in Forest City. And brother, if you go by one of 'em, if you hungry it sho' smells, that's the best smell. They taken that cotton seed oil out by pressing it, and then they press that inner part into cakes and they feed that to the cattle. Most people didn't raise corn to sell, though, they raised that for use. We raise quite a bit of that to feed the stock—hogs, mules and cows.

Well, it is two types of tenant farmers. One is what you call working on the halves. Everything you raise, if its cotton or corn or whatever crops you raise, half of it goes to the landowner. The landowner furnishes all the tools, the mules, and everything. And the sharecropper just furnishes the work. The other system is what they call, they call it "renting," but its third and fourth. We had our own stock, but we rented the land on thirds and fourths. That's like you raise three loads of corn, the landlord get one. You raise four bails of cotton, he sell it and he gets the fourth dollar out of the cotton and the fourth dollar out of the seeds. When we started, I was used to that. That's the way my Daddy farmed, givin' a third of the corn, and a fourth of the cotton. It was called thirds and fourths.

This is the difference of being a tenant farmer and a sharecropper: Third and fourth, you furnished your own stock and tools and seed, and you rented for so much an acre; you were a tenant farmer. For sharecroppers, they [owners] furnished all of the tools and mules . . . the landlord furnishes everything. The sharecropper didn't have nothin'. That's what you call workin' on shares or workin' on harvest, we call it. Sharecroppers . . . they get half, suppose to, of what was produced.

"Pitiful, Pitiful": Living on the Planter's Land

Although conditions forced John to move into the delta lands owned by rich planters, he still sought to maintain his family's economic independence. However, he soon found that the system worked against him and he began complaining of the very things that blacks in Elaine had tried to do something about. The huge Gennis Company on the Lakeside plantation wouldn't let its tenants or share-croppers sell their crop to anyone else. They kept the price of cotton artificially low for those who produced it, but jacked up the price of seeds, fertilizer, and food, while charging exorbitant interest rates for loans. John's family had always stayed out of debt and lived relatively well, but farming as tenants on the Gennis Company lands in the eastern Arkansas Delta now plunged them into misery. John could barely feed his extended family, and all around him he saw conditions more onerous than anything he had ever known before. However, as Handcox tells in this part of his narrative, he still maintained a sense of independence and refused to follow the dictates of whites when he thought they had gone too far.[21]

People was starvin' to death workin'. So many of them didn't get out of debt before they was right back in debt, more. It all depends on the year, what kind of crop they raised. If you had a bad year and you didn't make much, you didn't get out of debt. Where I was born and raised in Brinkley, just about all of the people owned their own little houses and farmed their own piece.

When we moved onto the plantation, we lived in a sharecropper house. The houses there you could lay in your bed and count all the stars, and you could look down through the floor and count your chickens! You might think that's a joke, but it's not. The floor cracks were so open you could count the chickens under the house.

My house I was living in at that time, I could walk under it. It was built for water, and water come up under it. It was on a hill and then it had 'bout five foot blocks up under it, wooden blocks. They cut some cypress blocks, and cypress won't rot so fast. They wouldn't rot enough for you to hardly notice in twenty years. They built them [houses] out of green lumber, and when green lumber shrinks, it draws up and you got a crack probably as big as you can see two fingers down there. You could see houses with old pieces of rags and paper shucked in the cracks to keep the wind out. But in the cracks when it got cold, we take card board boxes and lay 'em 'bout two deep on the floor and put somethin' over 'em to hold 'em down. We had one window to a room, wasn't too plentiful, with 12 inch glasses or so. If you had two windows to a room, you had a classy house! Windows was better than boarded up, because the wind wouldn' come through the glass. See, we didn't have big glass. We had windows with say about six panes, with partitions, about 12 inches of glass or somethin' like that.

That's the only time I lived in a house with a fireplace in it. I never liked a fireplace. I've seen people when it got cold near that fire, and when the winter's over, their legs peel off just like they're burnt. That fire would be done cook their legs! The next year I bought me a heater and some pipe and put this here pipe up, so the smoke would go up the chimney and heat. With a heater, you could be warm from the front all the way 'round, not just facing it.

When you was out there on them big farms, you never got no [news]paper unless you went to town on Saturday or something. You didn't know what was going on. It was before radio in the rural areas. The first radio I seen was in the fall of '35, a white fellow bought one and asked a bunch of us over to watch it: He had a windmill with a belt on it chargin' his battery. That's the way it was mostly, when I went on those farms.

The foreman, riding boss, whatever you want to call him, he had I think 'round three thousand acres he was ridin' around. We didn't see him much. One time I says "Mr. Hill, how come you don't come down and see us no time?" He say, "Oh hell, ya'll know how to farm." And so we never did have no trouble. We didn't see him 'till just about time we started pickin' cotton, maybe four or five times a year is all.

Pickin' usually starts somewhere in the latter part of September, and from then on until it's gathered. Some of 'em had cotton even after Christmas on those big planta-tions. It all depends on how much they had to harvest. They pull the cotton when it gets soft. And then sometimes after the frost fell the balls would open quicker. Sometimes the cotton would bloom late. You look for frost usually in the latter part of October. That frost [usually] would kill the leaves and burrs, and the cotton would open like that. But if the weather got cold or wet to where they couldn't harvest or couldn't pick it, then they would just go there and rake 'em off, just pull 'em off and put 'em in a sack and then carry 'em to the house. When you pull it in the rough, they'd call it, you get all the bolls and everything. Then the family could separate the lint and seeds and burrs. How long you would work then would depend on how quick you needed to get it done.

I never did do that, though I've seen it did. After we went down in the bottom we would hire some help to gather the crop sometime. In 1925, we had a pretty green crop, and it made good. I imagine some of it made three bails to an acre. When you make a bail and a half to an acre, that's a good crop. I picked five bails of cotton off of 12 rows. The cotton I planted they called it half and half: You plant 13–14 pounds, you get 500 and some pound bail of cotton off of that. Long staple cotton you had to put about 18 pounds to get a 500 some pound bail, and it's much different.

But we didn't live on that big farm but one year. In '26, after I made a crop and settled up, here come the top guy, they were going to change the plan and they wanted a third of the cotton, from a fourth to a third, and they wanted so much an acre for corn. I was the last one they'd come to. I said, "No, I can't, I won't do it. When I'm trading at your prices and ginin' at your gin, you're puttin' your hand too far in the pile then. Nope."

After he left, the foreman tried to make a bargain with me, by giving my corn land free, taking a third of the cotton. I said "Uh, uh, not mine. You just write me off your list, I won't do that." He tried to show me the place where the company was losing money and all that. I said, "Well, I can't help it. You can lose money. I won't do that. You want to take a third of that, you are sticking your hand too deep in the pile already when you takin' a fourth of it. And 'specially if I have to trade at your stoe, pay your prices, and take your prices for what you give for the cotton. No, not me."

And so I moved offa that place and went to another place and found work, about two miles from there, toward Forest City. And I rented 150 acres of land. Because I had the mules, the stock and the plows and everything to tend it with… We had the privilege to get up and move if we wanted, but on some farms, if you moved on there, you'd have to slip away. You couldn't just move off because they would find you and ca'y you back there, so they tell me. I didn't never live on one of those places [but] I met with a few of those people that lived on places like that and had to run away.

Here is what they would do if you lived on a place like that. They would claim you owed 'em so much, you see. I say 98 percent of the people didn't know what they owed or didn't owe, they just went and got what they let 'em have, and they never did get out of debt. In 1928 I farmed right across a fence row from a man, his son was as old as I was, and he hadn't been out of debt. The majority of people sharecroppin' was in that category. They didn't know how much they owe, a lot of em hadn't even heard of no itemized account, didn't know what it was. I think that if you didn't grow up on the big plantation you had a little more school.

Only buying I did from a commissary store was first year we moved to the bottom. We had to get some food. I think we got a little hay and corn and stuff like that from the landlord's commissary. No one knew anything about bills. They just go to the commissary. When I went there, I said, "I want a bill for this." I saved my bills.

I think the first time they ever got a statement or what, was when I went down there. I tried to keep my eye on things. I knew something was wrong, and so I just didn't let them get by with it. One time the bookkeeper made a mistake and I told him, I say, "you wrong." He went over it and just politely said, "here, you figure it out." I said, "there, your mistake is right there." I showed him where. "You right," he said. You know, a lot of people they just take it, and never look at it or nothin' else, never try, and if they wrong they wouldn't' tell 'em its wrong.

But I would. I don't know, I guess I was lucky I didn't get put in the river for that. I asked for an itemized account. The boss never did say nothin' to me concerning it, so I guess they just let it slip by or somethin.'

Lots of places you couldn't have a cow. They'd want you to come to the commissary. If you had a cow, you wouldn't have to get butter and milk from the commissary. And they wanted you to put everything in cotton. King Cotton was the financial part of the farming, you know. That [cotton] was about the only thing sold by the poor people. Lot of 'em I 'magine never did raise no corn because they didn't have nothin' to feed it to. The only thing they'd do is make meal or grits out of it. Lots of those plantations had gristmills. People preferred corn from the mill, say it taste better. It had a flavor, you know.

But I had mules and everything, with a little corn land. I had a crop of 12 rows, and my mother had a crop, too. I planted mine with some seeds I had. I was going to buy me an automobile, a Ford, and they wouldn't settle with me at the cotton gin. The foreman at the cotton gin said, "How come you got all of the crop, and your mother has all of the debt? I can't settle with you until your mother gets out of debt."I said, "OK, Mr. Taylor (his name was Mr. Taylor), I work for a living, and I'll die and go to hell about that. This cotton is the first pick, the best and clean, so I want the price that it is today." It was good I spoke up, because if I hadn't I'd have lost two or three hundred dollars in that deal.

So, after Mother had heard what I did, I went up to get a settlement. The old man, named Moses, he sat down and figured out my account. Cotton prices had gone way down by then. I said, "Oh no, Mr. Taylor said I'd get the price of the day I delivered the cotton." He says, "Go get Jake." I went out and said, "Hey, Mr. Taylor, you'd better go in there and tell that old man something." He saw that I was mad; he was crippled in one leg, and he was struttin'.' But he settled with me for what it was. 'Course, that was the biggest things about livin' on those farms and things, you had to stand up for your rights.

"Everyday seems like murder here"

The Mississippi Delta blues singer Charley Patton wrote "every day seems like murder here," and "I'm gonna leave tomorrow, I know you don't bit more care." [22] John Handcox didn't leave the Delta, but he never adjusted to sharecropping. Like his father, he considered it manifestly unfair that sharecroppers at the end of the year paid up to a half of what they produced and then usually ended up in debt for what they had borrowed at the start of the year. Like his father, John tried not to become ensnared in these arrangements. He saw people who owed money to planters and merchants pay as much as thirty to forty percent interest on their debts or who were simply lied to about what they owed. He saw farm laborers become peons, and those who left plantations without paying their debts arrested and imprisoned. Literate people like John could challenge their exploitation at the company store or the cotton gin, but they could also be thrown off the land, arrested, beaten, or killed merely for questioning a landlord or merchant's book keeping.

Life was already hard in the river bottoms due to this system of human exploitation, but the struggle to survive got much worse when nature intervened. In 1927, John married Ruth Smith, a Baptist several years younger than John whose family had migrated into Arkansas and settled into the same region where John's family lived. Ruth and John went on to have four children together, but as their family obligations increased, their conditions only worsened. During that same year, in April, a wall of water 20 feet high drove three-quarters of a million people from their homes, leaving many of them stranded on rooftops or floating on logs. The monumental Mississippi River flood drowned people and animals and turned plantations into lakes. Down in Mississippi, the National Guard created squalid concentration camps for blacks, forcing them to do unpaid labor while protecting whites in camps in the hill country. "So high the water risin', I been sinking down," Charley Patton wrote in his song, "High Water Everywhere." [23] John lost his crop in 1927 and most of the next crop as well, after more harsh rains in 1928. Then a terrible drought ravaged the crops in 1930. Nature seemed to be intent on driving cotton farmers out. John described the situation: [24]

And then we had a lot of places in low land, the water would rise and take and kill the crop . . . About three years, the farm I was tending had one hundred acres, but then the water destroyed our crop. We had just got through working it, in what we call laying it by, long in the latter part of September. The water come and destroyed it all. We didn't get nothin' but the cotton what was up on top of the hill. But those hills done washed down to the poor land where the cotton wouldn't grow very high; about knee-high was all it would get. Down in those valleys there, I've had cotton over head-high. But if that water come and rise in August or September and all, that would be it when the water would cover it up. If that cotton was opening, that cotton would wash out of the bolls. It would be just as clean as your yard is when that water went back down. And if it wasn't opening, for that water to stay for a couple of weeks it would be dead. That stalk would die. When that water went back down, seldom ever you could find a stack of cotton that would come back.

You could kiss that cotton good-bye!

So that's the way that went, and we lost the largest part of that cotton. I think we gathered some 25 or 30 bails. But I didn't owe but 150 dollars, so I made a clear crop. The way I made that crop that got washed out, I went over to where they gambled on Saturdays and Sundays, and I fixed sandwiches. I had me a truck and I'd go carry and sometimes I'd sell 75 to 80 dollars worth of hamburgers and lunches. I'd start to makin' pop, I'd make it with some poppy, and I got me some flavor I'd order from Carnation. I remember this boy, he was about nineteen, and he open the bottle with his teeth, and the gas from the bottle knocked the cap down his throat. He had to go to the doctor over it.

I bottled my own stuff. I was making home brew too. Well, I made a clear crop of that you might as well say. I would have made plenty money, or what we call plenty money, that year if it don't be for the water.

So it was 10 years I farmed in the delta. I did miss one year on the delta in there because I went and rented a little old place. The land was pretty rich, but it didn't have enough fertile on it. Problem was, we rentin' a small amount of land, and it was more people than it was land. Like it was my brother, he had a wife, and then my other brother, he had a wife and son, and my other brother he just had a wife. All on the same land. We had only two houses at that time. My older brother and I lived together and then my mother and brother next to me, they lived together, and I had two or three sisters wasn't married at that time and they all lived in that one house. My sister what was married, they had a little shack down there that they lived in. We bought a lot of food, sometime we'd buy as much as eight and 10 barrels of flour for the whole bunch. And we didn't do so good.

I never have done but one day work workin' out for somebody else out on the farm. That's the onliest day I ever just hired out to somebody to work. My wife was pregnant, and I thought I'd go out there and make 75 cents to get her something to nourish on, you know. That's the only day. But the terriblest experience I had ever, I think, is the foreman on this plantation that come by and asked me to come over and give him a hand . . . the next day. Went over, got there just about good sunrise. And he wasn't there, so I just waited until he come.

He come out, well, "Why ain't you in the field?" I says, "Nobody here told me nothing about what to do." He says, "well, I'm going to have to cut you." I say, "Cut me what, what you talkin' about cuttin' me?" "I'll cut your pay." "From 75 cents? Cut that?" I say, "It's already cut."

Yeah, 75 cents a day for workin'. I just jumped back on my mule. I had a mule, jumped back on him – good-bye. Went on back, I get the mule and went fishing. 75 cents a day and he was goin' to cut that!

It was about 10 years that I worked in the delta, from the first crop I made in the rich land in '25 to the last crop I made in '35. Ten years in the delta farming, where the land was rich, but you didn't make enough food to make a living. I was married in '27, and my first child [of four] was born in 1928. Two people couldn't make enough to feed four kids, when the landlord owned the land.

Angry at the abuses of the plantation system, he refused to move further down the agricultural ladder. He got angry and got going, as he would so many other times in his life.

*   *   *

By 1935, John's youthful years of relative independence were long gone, and his decade of working as a tenant and sharecropper on big plantation lands in St. Francis County had yielded little but basic survival. By 1935 he and Ruth had three children, John Jr. (1929), Maggie (1932), Vinnia (1934). A fourth child, Ruth, would be born in 1936. They also had John's mother and an extended family living with or near them, all in difficult conditions.[25] He had tried to maintain the deal for tenants that he grew up with in which the landlord took a fourth of the cotton and a third of the corn. But the cotton economy's downward cycle and the planter capitalists' monopoly over land, credit, and marketing crushed John's optimism and his enterprise. John's matter-of-fact way of telling his story understates the true chaos that he and his family endured, but he would later find a powerful way of expressing his experiences and observations in poems and songs. Labor songster Woody Guthrie later wrote, at the bottom of his hand-written first version of "This Land is Your Land," that "all you can write is what you see." And that's what John began to do.

After the failed harvest in the fall of 1935, John began protesting life's injustices in rhyming verse in poems and songs written under the pen name of John

Henry and published on flyers and in the newspaper of the STFU. He wrote one of his earliest published poems after observing the Memphis Cotton Carnival, which each spring celebrated the same cash crop of white gold that had fueled slavery and white supremacy across the South.

KING COTTON

The planters celebrated King Cotton in Memphis, May fifteen,
It was the largest gathering you most ever seen.
People came from far and near—to celebrate King Cotton,
Whom the planters love so dear.
Thousands of flags were hung in the street,
But they left thousands of sharecroppers on their farms with nothing to eat.
Why do they celebrate Cotton? Here, I'll make it clear,
Because they cheat, beat and take it away from labor every year.
Cotton is King, and will always be,
Until labor in the South is set free.
The money spent for decorations and flags,
Would sure have helped poor sharecroppers who are hungry and in rags.
Oh! King Cotton, today you have millions of slaves,
And have caused many poor workers to be in lonesome graves.
When Cotton is King of any nation,
It means wealth to the planter—to the laborer starvation.[26]

In verses such as this, Handcox would sharply define the crisis faced by tenant farmers and sharecroppers as a class question: why were those who produced the earth's wealth starving and "raggedy"? All across America, "raggedy" workers began joining together to fight the horrific conditions they suffered during the Great Depression. In the South, these conditions would finally cause whites and blacks to join together, in one of the most improbable places and one of the most improbable union movements in American history.

John called the 1930s "eye-openin' time."[27]

CHAPTER 3

The Planter and the Sharecropper: The Southern Tenant Farmers' Union

I wrote about the way the poor were being treated by the rich. I help to organize them so we all could get out of the ditches.

—John Handcox[1]

Hopeless circumstances in cotton country—debt peonage, floods, drought, and, finally, the Great Depression—caused many of King Cotton's victims to despair, turn to drink, or in other ways abandon their families. The economic crisis caused John Handcox, on the other hand, to find new meaning to his life. When he quit sharecropping at the end of 1935, he began to write. He also found a newspaper in which to publish, and most importantly, a movement to join. John's grandfather's stories of slavery, the music he learned in church, and the poetry he read by Paul Laurence Dunbar all had prepared him to join "the revolt of the sharecroppers," a phrase that rang through the labor reform agenda of the mid-1930s. In school, he had written songs and poems to amuse, but now he would use them to promote a startling historic departure, in which black and white tenants, both sharecroppers and renters, and wage laborers joined together in a union.

In one of his poems, "Landlord, what in the Heaven is the matter with you?," written in the spring of 1936, John described the plight of agricultural workers in cotton counry during the Great Depression and the early New Deal:

In nineteen thirty-three when we plowed up cotton,
Some of that money your labor have never gotten.
You pledged the government your labor you would pay;
You put it in your pocket and you went your way.

And in the AAA contract in nineteen and thirty-four
You chiseled your labor outa some more.
And in nineteen and thirty-five
The parity money your labor you deprived.
And in the AA in nineteen and thirty-six
You all are trying to fix.
We hope that it'll be so:
You'll get yours and no more.
Your labor you've always robbed.
Because they want their rights, you want them mobbed.
You disfranchise us and won't let us vote,
When we have all the load to tote.
Your labor never have had anything to do with what you join,
Neither broken into your meetings or your church or barn.
From none of your meeting by your labor have you ever been hailed,
Shot in the back, beaten with axe handles, or put in jail.
you are not honest enough to do right,
Your labor never shot in your homes neither throwed dynamite.
Now Arkansas would be a fine place to live you bet,
If the sod didn't have such a bad set.
Landlord, what in the heaven is the matter with you?
What have your labor ever done to you?
Upon their backs you ride,
Don't you think that your labor never gets tired?

John Handcox's fate would depend on the success or failure of a social movement. His memories, however, do not explain how and why this movement occurred. Much of this chapter fills in that void in his oral history, taking us into the context and the evnts that spurred the improbable rise of the Southern Tenant Farmers' Union (STFU).

The Richest Lands, the Poorest People

The revolt of the sharecroppers took place in the context of terrible conditions building up for over a decade—affecting not only agricultural workers, but also workers in textile, mining, timbering, and other so-called "sick" extractive industries. What was "wrong" with planters was the same thing that was wrong with other employers: throughout the 1920s, capitalists had built their fortunes based on low wages and no unions, impoverishing a working class that could not buy the goods it produced. In the "roaring twenties" Republican presidents supported the union-busting "American Plan" of big business, by which employers used company thugs, police, and vigilantes to attack labor organizers. Many Americans felt that something was fundamentally wrong with this picture.

Wall Street's stock market collapse of 1929 and the ensuing national depression showed that something else was wrong as well. Amidst the closing of banks, businesses, factories, schools, city bankruptcies, home foreclosures and evictions, mass unemployment, malnutrition, and actual starvation, there seemed to be no voice of reason among the rich. A few Wall Street bankers did jump out of windows, but most of the 1 percent that owned nearly 60 percent of the country's wealth simply enhanced their profits by buying up more assets and laying off more workers, while speeding up the work of those who remained. Treasury Secretary Andrew Mellon, one of the wealthiest bankers in America, escaped federal income taxes altogether, while the president of the National Association of Manufacturers blamed the unemployed for the depression, claiming they "don't want to work." Republican President Herbert Hoover claimed hoboes were "better fed than they have ever been."[2]

Alabama sharecropper organizer Ned Cobb said Hoover "just sat down on us" (blacks) while the President's conservatism played well to southern whites who wanted to "keep the dollar out of the nigger's hands." However, many workers turned against America's corporate elite. Once regarded as folk heroes in the mass media and Hollywood, wealthy business owners now looked to many working people like common criminals. Woody Guthrie popularized this sentiment when he sang, "some will rob you with a six-gun, and some with a fountain pen."[3] Yet, even in the supposedly conservative agricultural hinterlands spreading from Arkansas to Oklahoma and Nebraska, remnants of a previous era of "grassroots socialism" still existed.[4] In the Great Depression, radicalism sprouted once again. Members of the Socialist Party (SP) and the Communist Party (CP), which had begun as a splinter of the SP, as well as Christian Socialists, evangelicals, and even some conservative farmers went into revolt.[5] The president of the National Farmers' Union told a Congressional committee in 1933 that "the biggest and finest crop of revolutionaries you ever saw is sprouting over this country right now."[6]

Victims of the depression increasingly took matters into their own hands. The unemployed and hungry marched in urban centers, even in Deep South cities like Birmingham, Alabama, while rent strikers blockaded eviction proceedings. World War I veterans encamped in the nation's capital demanding early payment of their military bonuses to tide them through a period of mass unemployment. Shamefully, federal troops responded to their protests by beating, tear gassing, and killing people, while police likewise shot and beat demonstrators in Detroit, Chicago, New York, and elsewhere.[7] In the South, National Guard troops in 1929 killed striking textile workers in Marion, and police murdered labor singer and mother of five Ella May Wiggins, in Gastonia, North Carolina. At Camp Hill, Alabama, in 1931, police raided a meeting of black sharecroppers; a year later, authorities killed and imprisoned others in nearby Reeltown for organizing an agricultural workers' union. Ned Cobb went to prison for 12 years for defending himself. Atlanta authorities arrested black Communist organizer Angelo Herndon and sentenced him to 20 years at hard labor on a chain gang, merely for passing out leaflets.[8]

Repression of labor organizing happened almost everywhere, but it did not fill people's empty stomachs. Even in the isolated eastern Arkansas plantation districts where John lived, increasingly desperate people demanded government action. Poll taxes and Jim Crow laws disenfranchised most southern blacks and many poorer whites, but the majority of southerners who could vote helped to elect Democrat Franklin Roosevelt, the one rich man who seemed to care, as President in 1932. Roosevelt experimented with programs to restart the banks, rebuild the nation's infrastructure, create jobs, increase wages and incomes, and provide relief to home owners whose property values had collapsed.

Tragically, however, the administration's Agricultural Adjustment Administration (AAA), enacted in 1933 as part of Roosevelt's "first" New Deal, made things worse for agricultural workers. Some economists held that the price of crops had dropped because farmers had produced "too much." To drive prices up, the AAA sought to create scarcity by paying millions to farmers to plow under ten million acres of cotton, and to slaughter pigs, pour milk down sewers, and burn food crops. Economic historian Broadus Mitchell called this the "imbecility, to which the depression had brought the nation's economy," and Socialist Party leader Norman Thomas called it "an illustration of the folly of the capitalist system." H. L. Mitchell, who would help to create the STFU, asked, "Was there ever a time when avowal of production for use, rather than for private profit, was more appropriate?"[9]

If people were raggedy, hungry, and homeless, John Handcox and others asked, how could there be *too much* cotton and *too much* food? Many sharecroppers and tenants in the Delta saw their problem not as one of overproduction, but of under-consumption by the people, and greed and disproportionate power in the hands of plantation capitalists. Federal regulations required planters to share subsidies with tenants. Instead, they threw tenants off the land and kept the subsidies for themselves, or let tenants stay but coerced or hoodwinked them into signing waivers that gave away their share of the subsidy and further inflated their debts. Landlords administering the local AAA boards looked the other way. The AAA finance director, one of the country's largest cotton planters, ran a payment plan directly benefiting his own wealth. Arkansas' Joseph Robinson, majority leader of the US Senate and one of the most powerful Democrats in Congress—himself a large plantation owner—threatened to hold up all New Deal legislation if anyone interfered. By 1934, the world's richest lands in Arkansas and the Mississippi River delta region now contained some of its poorest people. A survey that year by University of Tennessee Medical School Professor William Amberson in Memphis found that farm workers in the most fertile lands of the lower Mississippi Delta had the lowest incomes in the country—averaging a star-vation wage of about ten cents per day.[10]

This area included St. Francis County, where John lived, and nearby Crittenden County, where African Americans composed 70 to 80 percent of the tenants and sharecroppers. Tenant and sharecropping families in eastern Arkansas averaged about $262 a year in income, and each year the great majority of them ended up further in debt. Eating (at best) salt pork, corn bread, and molasses, or just boiling mustard greens, children grew up malnourished and suffered pel-lagra, their skin lesions and ill health caused by a lack of vitamins obtained in vegetables and fruit; and for lack of screens and plumbing, children died from malaria and dysentery. No images brought Depression hardships into clearer focus than the era's stark photographs of the gnarled hands, care-worn faces, and disheveled bodies of both black and white sharecroppers.[11]

With the AAA subsidies, things got even worse, as planters took the money and forced an estimated 900,000 Delta agricultural workers off the land by 1936. The AAA investigated illegal evictions, but did little to stop them. When Gardner Jackson and other liberal New Deal staff members in Washington, D.C., pro-tested the fraud, the Secretary of Agriculture Henry Wallace fired them. The suppression of dissenting voices was worse in the Arkansas delta. "The land-owner in the rich plantation country wants a man who can be subjected to his will by means of fear and intimidation," wrote Erskine Caldwell. Planters and the "small town rich," as journalist Ralph McGill called them, teamed up with bankers, cotton brokers, and mass media publishers and politicians throughout the region. The Cotton Exchange and the National Cotton Council in Memphis coordinated their cotton plantation empire. With so many vested interests on the side of King Cotton, few thought that anyone could change the relationship of workers to landlords, or blacks to whites.[12]

The Sharecroppers' Revolt

In this context, it came as a big surprise when fierce resistance to King Cotton broke out among the rural working poor. Their revolt proved especially strong in the majority-black districts of the eastern Arkansas Delta, where the largest number of evictions occurred and where John Handcox and his extended family lived. Their fate would, improbably, become tied to the actions of a few dedicated white Socialist Party members. Nearby, in the little town of Tyronza, lived Clay East, a gas station owner, and Henry Leland (H. L.) Mitchell, a dry cleaner. These two white small-town merchants had been avidly reading Socialist publications and identified with the militant and revolutionary politics gestating in the depres-sion era. East, elected as constable of the town, carried a gun and some authority. Mitchell, who grew up working in the fields of West Tennessee as a youth, had followed his parents to Arkansas when his father tried his hand as a barber. In the wake of the stock market crash Mitchell and East believed capitalism no longer served the needs of humankind.[13] They organized a tiny chapter of the Socialist Party in 1931, and its membership leapt to 2,000 by 1933 after a visit by SP leader and presidential candidate Norman Thomas. On another visit, speaking to 500 people at an outdoor meeting on February 16, 1934, Thomas called for the government to take over plantations and distribute them to producers, much as freed slaves had demanded after emancipation. Thomas also suggested a more practical idea: sharecroppers needed to organize a union to represent their interests.[14]

Small town merchants Mitchell and East knew nothing about how to organize trade unions, but plantation owner Hiram Norcross touched off a movement to do just that. In January of 1934, he evicted about two dozen families from his 5,000-acre plantation. The AAA had made it more profitable to take payments not to grow crops and dispense with the expense of advancing funds to sharecroppers. Other landlords also refused to sign annual contracts with their sharecroppers, leaving increasing numbers of now landless people with no means of subsistence. Starvation and distress spread throughout eastern Arkansas. In response to this roiling crisis, Mitchell and East organized a meeting of 11 white and 7 black men on July 13 at a schoolhouse called Sunnyside, in Poinsett County. This group took up the challenge of organizing sharecroppers, tenant farmers, and wage laborers into one unit. Some called for a secret organization with separate units for whites and blacks as a way to avoid planter reprisals. But, according to Mitchell, Isaac Shaw, a black survivor of the Elaine massacre, argued forcefully for a broader form of unity:

> We colored can't organize without you . . . and you white folks can't organize without us . . . For a long time now the white folks and the colored folks have been fighting each other and both of us has been getting whipped all the time. We don't have nothing against one another but we got plenty against the landlord. The same chain that holds my people holds your people too. If we're chained together on the outside we ought to stay chained together in the union. It won't do no good for us to divide because that's where the trouble has been all the time

Mitchell provided the only eye-witness account, and he may have partly embellished this foundational story with his own desire for a coalition between whites and blacks. In any case, we know for sure that Sunnyside participants decided to operate in the open and to form a single, nonsegregated union. They elected white sharecropper Alvin Nunally as the chairman and black minister C. H. Smith as the vice-chairman, and incorporated the STFU with the State of Arkansas on July 26, 1934.[15] East and Mitchell sent out a "call" for help, and SP activists far and wide responded. Ward Rogers, Claude Williams, and particularly Howard Kester—all of them white Social Gospel preachers—would play key roles in building the union. Born in 1904, the same year as John Handcox, Kester's grandparents had migrated to the South after the Civil War and his father became a successful merchant in Martinsville, Virginia. His business collapsed, and they moved to Beckley, West Virginia, where Howard witnessed poverty and racial and class oppression. This college-educated, middle class, religious, and Socialist white man during the depression years increasingly became a bold advocate of racial equality and working-class emancipation and a key organizer for the STFU.[16]

But the support of white Socialists would have meant little without the clear involvement of sharecroppers, tenant farmers, and day laborers. According to Southern poet John Beecher, workers in the cotton country had come to realize that "white men and black were getting beat with the same stick."[17] This realization would help to create one of the most remarkable experiments in interracial unionism in American history.

Although East and Mitchell thought they saw the basis for a revolutionary movement, STFU members primarily wanted to achieve a viable standard of living and to reduce the exploitation of the landlords, and knew little if anything about socialism.[18] Nonetheless, as historian Jarod Roll shows, agricultural workers who demanded rights where none existed could be a powerful force for social change and produce a radical critique of the existing order.[19] The sharecropper revolt emerged in the midst of disruptive worker upsurges and radicalism that surged across America in 1934. Congress had enacted the New Deal's National Industrial Recovery Act (NIRA), as a companion to the AAA. Section 7(a) of the NIRA guaranteed workers the right to organize unions. It had few enforcement powers and did not apply to agricultural or domestic workers, yet the mere fact that the federal government openly supported union rights set off an avalanche of organizing.

In 1934, nearly 400,000 textile workers went on a general strike, most of them in the South (the strike ultimately failed and numerous workers were killed). General strikes also shut down San Francisco and Minneapolis and workers in various other places gained union contracts through direct action. East and Mitchell and other SP members in the South avidly read about all this in their Socialist publications. At nearby Commonwealth College, in Mena, Arkansas, students and teachers gave picket line and organizing support to coal miners, sharecroppers, and others forming unions. Communists and many Socialists as well brandished the slogan "Negro and White, Unite and Fight." Throughout the 1930s, the CP took up the historic fight against Jim Crow and lynching, starting with the defense of a group of nine young black men in Scottsboro, Alabama, against bogus charges of rape. Communists supported "full equality," including interracial marriage—the advocacy of which could get you killed in the South.[20]

Employers, and especially planters in the Mississippi Delta, had used "the production of difference"—racism—to divide and conquer, often aided and abetted by worker claims to "whiteness" and its privileges.[21] How to join whites and blacks into the same organization under conditions of segregation remained the most difficult question for any southern union. Some examples of how to do this already existed. Following Congressional passage of the NIRA's 7(a) in 1933, the United Mineworkers of America (UMWA) took its guarantee of the right to organize union seriously, and its ranks blossomed in Alabama. With a 60 percent black membership in the Deep South, the UMWA formula of electing whites for top posts as presidents and secretary treasurers, and blacks as vice-presidents and in other secondary offices, provided a means to enable black and white cooperation.[22] STFU members followed this pattern, electing J. R. Butler, an SP member and white former sharecropper, teacher, and sawmill hand (a "hillbilly," he called himself), as the first STFU president, and E. B. McKinney, a follower of Marcus Garvey and a firebrand black preacher, as vice president. They made H. L. Mitchell Secretary and the primary organizer of the union.

Similar to the UMWA, the STFU created a bi-racial union with a majority-black membership, but with white leadership at the top. George Stith, a black STFU activist, explained, "A black man wasn't recognized enough to get into the places where he needed to go, even if he had enough education . . . So a black person as president could not have been too successful in getting a lot of outside help." Stith explained that some plantations were almost all black and others all white, and each local reflected that racial composition. Blacks clearly were the majority of union members, but "we decided," said Stith, "and it was partly my decision along with others, blacks and whites, that if a black man got to be president it might divide us. So we decided, well at least we'll put him in second spot, make him vice-president."[23]

Butler remarked that many blacks felt comfortable with this white leadership model, because "if they had a meeting with just black people there, they wouldn't have any protection whatever, but a few white people might have protective influence"[24] Organizers also adapted pragmatically to the reality that white workers almost everywhere typically looked for clear signs of white leadership before they would join a union.[25] Using the UMWA formula for governance, in the summer and fall of 1934 the STFU held numerous interracial meetings and marches, establishing a new kind of movement few had ever dreamed of in the heart of the planter's domain.[26] According to Butler, in the eyes of plantation owners, "The whites were niggers too. There was no difference, and some of 'em were beginning to see that there was no difference. Of course, there was still a lot of prejudice among white people in those days, but hard times makes peculiar bedfellows sometimes, and some of them were beginning to get their eyes open" The union created an executive council to coordinate activities, and people at the local level began to organize STFU chapters. The idea of unionism quickly spread.[27]

Planters immediately attacked the STFU as a "nigger union." Said Stith: they "tried to separate people by class, and they tried to do it by race. Whichever was best to use, they used it. It worked on a lot of people, and some people it just didn't work on."[28] If race-baiting and racial division did not always work, planters thought that violence certainly would. Throughout the next year, planters, riding bosses, and local sheriffs waylaid union supporters on the back roads, beating, threatening, and shooting them. Planters evicted suspected union supporters from their shacks and threatened to revoke their credit. In Tyronza, white church women organized a boycott of Mitchell and East that forced them to close their businesses and leave for Memphis, where they set up STFU headquarters at 2527 Broad Street.

In the midst of an accelerating campaign of racial intimidation and violence, the STFU won its first significant victory. In August, 1934, black preacher and sharecropper C. H. Smith, one of the founders of the union at Sunnyside, along with white Socialist minister Ward Rogers, led a meeting to protest evictions in Crittenden County. Two days later, a mob dragged Smith out of a car and into the woods, severely beating him. Authorities then threw him in jail in Marion, and unionist feared he would be imprisoned indefinitely or lynched. But a white Arkansas attorney named C. T. Carpenter took the union's side, and, on his advice, 40 to 50 white union members filled the courtroom when Smith went before a judge. They carried long walking sticks into the courtroom to defend themselves in case anyone tried to stop them.[29]

This surprising show of determined white support for a jailed black minister caused the judge to drop the charges. At a union rally after his release, Smith declared to an interracial crowd his willingness to bear the union "cross" (in fact he never fully recovered from his injuries). The power of numbers to affect the judicial system alerted unionists to the importance of labor solidarity. Whites would have to stand up for the rights of blacks, for if they did not, they could not expect blacks, the majority of sharecroppers and tenants in the region, to stand up for them; interracial solidarity provided strength rather than a weakness.[30] In another incident, blacks faced down vigilantes who invaded a union meeting in their church, proving they could organize without getting massacred. Such small victories over racism and anti-union terror spurred rapid expansion of union membership.[31] In some cases, the union posted armed guards outside of meeting places; Stith heard unionists comment to the effect that, "'We're not gonna let them do us like they did in Elaine, just come and kill us out. So we gon' be prepared.'" Union members made their way to meetings in small numbers to avoid detection, and the union advised them "if they wanted to sing, that was alright, but they should keep their voices low," recalled Mitchell.[32]

As union members gained confidence, however, they raised their voices, increasingly animating the union with group singing and interracial mass meetings and taking first steps toward converting a segregationist labor movement in the South into an activist and egalitarian one. The STFU took on the appeal of an evangelical movement. "When they first started talking about a union, I thought it was a new church," one female member of the union remarked. And in a sense, it was.[33] To avoid attacks on them outside of the view of the public, unionists took to holding meetings outdoors, with leaders preaching and members singing. "Jesus is my captain," an old camp meeting hymn, became "the union is my leader." A. B. Brookins, a black preacher from Marked Tree in eastern Arkansas, became chaplain of the union and unified members by teaching them to sing in unison, as his congregants sang in church. He taught them "We Shall Not Be Moved" and turned "Climbing Jacob's Ladder" into "We are building a strong union." In November, 1934, police struck back. They arrested Brookins and other union leaders in Cross County and imprisoned them for 40 days.[34]

Defying planter violence, the STFU became a preaching and singing movement. STFU member J. W. Washington recounted a local meeting that began with "I shall not be moved." Long used by the United Mine Workers union and sometimes sung as "I shall not be moved" in country music, this song seems to have first originated in the black church. Washington recalled how preachers in this meeting echoed Moses in calling people to the Promised Land, and urged workers to be like the Good Samaritan by helping a robbed and wounded man by the side of the road. As one preacher after the next condemned the planters for their greed, euphoria swept the room.[35] Often sung at the beginning or end of a meeting, "We Shall Not Be Moved," became the theme song of the STFU and the power of preaching and singing multiplied the power of small bands of workers. In a number of instances, white union members responded to anti-union terrorism by marching through plantations and small towns, spreading out to make their numbers look more impressive, and singing:

> We shall not, we shall not be moved,
> We shall not, we shall not be moved.
> Like a tree that's standing by the water,
> We shall not be moved.

Congregational singing had long provided a powerful vehicle for getting people together in the black church, and it did so in both the STFU and in the civil rights movement of a later era.[36] Black oral traditions played a special role in the STFU, as preachers of the social gospel of economic and social justice provided a narrative of inspiration, while black spirituals and freedom songs provided powerful melodies and a call-and-response structure that begged for collaboration. As a song leader called out a few words to give substance to each verse, other singers responded and built the song to an emotional peak. Rhythmic meters, percussive hand clapping, and foot stomping brought workers together in unison.[37] Blacks and whites came from markedly different religious styles and traditions, yet many of them participated in Pentecostal and other grassroots religious movements in eastern Arkansas and Southeast Missouri, where the STFU built its base from 1934 to 1937. They met separately in church and sang and preached differently, but it was not difficult for whites to adapt black religious and song traditions into a movement. Music and religion helped agricultural workers to cross the barriers of "black" and "white" racial designations.

Agricultural workers trying to shield themselves from planter repression often met in secret and adapted signals and signs from the Masons to identify each other. Recognizing a sign from a fellow unionist, a member would offer his or her hand, extend the full length of an arm with the thumb in the palm, and say "I am for a worker's world." A dialogue people used to identify each other, based on the union insignia, was this one: "The plow and hoe that you see shows the tools which we use in making the riches for the world, but we do not share in the happiness derived from it." According to the union book of rituals, the STFU stood for "a band of workers united together, they realize that they have been robbed of the proceed of their labor and that has left him, his wife and children to perhish." Initiation rituals sometimes featured a member with his or her hands tied behind their back, pledging not to betray any fellow union member to the planters. The union pamphlet, "The Disinhereted Speak," also pointed out the importance of "interracial tolerance," saying that "for the first time, an important Southern organization has drawn no color lines in its membership requirements and activities."[38]

It seemed unbelievable to many observers that whites, some of them former KKK members, and African Americans, some of them former racial separatists, could join together in the STFU. But they did.

Black and White, Together?

Not surprisingly, though, race relations remained a thorny matter. In plantation areas, blacks constituted 80 to 90 percent of the population, while whites dominated in other areas. "Even though whites and blacks organized together, it was set up on the basis of race," George Stith explained. "It was a community thing. Naturally, the communities were segregated. That's why we had segregated locals, because whites and blacks usually didn't live on the same farm together." Blacks couldn't even travel through some of the northernmost counties in Arkansas, unless accompanied by a white man.[39] Thus, in some communities, the union built separate black and white locals; in others, bi-racial locals. According to one statistic, of 103 locals organized in the next two years by the STFU, 73 were either all white or all black; either whites or blacks dominated most of the remaining 30 locals, where people proved willing to organize bi-racially even if it meant they themselves were in a minority.[40]

Segregation laws and segregated community patterns caused the union to typically use white organizers among whites and black organizers among blacks. White union leaders sometimes glossed over the racism afflicting African Americans and the union's newspaper, the *Sharecropppers' Voice,* eschewed "social equality" in its editorials. But new relationships also emerged. In Marked Tree, whites and blacks established two separate locals, but since a lodge hall in the black community provided the only accessible building large enough to accommodate mass meetings, they soon held their meetings together and more or less merged. Black preachers played a special role in offsetting the reluctance of whites to accept blacks. STFU Vice-president E. B. ("Britt") McKinney rode from place to place, providing both dynamic oratory and common sense preaching that helped to win many skeptical whites over to the union. As a powerful symbol of black leadership, he also travelled to the North to garner financial support.[41] His incessant travel wore him down and later forced him into a hospital for exhaustion. McKinney belonged to a more or less secret underground network of former followers of Marcus Garvery, the Jamaican-born leader of the Universal Negro Improvement Association (UNIA), who in the 1920s recruited the largest mass movement in African-American history. At one point, the UNIA had some 400 members in Arkansas, concentrated in the very majority-black counties that provided the core of membership for the STFU. McKinney, both a farmer and a pastor, serviced 35 or more congregations and combined Black Nationalism, biblical oratory, and union organizing. He gave the STFU an incredible jolt of energy and provided strong black leadership.[42]

Unlike craft unions in the American Federation of Labor (AFL), the STFU did not follow the rules of segregation. Union members did not call black men "boys" and black elders "uncle" or "auntie." STFU leaders pointedly rejected racist terminology by making a practice of using the title of "Mr." or "Mrs." when people addressed each other in meetings, a practice that infuriated racists.[43] Blacks at the local level exercised meaningful leadership, Mitchell concluded. "[I]t is all right for the two races to organize into separate locals so long as they are in the same union and fighting for the same thing."[44] Mitchell wrote to one of the union's white organizers, "There are no 'niggers' and no 'poor white trash' in the Union. We have only Union men in our organization, and whether they are white or black makes no difference."[45] The union's practices of respect meant a great deal to black members of the STFU. Scholar Donald Grubbs points out, "all important action was taken at integrated mass meetings" in a union that was "from half to two--thirds black."[46] He felt the union addressed the South's endemic racial divisions "as well as any realistic observer could expect."[47]

By its very existence, the STFU demonstrated to other unionists that a movement of white and black working folks could join together, and this could potentially unleash powerful forces for change in the South. Breaking the color barrier remained crucial to organizing unions in the mid-1930s in nearby Memphis and many other places.[48] Despite the ever present strictures of legal segregation almost everywhere, most observers understood that the strength of the STFU and of many emerging industrial unions, especially in the South, depended heavily on African American participation. Through the black church and informal community networks, southern blacks had strong traditions of group solidarity and resistance to exploitation going back to slavery. By contrast, most southern whites did not experience those traditions, often proved less literate, and remained more wedded to an evangelical religion that emphasized individual salvation over collective deliverance. Clay East remarked on the difference: "[T]he colored guys back there, if anything, were more solid than the whites. They'd go ahead and sacrifice and get killed or beat up or anything before they'd give up."[49] Black churches provided most of the meeting places for the STFU. George Stith observed that where white sharecroppers and tenants belonged to a church "the higher ups also belonged, and they couldn't get the church to have a meeting. So they had to come to a Negro place"[50] Few "higher ups" existed in small black churches in poverty-stricken eastern Arkansas, and people like John Handcox remained quite ready to criticize anyone who got too high and mighty.

To weld its unwieldy group together, the STFU first organized the preachers, black and white, and they proved crucial to its early success. McKinney, along with Brookins, Stith, Isaac Shaw, F. R. Betton, Henrietta McGee, and many other black unionists were self-ordained preachers.[51] Religious themes remained integral even to the discourse of Handcox, an anomaly because he didn't often go to church.[52] Whites also shared common ground with blacks by their familiarity with a body of Christian hymns and Biblical learning, even if they interpreted the Bible somewhat differently. White Socialist preachers that came to aid the union, particularly Claude Williams, Ward Rogers, and Howard Kester proved invaluable, while a small number of "jackleg" white preachers also participated in locals. Religious fervor marked STFU gatherings so often that participants weren't always sure if they were attending a religious revival or a union meeting.

Black women like Henrietta McGee also played a powerful role in the union. They "were very active and made a lot of the decisions. Women decided to do things that men felt they couldn't do," Stith explained. In one local near Cotton Plant, planters threatened to kill black men who stood for the union, so black women took the lead and held all the positions as officers. Black women, afflicted by sexual attacks by white men and other atrocities rooted in the South's history of slavery and segregation, had every reason to be timid and quiet. Instead, they were often bold and militant. Stith said "women look like always were apt to move out. They would walk up and say to the plantation owner, look, this is what I ain't gonna do."[53] McGee, a widow and mother of nine children, served as a powerful speaker in the union and at fund-raising events to support the union held in the North. White women played an important role as well. Evelyn Smith, a young white Socialist Party member from New Orleans, became the crusading secretary for the union. Myrtle Lawrence, a desperately poor but tough white woman from the hill country near where John was raised, became a strong advocate for black civil rights and women's rights in the union.[54]

Crucially, Butler said, "we considered the whole family members of the union."[55] Family participation provided the STFU with a special strength, especially compared to many other unions where only the breadwinner, usually a male, belonged. Said Stith, "[W]here there was a man and his wife involved, she was a member too. She had a voice when it come down to talking or voting"[56]

"Acts of Tyranny and Terror"

Its diversity strengthened union ranks enormously and the STFU got off to an auspicious start in the summer and fall of 1934. As word spread and more people joined, however, the planters accelerated their terror. The white Social Gospel minister Howard Kester, who had investigated the gruesome torture and lynching of African American Claude Neal in Florida, came to Arkansas from his home in Nashville. He wrote up the anti-union terrorism, first in a report titled "Acts of Tyranny and Terror" and later in a pamphlet titled "Revolt Among the Sharecroppers." He recounted instances in which planters and their henchmen padlocked black churches and schools or stuffed them with hay so no one could meet; evicted tenants and sharecroppers and threatened others who might join the union; and beat people with clubs, axe handles, and leather straps. As word spread of planters purchasing machine guns, some sharecroppers openly carried a shotgun with them for protection.[57]

Mobs targeted all union organizers or sympathizers. In January, 1935, authorities arrested the white Socialist preacher Ward Rogers for giving a speech in Marked Tree, a bastion of repression in eastern Arkansas, where authorities sentenced him to six months in prison for "anarchy." The city's mayor vowed that only such measures could protect "white supremacy, Christianity, the American flag and the sanctity of home and family ties." He drew upon a popular book published in 1934, Elizabeth Dilling's *The Red Nework: A 'Who's who' and Handbook of Radicalism for Pariots,* which fanned the flames of racism and anti-communism for years to come. In another incident, police held Rogers and other organizers in a jail flooded with sewage and threatened them with lynching. Mobs attacked white organizers Robert Reid and Lucien Koch from Commonwealth College. A mob in Marked Tree tried to lynch Rev. Brookins and riddled his home with bullets in the night, forcing him, at age 70, to flee to Memphis for his life. Mobs threatened the union's white attorney at his home; forced out John Allen, black secretary of the union at the Twist plantation, who traveled through the woods and swamps by night to escape to Memphis; severed the ear from the head of a black woman; shot up black churches and various homes; and terrorized the family of Rev. McKinney, shooting into his home and wounding several people huddled there.[58] Norman Thomas, who came to the plantation districts to publicize these attacks, was nearly beaten by a mob at a March, 1935 meeting in Birdsong, also in eastern Arkansas.[59]

Planters, the police, and the KKK worked together in this Mississippi River Delta region where the extended Handcox family resided. The white preacher Ward Rogers saw it as a coordinated class war, with all of the military power on one side. On a speaking trip to raise funds for the union in Boston, he wrote to Kester, "I have received no word from Arkansas in a week now, how many are dead or wounded? Shall I return immediately to preach their funerals?"[60] Planters in some places set up set the equivalent of company unions, designed to trap agricultural workers who wanted to organize into groups controlled by the planters.[61] The union had virtually no funds, so that organizers sometimes had to hitchhike to meetings, exposing themselves to lynching parties. Organizers lacked not only vehicles but money for stamps and paper to report on their work. Lawmen rounded up African American members in particular, charged them with "vagrancy," and put them to work on the dreaded county farms of Arkansas, a variation of the old convict lease system that the courts had ruled illegal.[62]

The union's success or failure began to take on national significance as a struggle for the right to exercise Constitutional First Amendment freedoms to speak and organize. The struggle to organize unions in Harlan County, Kentucky, where mine owners and company thugs constituted a law unto themselves, took on similar national significance. Union organizing in the 1930s represented a battle to uphold quintessential rights that presumably every American had a stake in defending. Mitchell and East, Kester, McKinney, and others went to Washington and New York to appeal for media publicity, and union allies like Gardner Jackson, and above all Norman Thomas, continually called on the federal government to stop violations of civil liberties occurring in the South.[63] Much as southern civil rights activists did thirty-some years later, Mitchell, as secretary of the union, called for federal intervention and attention by northern religious leaders and the mass media, in hopes to create some semblance of civil liberties and rights to organize unions.[64]

Also parallel to the civil rights movement of the 1960s, union officials—knowing they could not compete militarily with the planters and the state and remembering Elaine—continually urged members not to shoot or fight back, no matter how outrageous the violence against them. The STFU held many of its meetings outdoors so that everyone could see what was happening, even when surrounded by deputies who shot their guns over the heads of union members to intimidate them. In some cases, individual unionists effectively used guns to guard meetings or protect themselves and their families from vigilante attacks, but the union hewed strictly to nonviolence in public demonstrations and responded with legal actions in the courts when it could. Arkansas planters tried to take away the union's state charter but failed, and the union pushed back by suing plantation owner Hiram Norcross. Despite violent attacks against them, unionists kept organizing.[65]

Strike in Arkansas

John Handcox would respond to the repression in eastern Arkansas by writing, "Landlord, what in the Heaven is the matter with you?" The union would respond with a strike. In June of 1935, nearly one year after its founding, the STFU executive committee held secret meetings in Memphis to prepare for a frontal challenge to the planters. "Strikes were talked about all the time, all the time," recalled Stith. Mitchell, McKinney, and Howard Kester served on a central coordinating body to set up strike committees in five areas that would in turn coordinate secret smaller committees on various plantations. The executive committee planned on creating a strike fund for which members would pay 5 cents for each 100 pounds of cotton they picked on the day before the strike, but no one knew how the union would collect the funds or whether a strike in Arkansas had a chance of success.[66] However, the Alabama Sharecroppers Union, led by Communists, had proven that it could be done: starting on May Day, it began a rolling strike that affected 35 plantations in Lowndes, Dallas, and Montgomery Counties, all areas where major civil rights activity would later occur. The union openly stressed interracial cooperation, with flyers appealing to "All White and Negro Farm Women and Youth." Despite arrests and beatings, the union in a few places raised wages for cotton picking to $1 per one hundred pounds, the equivalent of one dollar a day.[67] Organizers considered it a modest success.

The New Deal in far-away Washington that summer also encouraged labor organizing. On July 5, 1935, Congress enacted the National Labor Relations (Wagner) Act, which spelled out the legal rights of workers to speak and vote freely for or against unions, protected by the National Labor Relations Board (NLRB) and the US Justice Department. Unfortunately, the US Senator and plantation owner Joseph Robinson from Arkansas and other Southern Democrats threatened to block other New Deal legislation unless Congress excluded agricultural and domestic workers from Wagner Act coverage. Workers accelerated their organizing in the face of violence from company unions, police, troops, and gunmen and mobs, and the Supreme Court would uphold the Wagner Act in 1937), but the law's exclusion of agricultural and domestic workers left millions of oppressed, black, Hispanic, female, and poor white workers without federal labor rights, locked into a low-wage labor pool.[68]

To make matters more difficult for the STFU, during the summer of 1935 the unity fostered by the union almost came undone. A poverty-stricken white sharecropper named W. H. Stultz, who had replaced J.R. Butler as union president when he stepped down, campaigned to more or less segregate the STFU and make it into a white man's union. The STFU Executive Committee averted a racial split in the union's ranks by expelling him and temporarily replacing him with Rev. McKinney. Butler returned as president, but the conflict could easily have destroyed the union and racial disunity certainly would have made a successful strike impossible.[69]

The executive committee consolidated its ranks and tabulated votes from 90 councils of the union: 11,186 members had voted to strike for $1 per 100 pounds of cotton picked and 450 had voted against; 7,736 had voted to demand 75 cents per 100 pounds and 2,513 had voted against.[70] On September 1, the committee took a secret vote to authorize a strike. After the vote, McKinney gave a benediction, predicting that some strikers would be jailed, some would be driven from their homes, and some would be killed for going on strike. As Howard Kester described McKinney's words, he "prayed for the men to be guided to the right cabins and along the unguarded roads, for all the organizers to escape from the hands of the law, to give all the people courage when they needed it and to seal their struggle with victory." The union printed up bundles of flyers and hid them until Sunday night, September 11, when the STFU put its plan into effect.[71]

Carrie Dilworth, the black secretary of an STFU local—who would provide support for the Student Non-violent Coordinating Committee (SNCC) in the 1960s—described how organizers drove the back roads through the night, scattering leaflets on the road to be picked up and used by local union members. In a carload of four women, with the lights out, Dilworth lay on the floor in the back seat, pushing out the leaflets. "If they had caught us, I don't know what they would have done to us. But, they couldn't tell where we was. White folks thought a plane had flown over there and spread all them leaflets," she recalled. The leaflet demanded $1 per 100 pounds of picked cotton.[72]

At the height of the harvest season, at a time when planters desperately needed agricultural workers to pick cotton before the bolls started to rot, as many as 5,000 tenant farmers and day laborers refused to go into the fields. Many sharecroppers just sat on their front porches and refused to budge. It was a classic example of noncooperation but one that largely avoided confrontation with authorities. The STFU "sit down strike" proved powerfully effective because the union had kept its plans utterly secret, and surprised the planters, who stood to lose the entire year's crop. The police responded by arresting people and putting them into the custody of their landlords, jailing people, threatening them, and breaking up union meetings. But the strike continued.[73]

Without the time or organization needed to compel workers to harvest their crops, various planters began to grant wage increases of 75 cents to $1 an hour, a 25 to 50 percent improvement. On October 4, the STFU declared victory and everyone went back to work. The last time cotton workers in Arkansas had gone on strike authorities responded with the Elaine Massacre.[74] Now, after a year in which the STFU had struggled for mere survival, the surprise strike of 1935 finally provided leverage to change the seemingly hopeless plight of agricultural workers. Day laborers, who streamed into Arkansas from Memphis by the thousands at picking time, benefited from the wage increase for cotton picking, but sharecroppers and tenants also gained a higher price for their cotton. Norman Thomas wrote to Mitchell at the end of 1935 praising the union for surviving terror and racial division, for raising wages for cotton pickers, and for even getting signed written contracts for sharecroppers and tenants with some planters. Mitchell reported that membership had shot up to over 40,000 after the strike: he listed 22,742 members in Texas, Tennessee, Mississippi, and Missouri; nearly 12,000 members in Arkansas; and nearly 10,000 in Oklahoma, where Native American-identified Odis Sweeden played a leading role.[75]

Howard Kester went to the AFL national convention to report this success and ask for the federation's financial support. A. Philip Randolph, President of the Brotherhood of Sleeping Car Porters, got a resolution passed endorsing the STFU (though not "recognizing" it, which would have made the union a member of the AFL). In Little Rock in January of 1936, the STFU held its own convention, an optimistic and joyous affair. Delegates sang "We Shall Not Be Moved," drafted a constitution, and heard exciting news about the formation of the new Committee for Industrial Organization (CIO). Many women attended, and the convention declared them equal members of the union and allowed them to form their own locals; one black and one white woman joined the STFU executive council. The convention also adopted a proposal by H. L. Mitchell and William Amberson to undertake a cooperative farm movement.[76] Their work at this point appeared to be a spectacular success.

John Handcox did not participate in this strike or the convention, but he watched all of these developments with growing enthusiasm. When he first became aware of the STFU, he exclaimed, "That's what we need, a union!"

From Sharecropper to Organizer

Handcox at this time lived in St. Francis County, adjoining Crittenden County—the two places where the union gained its greatest numbers and suffered its worst repression. He watched "snitches," who ran to the planters to report any organizing. "*On all the big plantations I have lived on there was always someone that would not let his shirt tail touch his back until they would tell the boss what everyone said and did,*" he recalled.[77] His own crop in 1935 was a financial disaster and, as recounted in the previous chapter, when he had tried to supplement his sharecropping by working for a pitiful 75 cents a day as a laborer, a riding boss tried to cut even this measly pay. He realized he was getting nowhere:

> *I [had] rented except for the last year. That was the only time I'd ever sharecrop. We*
> *give up farming and went over on this plantation and made one crop, that was in*

'35. That was when I gave it up. I made my last crop that year in '35, and I sat down and counted up peanuts, popcorn, cotton, and corn, and I figured why? My wife had worked for $200 or $250 that year. Of course, I didn't owe but $18; [but] when I picked my first bale of cotton, I owed $18! You didn't make enough money to make a living. Two people, including everything we could produce, only made 150 dollars, and we had four kids. And then there was the subsidy problem. You know they had some whole lots of trouble in different places about the way your landlord was handling it. Lot of people never did get anything. The landlord takes it and place it on his account.

So I just gave it up and went fishin'. Bought me a net, and I went to fishing and mushelen, selling the shells and I was selling fish. Well I made more in a month selling fish than I made a whole year out of the crop that I made. Two months, I had made better than $250 selling fish at eight or ten cents a pound. So then I told my wife I wasn't going to farm anymore; I was going to get in the river and fish and catch mussels. So I give it up. I'd go from one plantation to another, sellin' fish and mussels. Never sold them in town. You go round the road and holler "fish!," and after you get your route establish they'd be looking for you, listening for you to say fish. I would keep the fish alive in a net in the water, and when I get enough to sell I just take 'em around from house to house.

For a time, "*I must admit I did not know nothing about the union,*" Handcox later wrote, and he seems to have harvested his crop in 1935 without any involvement in the strike. "*But I did know how the people were being treated by the landlord and their bosses,*" he wrote. In fact, he was already supporting the union. *I would tell people about the organization everywhere I went and talked with 'em. I [had] found out about the union in the fall of '34 or spring of '35, when I heard 'em talkin'. It come from Earl down there. A friend of mine he had been over to a little ole grocery store, and he come back talking about the union. So I talked with him and I told 'em that's exactly what we needed. "That's what we need, a union!" And we started working from there. He managed to get a paper, the Sharecropper's Voice, and the address of where the union was located, in Marion. Then it moved to Memphis, and we went over there several times to pick up literature and ca'y [carry] names of people that had joined. I didn't meet too many of the top officials of the union.... I would get a few names, and I would go to the office and turn it in, and pick up the union papers.*

John's new occupation of selling fish presented him with the opportunity to spread the word about the union. While riding a horse from plantation to plantation selling fish, popcorn, and homemade pop, John became a roaming salesman for the STFU. In his travels, he witnessed the disastrous situations of other people and became dead set on bringing them together to represent their rights. He quickly experienced threats, merely for talking union:

I went around from house to house and talk with the people, and we told 'em 'bout the union, what we should get together, and we managed to set us up a union so we could demand our rights. 'Course, I knew a lot of 'em that wasn't getting their rights. I wasn't exactly hurt by it as much as some of 'em, especially the sharecroppers. You see, I knew people that had sons older than I was and daughters older then I, they say they hadn't been out of debt in that many years. And I was old enough to be done married and had three or four kids at the time.

A guy lived across the river from me, he called me over there, made like he didn't understand what was happenin.' Said, now you've been to school more than I is, and I don't understand what they trying to do. And me being good hearted and wasn't thinking, I saw they had give him his check, then turned around and charged him twice for it. So I told him, here's what they did, they paid you the subsidy but turned around and charged you twice for it.

He claimed he didn't know what happened. So that night or the next night or two, here come the riding boss, him, and three or four guys. They knocked on my door, and he made like he wants a glass to get some water. I had my little gun in my hand, and I opened the door and give him the glass, and said "just set it down when you get through with it." I still believe when they come there they was gonna ca'y me out there and beat me up for telling 'em. That's what I'm thinkin.' That time of night—I'd gone to bed and they wanted to get a glass of water! They had their own water. I don't know if they seen the gun or not.

I didn't have too much success in Arkansas setting up locals. Course one thing, the people didn't have the money, the twenty-five cents. I know when I was organizing I pay more twenty-five cents than the majority of the people. When I was organizing in Arkansas it was during the spring and summer [of 1936]. You know, people didn't have no money. When I [later] went up to Missouri it was a little better in a way because it was cotton picking time when I was up there.

One time I went down on this plantation [in Arkansas] and I stayed all night with my sister-in-law's sister, my oldest brother's wife. Well, I went to several of the houses there talking 'bout the union. I met with some of them and I told 'em, I says "y'all get together and let me know and I'll come by and set up a local whenever you get together." So my wife's sister, she happen to be in town that next Saturday, and she says a fellow that lived near me said "tell John I say don't come back down here." He says, "the bossman told 'em if I come back down there, they'd be sure to put me in that river." So I didn't go back down there.

"Landlord, What in Heaven is the Matter With You?"

In February of 1936, John was working out of Forest City and describing himself as a "business agent," handling affairs for three STFU locals. Mitchell wrote to him "we want you as an organizer to make us a weekly report of each place you attempt to organize each week," but there is no record of his field reports.[78] John's role in the union soon took on greater importance, however, as a writer.

Sometime in 1935, according to Mitchell, he had first met John when he had walked into his STFU office in Memphis with four lines of poem on plain ruled paper: "When a sharecropper dies, he is buried in a box/without any necktie/ and without any socks." He titled his poem "The Rich Man and the Poor Man." Mitchell asked John to "write some more like it—show in so far as possible life in Arkansas." Mitchell, in his words, "rearranged" the poem and changed its name to "The Planter and the Sharecropper." In March of 1936, John's poem appeared in the *Sharecropper's Voice*. To protect his identity, he published under the pen name of John Henry, the mythical steel-driving man who could defeat the boss man's machine, celebrated in literally hundreds of versions of the song "John Henry."[79] The union's fledgling newspaper, edited by Howard Kester, provided perhaps its most important organizing tool. Passed from hand to hand, it reached an estimated 5,000 people. Donald Henderson, a former Columbia University college professor organizing a national agricultural workers union to which the Alabama Sharecroppers Union belonged, later read it and praised its poetry.[80]

John's first published poem demonstrated his keen eye, sharp words, and genius in making a story come alive. He neatly summed up how the system of plantation capitalism devastated the lives of agricultural workers. This is how his poem appeared in the *Sharecropper's Voice*, March 1936, credited to "John Henry, Union Organizer, Southern Tenant Farmers' Union":

> *The planter lives off the sweat of the sharecropper brow*
> *Just how the sharecropper lives, the planter care not how.*
> *The sharecropper raises all the planter can eat,*
> *And then gets tramped down under his feet.*
> *The sharecropper raises all the planter can wear*
> *While he and his family have to go bare.*
> *The sharecropper works, toils and sweats*
> *The planter brings him out in debt.*
> *The planter has good and wholesome food to eat*
> *The sharecropper has cornbread, molasses, and fatback meat.*
> *A lots of good things the planter have to waste,*
> *But the sharecropper knows not how it taste.*
> *The sharecropper wife gods to the washtub, kitchen and field*
> *While the planter's wife enjoys herself in an automobile.*
> *The planter's children dresses up and goes to school*
> *While the sharecropper's puts on rags and follow a mule.*
> *If you ask the planter for your right*
> *You might as well just spit in his face and ask for a fight.*
> *The planter says he inherited his wealth from birth,*
> *But it all comes from the poor man who tills the earth.*
> *The planter get together and they plots and plans*

You can bet your life it's all against the poor man.
The planters take the sharecropper's mule, wagon, or plow.
He don't allow them to have a hog or cow.
The planter lives in a house as fine as the best
And wears good clothes and all the rest
Makes no difference how much the sharecropper raise
The planter gets all the praise.
When the sharecropper dies he is buried in a box
Without a necktie or without any socks.
The sharecropper works hard and wears cotton sacks
And live in raggedy, filthy broken down shacks.
The poor man has fought all the rich man wars
And now we are being punished without any cause
The sharecroppers labor the planters pockets to swell,
But the planter's unjust deed are seeing him straight to Hell.
Now no rich planter to be ever do I crave
But I do want to be something more than a planter's slave
If anyone thinks that this ain't the truth,
He can go through Arkansas and get the proof.

Seeing his words in print, John quickly came to the idea that you can say more in a poem or a song than you can in a speech. His experiences in the union also soon taught him that music can move people into a more powerful sense of emotional unity than words alone:

When the union picked up, that's when I started on the songs. I used to write poems for the closing exercises of school each year, something funny. The union poems weren't funny, but they were about things that were happening at the time. Like "Raggedy, Raggedy." "Raggedy, Raggedy" was describin' the conditions that the people was livin', was workin' but yet and still they wouldn't getting' paid enough for the work or wouldn't gettin' paid anything for the work—so they was raggedy.

The union leaders were trying to tell the people that they weren't being treated right, that they were being taken by the landlords. At first I would sing songs at the meetings, then after I wrote one or two, I started sending them to the union head-quarters. Then they would come out in a little paper called The Sharecropper's Voice. It was being sent out to every local.

In the union, I tried to write something interesting about the conditions that people were living under and what's happenin'. Pointing out to people when they're working hard, and they ain't gettin' anything out of it. Like "Mean Things" and "Mr. Snow." Another example of the things I wrote it this here poem, "Landlord, what in the Heaven is the matter with you?" [recites:]

Landlord, what in the Heaven is the matter with you?
What has your labor ever done to you?
Upon our backs you ride,
Don't you think your labor never get tired?
Landlord, what in the Heaven is the matter with you?
For many years you've been so degrade.
You've taken all that labor made.
You've taken this cotton and this corn
and left them nothing to live upon.
Landlord, what in the Heaven is the matter with you?!
You treat your labor all so mean, that they have nothing to eat but motherless
*   greens.*
I'll tell the world what the labor has to eat—
It's motherless greens without any meat.
Landlord, what in the Hell is the matter with you?!

"Motherless greens' was my expression, greens without meat. People growed up down
there and didn't know what a ham was.

****

John began seriously building the union's network as a plantation organizer in the winter of 1936. But his greatest historical legacy would be his role as a poet and songwriter. By providing words and a voice for the union's historic departure, John would carry forward black oral and musical traditions and create new ones. He would use songs and poems like editorials to criticize and mock, to expose the perfidy of the planter class, whose values had been twisted by the privileges granted by racial plantation capitalism. John would sketch indelible word-images that detailed exactly the relationship between the planter and the sharecropper, often in tones of barely concealed outrage. He kept asking the landlord, in various songs and poems, "what is the matter with you?" As he developed his poetic imagination through poems published in the union newspaper he also developed his singing voice in union meetings and came to see the power of song as a way to get the union message through to people and help them to join together:

All of my songs and poems point directly to the conditions in which people was livin.'
That was my object of writin' songs, was trying to appeal to the people, the way they
was livin' and what was causin' 'em to live that way. That was why I wrote songs, to
get it over to the people, the workin' class.

*   Oh, I used them to inspire the people. I found out that singing was more inspi-*
rational than talking. A lot of them, they didn't know anything about the union. But
in church, they usually open up the church service with singing to get the people all

inspired up before the preacher starts with his sermon. So I found that through life it was the best policy to try to get the attention of the people.

With almost no finances and representing desperately poor people, the STFU broke all the racial and gender stereotypes of the South and appealed to the hearts of many people across the country. As the union tried to consolidate its gains from the cotton harvest strike of 1935 during the winter and spring season of 1936, John Handcox would become its troubadour and poet laureate.

1. A sharecropper's dwelling in Marked Tree, Arkansas, 1935. Photographer unknown. Howard Kester collection, Wilson Library, University of North Carolina.

2. Sam Nichols, a tenant farmer in the upcountry of Boone County, Arkansas, in a 1935 photograph exemplifying John Handcox's song "Raggedy, Raggedy Are We." Photograph by Ben Shahn. Library of Congress, Prints & Photographs Division, FSA/OWI Collection, LC-USF33-006037-M3.

3. The predominantly white 18 founding delegates to the first convention of the Southern Tenant Farmers Union in 1935 in Marked Tree, Arkansas. Isaac Shaw is kneeling on the left of the front row and H. L. Mitchell is eighth from the left in the back row. Photographer unknown. Howard Kester collection, Wilson Library, University of North Carolina.

4. Working in the cotton fields, Phillips County, September 1938, near the scene of the 1919 Elaine Massacre. Library of Congress, Prints & Photographs Division, FSA/OWI Collection.

5. In January, 1936, sharecroppers evicted from their homes by the owner of the Dibble plantation near Parkin, Arkansas. Photograph by John Vachon. Library of Congress, Prints & Photographs Division, FSA/OWI Collection, LC-USF34-014009-E.

6. Some of the sharecroppers evicted in Arkansas ended up in a cooperative farm near Hill House in Mississippi, July, 1936. Library of Congress, Prints & Photographs Division, FSA/OWI Collection, LC-USF34-009549-C.

7. Women—particularly black women such as this sharecropper from Pulaski County, Arkansas—played a powerful role in the STFU at the local level. Photograph by Ben Shahn, October 1935. Library of Congress, Prints & Photographs Division, FSA/OWI Collection, LC-USF3301-006020-M5.

8. Workers listening to speakers at an outdoor STFU meeting in Arkansas in 1937. Photograph by Louise Boyle. Kheel Center for Labor-Management Documentation and Archives, Cornell University, 5859pb2f26kc.

9. These refugees in Charleston, Missouri were among those who fled a massive flood in January of 1937. Library of Congress, Prints & Photographs Division, FSA/OWI Collection, LC-USF33-009212-M1.

10. A line of tents at a flood refugee camp in Forrest City, Arkansas, January 1937. Photograph by Edwin Locke. Library of Congress, Prints & Photographs Division, FSA/OWI Collection, LC-USF33-004206-M4.

11. Thousands of laborers such as the ones pictured here in 1939 went across the bridge from Memphis to Arkansas during the cotton harvest season. Photograph by Marion Post Wolcott.

CHAPTER 4

There Is Mean Things Happening in This Land: Terror in Arkansas

On the 18th day of May, the union called a strike
But planters and their bosses throwed the people outa their shacks.
There is mean things happening in this land.
There is mean things happening in this land.
But the union's going on and the union's growing strong.
There is mean things happening in this land.
The planters throwed the people off the land where many years they had spent,
And in the cold hard winter they had to live in tents.
There is mean things happening in this land . . .
The planters throwed their people out without a bite to eat.
They cursed them and kicked them and some with axe handles beat.
There is mean things happening in this land . . .
Their people got tired of working and that from sun to sun,
But the planters forced them to work at the point of their gun.
There is mean things happening in this land.
There is mean things happening in this land.
But the union's going on and the union's growing strong.
There is mean things happening in this land.

—John Handcox

I was doing pretty well until a friend of mine was up at the store and said some men
had a rope and the limb and all they needed was me!

In January, 1936, when the Southern Tenant Farmers Union (STFU) met in
convention in Little Rock, union leaders had pledged to increase membership to

100,000. Six fiery working-class preachers helped to lead the union's 14-member executive council. The movement remained strongest in John Handcox's St. Francis County, where nearly 7,000 STFU members reportedly belonged to 81 locals; predominantly black locals in St. Francis and in nearby Crittenden County had strong women leaders. The new year seemed to herald the onset of a new era.[1] However, John Handcox's song, "There is mean things happening in this land," explained how events burst STFU optimism in the winter and spring of 1936.

Planters terminated annual contracts with sharecroppers and tenants at year's end and renewed them in January, and in 1936 this became the occasion for another wholesale disaster for people who worked the land. Planter C. H. Dibble near Earle (in Crittenden County) had been meeting with the union's attorney to negotiate an agreement based on a "model contract" the STFU had proposed. It allowed tenants to choose their furnishing merchant at the start of the year and also who they would market their cotton to at harvest time, and upheld their right to get the best income for their labor.[2] Dibble seemed sympathetic but H. L. Mitchell at the union convention had perhaps unwisely threatened to picket him if he didn't sign the contract. Meanwhile, the local bank threatened to foreclose on Dibble's mortgage if he made any agreement with the union. On January 16, against his own feelings of sympathy for his tenants, Dibble evicted everyone that he thought belonged to the union,. He put out 21 tenant families—105 people, 28 of them under 15. They had no place to live in the freezing winter weather.

Union supporters took them to a nearby Baptist church, where people created makeshift tents out of quilts and cotton sacks, and huddled in the church yard exposed to the elements, wearing scanty clothing and with little to eat. Union members organized a protest meeting that very night at a nearby Methodist church. Then things got much worse.[3]

Crittenden County Sheriffs Everrett Hood and Paul Peacher busted into the church without a warrant, carrying shotguns and ordering people to leave. People started to run, and an African American named Jim Ball, the union's doorkeeper, grabbed Hood's gun to keep him from shooting them. The deputies beat Ball senseless and took him to jail. The workers who remained tried to carry on the meeting, but the officers came back and broke it up, shooting two men in the back as they tried to escape.[4] The atrocities did not stop. Some 450 people held another protest rally at the Providence Methodist church, near one of the tent colonies for the people evicted from the Dibble plantation. Deputy Hood again appeared, leading a mob of white men armed with guns and axe handles. They broke into the meeting, randomly beating people, some of whom leapt out of the windows. Hood and the mob confronted the white Socialist minister Howard Kester as he tried to speak from the podium. Hood leered at Kester and muttered, "There's going to be another Elaine Massacre, only the next time we'll kill whites as well as niggers."

Kester tried to carry on but the posse seized him along with union attorney Herman Goldberger and forced them into the attorney's car, where the frightened STFU secretary Evelyn Smith, a young Socialist Party member from New Orleans, was waiting. They then kidnapped Kester. With a pistol to his head, they took him to the woods near Earle and dangled a hangman's noose in front of him. Having witnessed the lynching of Claude Neal in Florida, Kester knew to act quickly. He pointed out that he had crossed state lines to get to Arkansas, and that the Federal Bureau of Investigation (FBI) would investigate if someone killed him. Realizing the danger to themselves, the assailants eventually let him escape across the river to Memphis, with the warning that they would kill him if he returned. Union supporters had already telegraphed word of Kester's kidnapping to his wife in Nashville, who thought he had been murdered.[5]

This deadly conflict based on the events in the churches played out further nearly two months later, on March 12. Two masked men, who looked distinctly like Hood and Peacher, invaded the home of sharecropper James Williams. His friend Willie Hurst, a witness to their January attack on Ball, was there. The sheriffs had already tried to force Hurst to sign a statement that exonerated the deputies for the church shootings but he had refused, vowing to testify in court that Ball had acted in self-defense during the sheriff's raid. Mitchell succinctly summarized what the masked men did next: "Hurst was murdered in cold blood, before the eyes of Williams and his wife." When a minister later came to console Hurst's widow, her landlord ran him off with a shotgun, yelling at the minister, "I'd shoot you if you was Jesus Christ himself!" A judge, who was also a landlord, sentenced the hapless Ball to seven years in prison. The Arkansas Supreme Court later reduced that to a year in prison, leaving Ball's five children and his wife without a father, husband, and breadwinner.[6]

The Dibble plantation eviction and its aftermath signaled an intense new round of terror. The government's AAA payments not to grow crops went directly to Arkansas planters, who were supposed to share the money with their tenants and sharecroppers. Instead, landlords consumed federal subsidy payments to the tune of $73 million between 1933 and 1938, sharing almost none of it and making no complaints about the money spent on their behalf by "big government." In St. Francis and Crittenden Counties, the number of farms with over 1,000 acres shot up by 200 to 300 percent. The number of tenants dropped more than 20 percent, and nearly 3,000 tenant families lost their homes. The number of landless wage earners in the five counties of northeastern Arkansas tripled.[7] As evictions proceeded, mob attacks, arrests, vigilante gangs, and lynch mobs continued to plague STFU members and their supporters.[8]

Remarkably, following the Dibble evictions, the union reported that 71 white men and 52 blacks applied for membership in Earle. Some of the whites offered to protect union locals with guns. Possibly this might have stopped some of the attacks but STFU leaders felt armed self-defense would certainly lead to a conflagration like Elaine and destroy any hope of organizing.[9] The union argued that everything it did was nonviolent and legal and that the civil liberties of all Americans were at stake in Arkansas. "This is in 'America, Land of the Free' where men are beaten, shot, blacklisted, jailed and starved for daring to organize a union," declared *The Sharecropper's Voice*. On March 26, Norman Thomas read a press statement on the National Broadcasting Corporation network, decrying Hurst's murder and urging President Roosevelt to intervene. "The ultimate escape of America from Fascism requires the end of the brutal slavery of the cotton country," Thomas told his national radio audience.[10]

STFU leaders and their Socialist Party allies used each terrible incident to get national attention and to press for investigations by the US Justice Department, which had the power to protect witnesses.[11] However, the Supreme Court upheld the Wagner Act as Constitutional, and anti-union employers everywhere still believed they could get away with murder, not only in Arkansas but in Harlan County, Kentucky, and in other places where workers organized.[12] Prompted initially by publicity about the incidents in Arkansas, US Senator Robert La Follette of Wisconsin in the spring of 1936 held extensive hearings on civil liberties violations against workers that produced startling testimony on bloody repression in the southern coal fields and in workplaces in many locales. His committee, however, never got around to investigating the repression in Arkansas.[13]

Much like civil rights movement activists in the 1960s, STFU organizers spent much of their time seeking national publicity and appealing to federal authorities to stop gun-toting, axe-wielding thugs from killing people. Mass media attention brought pressure on President Roosevelt, who brought up the Arkansas situation in his March 6, 1936, cabinet meeting.[14] He seemed concerned, but in early June the President would nonetheless go to Arkansas for its Centennial celebration to publicly embrace Senator Robinson and refuse to see union representatives.[15] Terror continued and Howard Kester compared eastern Arkansas to Hitler's Nazi Germany. He described it this way:

> Hundreds of Union members have been evicted from the land and are today without homes or jobs. Members and leaders of the Union have been mobbed, beaten, illegally arrested, jailed and shot. Meetings have been broken up and homes have been riddled with bullets . . . Black terror stalks the cotton fields as the Southern Tenant Farmers' Union fights for the elemental rights of freedom of speech and of assembly—the very foundations upon which all free government stands.[16]

During the winter and spring of 1936 hundreds of people lived in tents in the backwoods of Arkansas in a starving condition. They besieged the union with heart-rending pleas for relief. Poorly clad, starving families became sick with pneumonia, pellagra, and worse. Socialists and supporters from the Midwest to

Harlem and Washington, D.C., via the union sent tons of canned food and clothing to these suffering families much as northerners would during the civil rights movements of a later era. Young Socialists began applying to come South to support the union but it barely had money to pay for postage and could not provide food or shelter for outsiders. [17] National union supporters paid Howard Kester and the Socialist Party paid Mitchell 40 dollars a month, but organizers in the field like Handcox went mostly unpaid, although it appears that they were allowed to take a small organizer's fee when workers paid their union dues, which was not often. [18]

"The Disinherited Speak"

The Worker's Defense League in New York City, established in 1936 by the Socialist Party to aid the labor movement, published Howard Kester's pamphlet, "The Disinherited Speak: Letters from Sharecroppers." Drawing on the heart-rending letters Mitchell received in the STFU office every day, Kester presented a shocking picture of misery in the cotton fields. One family recounted that the plantation boss "said that anybody on his place that belong to the union will have to look for a home," and that their children "went on half feed and naked all year." One man wrote that his family had nothing to eat but hickory nuts. Isaac Shaw, one of the union's founders, wrote from Earle of union members eating long-dead road kill. A woman who still had a plantation job complained of massive overwork "that just keep me on a stair I has to be movin' all the time," at starvation wages.[19] Union members complained of beatings with axe handles and revolvers, of having letters from the union tracked by postal officials, of planters who placed traitors within the union movement. George Handcox, John's older brother, wrote from Kinton, Arkansas, to inform Mitchell that "One of our So Call Brothers Become a Judas and Betrayed the union to our Land Lord," who promptly kicked STFU members off the plantation.[20] White workers proved especially fearful of joining the union, and when they did, blacks often suspected them of secretly working for the planter. One union member wrote, "My Boss man told Some of the tenants Here on the place there was Going to Be another Elaine Raid." Another picked up a common theme: "I am tired of working for nothin it is worser now than it was Slavery."

Those who stuck with the union knew they risked their lives to do it. Union members wrote, "We truly mean to stay with union until it go Down"; "We are in the Union to live or Die"; "You may count on me until death." Authorities near Forrest City jailed Henrietta McGhee for calling a strike on her plantation. She wrote to the union that her husband had been run off for joining the union, but "i am still Working for the union and I going to fight until Death." Another worker wrote, "They want us to quite the union and I am not goin to do it," but he also pleaded, "please fix some way for us to git something to eat or give us some work for we cant live this way."[21] Lula Parchman, a black woman in the St. John's local, summed up conditions: "We are Starveing, being driven from place to place, and pressed down by The unjust laws of man. The Union is needed. Through out The universal world among The poor classes. Regardless of color or creed"[22]

In 1953, anthropologist and folklore scholar John Greenway would publish a book in which he interviewed John Handcox, the "Negro organizer, sharecropper, and songwriter for the Southern Tenant Farmers' Union during its early days." Handcox described the situation in 1936 to Greenway this way:

> *When the planters in East Arkansas saw that the people were joining the union they told them to git off the land. They didn't wait for some of them to git—they threw them off. It was a cold winter. The hungry people had no place to go. When they held union meetings the laws clubbed them till they lay like dead on the ground. It didn't make no difference if they was men or women. They killed some union members and threw some others in jail. This was in the winter, in 1936.*[23]

Another Strike in Arkansas

The union executive board worried that without some progress the union would die. By the end of February, 1936, funds it had raised to help feed the starving, evicted families had evaporated. Many evicted tenants and sharecroppers had become day laborers paid at 75 cents a day, if they could get employment at all. The board talked of initiating a strike to demand a 10 hour work day for $1.50 and contracts that would provide laborers with some job security beyond hoeing and harvest times.[24] Wanting to know more about the somewhat successful cotton chopper's strike of the previous spring in Alabama, Mitchell went to see The Alabama Sharecropper's Union (SCU) about making an alliance. However, he decided the SCU was badly organized by unrealistic and over zealous CP members. They sought to highlight black leadership, but Mitchell thought this could only isolate the union from possible white allies and make black workers even more vulnerable to repression. Mitchell rejected an alliance.[25]

The STFU executive board meanwhile formed a strike committee and canvassed locals to decide whether they would support strike on the eve of the spring planting season. A number of local leaders responded that they were not ready to strike. Most locals remained small and weakened by evictions, with members scattered across various plantations with little coordination.[26] Nonetheless, nearly 12,000 members in St. Francis, Crittenden, Cross, Poinsett, and Woodruff counties, where the union had grown the fastest, could provide the basis for a successful strike. The strike committee called for a vote.[27]

When the Executive Council met to tabulate results in Memphis on March 15, it found that most members had not voted. The canvassing went out through the mail and some locals did not get notification of the vote or could not respond. Nonetheless, of those who had voted, 6,118 had voted for a strike and only 384 had voted against. The STFU alerted locals that it would call for a dollar a day for 10-hour days of cotton chopping, and 15 cents an hour for overtime, which could in many cases average out to a pay of $1.50 a day. By contrast, one organizer wrote that people in his area made 75 cents for a 14-hour day, and some people made as little as eight cents an hour.[28] The union believed it had 150 active locals in Arkansas, 60 in Oklahoma, and a dozen others in Tennessee, Mississippi, and Missouri. Mitchell pledged that the union would get "the support of labor organizations all over America" and possibly from "the treasury of that powerful and fighting labor union," the United Mine Workers of America (UMWA).[29]

Mitchell felt optimistic, in part due to the changing national climate for labor. By the winter of 1936, the formation of the Committee (later, Congress) of Industrial Organizations (CIO) had opened the floodgates to a grass-roots movement of working people to democratize the workplace. "We thought . . . the CIO was going to sweep the whole country and organize all the unorganized," Mitchell later recalled.[30] The CIO would help to overwhelmingly reelect Franklin D. Roosevelt as President in November, 1936. CIO unions included all workers regardless of race, creed, gender, or nationality, and thereby opened a vast new terrain for organizing.[31] In contrast, AFL unions had largely ignored noncraft workers, discriminated against racial and ethnic minorities and women, and failed to organize the unorganized. Predictably, appeals to the AFL by the STFU produced nothing but a resolution of sympathy, but the CIO and even the United Mine Workers union also failed to help. They all realized that STFU members could hardly pay any dues, and that since no federal laws protected agricultural and domestic laborers, the STFU would probably lose this strike.[32]

As to the wisdom of going on strike, John Handcox thought there had not been much choice. He later told John Greenway:

> *In the spring, at cotton chopping time, it didn't make much difference if we was working or not—our young ones was still hungry. So we began to talk about a strike. Most of us was workin' from sun up to sun down and making less than 70 cents a day. We wanted $1.50 a day for 10 hours' work. We made handbills and posters and signs telling what we wanted, and plastered them up all over the place. There was about 4000 altogether who said they would go out on strike.*

Unfortunately, the planters were several steps ahead of the union. An organizer wrote to Mitchell that employers had created a Planters Union Lodge and offered to pay five dollars "for organizers to join them." Across America, employers used company unions as a way to divert people from joining real ones, and the planters thought, why not?[33] The planters circulated a bogus newspaper called, absurdly, *The Southern Liberator*, that advised people, if they had complaints, "take it to your boss and you will get more consideration than joining some Radical movement—DON'T BE AN INGRATE!" In a poem, "Landlord What in the Heaven is the Matter With You?," published in the May 1, 1936, edition of *The Sharecroppers' Voice*, Handcox derided this newspaper that seemed to use the black labor movement as a front for some of the worst employers, such as those at the Twist Brothers plantation. John wrote:

> You landlords get together and have some black hearted "Nigger" to print a paper
> Its known as the Southern Liberator which says the man who works gets what he
>   wants
> That's a stinkin' lie "You know he don't"
> Further you advise Labor not to buy Baloney, sardines and cheese
> You want them to continue to buy corn bread and peas.
> You have taken all you Labors Rights now you want to take his appetite.
> You say move away from landlords who are unfair
> You must want us to live up in the air.
> You said landlords like Beck and Twist and such
> Pay their money for long term schools
> You must think all of us workers are fools.[34]

Whether they thought the workers were fools or not, planters proved well prepared, in contrast to the strikers. The STFU had warned workers to keep local meetings closed to outsiders, for "above all the planters must not know just when we will strike or anything about it."[35] But, as John complained, some people wouldn't "let their shirt tail touch their back" before running to tell the landlord what the union was doing. Perhaps more damaging, Mitchell himself let the word out to newspapers, apparently thinking that unfavorable publicity and the threat of a strike might cause the planters to sign contracts. "A general strike looms in the eastern part of Arkansas," reported New York City's *Amsterdam News*, published in Harlem, on March 7, 1936.[36] Not only did the union tip off the planters to its plans, but it also was almost penniless and had no strike fund. Even more ominous, eastern Arkansas had a serious drought, so that the planters would not need people to chop weeds and plant cotton as urgently or in the numbers normally required.

Even under these unfavorable conditions, the union began a strike on May 18, 1936, at the start of the Memphis Cotton Carnival (described by John in his "Strike in Arkansas" poem in the previous chapter). Handcox recalled the tough circumstances that provoked the cotton chopper's strike:

The Arkansas sharecroppers' union strike in 1936 was brought on because some of those planters . . . would go into the little towns and try to get people to come out on the plantations and chop cotton by the day. They told all of them that lived on the plantation to not go in the field, and brought these town people out and paid them by the day, instead of payin' the tenants. See, we was supposed to have been strikin' for, I think, a dollar a day, what we was asking for day labor, you know. A dollar a day. 'Course now, what it was, we didn't work hours. It went from sunup to sundown, from the time you can see 'till you can't see. This is a poem I wrote after the union decided to strike in Arkansas in '36. It mentions some of the things that went on during the strike, and it goes like this:

> *On the 18th day of May, the workers called a strike,*
> *For they could not live on what the planters pay.*
> *They asked people in Memphis not to come out on the truck,*
> *But the picketers found that the jailhouse was their luck.*
> *The union, having many friends and good support,*
> *Had to pay a $10 fine to the unjust Memphis court.*
> *In Earl, Arkansas they threw so many in jail,*
> *That anyone would declare such an arrest "wholesale."*

The union claimed that on the first day of the strike nearly 5,000 cotton choppers stayed out of the fields, although other observers placed the figure at around 2,000.[37] As John's poem tells, the planters responded with immediate arrests. David Benson from Ohio, a member of the Workers' Alliance, a national united front organization formed by labor leftists, picketed the Hanrahan Bridge in Memphis to stop day laborers from going across the Mississippi River to work in Arkansas. The picketers succeeded in stopping 40 truckloads of potential cotton pickers and turning back 700 day laborers, until Memphis Police Chief Will Lee jailed four of the picketers and shut the picket line down. The picket line had mostly stopped day laborers from crossing the bridge that day, but the chaos unfolding in eastern Arkansas overshadowed this small victory, as John indicated in a poem: [38]

> *Some planters forced laborers into the field with guns,*
> *And drove them like convicts from sun to sun.*
> *The planters were using pistols, whipping the labors*
> *'cross the head,*
> *Tellin' them, "If you don' get out there in my field,*
> *I will kill you dead."*
> *Planters say, dollar and a half a day is unfair.*
> *He never mentioned high prices the labor had to pay him for what they eat*
> *and wear.*

> *Everybody know the union doesn't even ask enough,*
> *If you remember how the planter sells his beans and stuff.*

The Shadow of Slavery

Paul Peacher, the infamous sheriff of Earle, a majority-black town of 2,000 souls in eastern Arkansas, boasted to planters gathered in the town square, "I'll break the strike." He took off in his car through the black section of town, and first arrested John Curtis, a 26 year-old-black man on his way to work in the fields. He picked up another young African American and dumped them both in jail. After that, he arrested Winfield Anderson, a timber worker whose arm had been injured by a falling tree, for the crime of sitting on his porch. He charged 35 city workers with vagrancy, a charge that had been frequently used to in effect re-enslave freedmen after the Civil War.[39] The town's mayor, who had listened to Peacher in the street earlier that day, sentenced the men to 30 days labor on land owned by the Earle School District—a property farmed on a lease by Paul Peacher. Most of Peacher's previous workers had quit. None of the men he arrested were on strike or members of the union.[40]

On May 21, at the invitation of H. L. Mitchell, the evangelical preacher Sherwood Eddy came to Arkansas and managed to get into the labor camps and talk to the prisoners. Eddy then went to Peacher and demanded to see court records and warrants of arrest. Instead, Peacher threatened Eddy and put him in a jail cell for a few hours before running him out of town. Eddy returned to Memphis to contact a former classmate at Yale—who was now the Attorney General of the United States!—and reported that Peacher was holding workers in an illegal state of peonage, imprisoning them, and forcing them to work at no wages.[41]

On May 22, two white women, Evelyn Smith (the STFU secretary) and Maxine East (married to union founder Clay East) also came over from Memphis and snuck onto Peacher's plantation at night. They found 13 black men in miserable conditions in a stockade. Peacher's men apprehended the two women, smashed their cameras, and ran them out. Union attorney Newell Fowler and the Socialist Party's Workers Defense League activist Aaron Gilmartin, who had arrived from New York City, also went to Peacher's stockade to demand the release of his prisoners. Instead, a deputy and Fowler got in a fistfight and Peacher arrested the two "outsiders" for "disturbing labor." When they were released, they appealed to the US attorney in Little Rock for help, but discovered he was yet another plantation owner, and he would do nothing.[42] John described these events in his poem:

> *Planter rides 'round cursing and raising sand,*
> *When it's well known he sold baking soda for fifty cents a can.*
> *They 'rested Gil Martin and his New York guest*

Who were investigating the people in a distress.
On the 22nd of May, the most terrible thing happened,
Police attacked Evelyn Smith and Mrs. Clay East.
Told them to leave there at once for disturbing the peace.
The women had taken pictures of the union people in stockades,
Only wanting to seek some way to give the union people aid.
Police took the Kodaks and tour up the film, saying,
"You'd better leave Arkansas or you'll be hung to a limb.
The planters' laws in Arkansas was raising cain, they had no respect for a
  woman or man.
Makes no difference if you're white or black; if you're not in the ring, you all
  looks alike.

Handcox explained the last phrase: *"What that means, if you were one of them big planters, you were in the ring, like a courthouse ring . . . They put Evelyn and Mrs. Clay East in jail. They had taken Evelyn's camera that day. Then they started arresting everybody they thought was an agitator or helping the union people, almost every farm person."* In plantation country, landowners told people who to vote for and put people in power – the courthouse "ring"—who would do their bidding. "The plantation was actually like a state," George Stith recalled. "It had its own government and it even had its own courts"[43]

On May 23, Deputy Peacher began systematically hunting down union members. The union sought to rally people through a series of small meetings, but Peacher's vigilantes boldly charged in to disperse or arrest them and attacked marchers in the street. In one case, Memphis Police Chief Will Lee joined in apprehending a union man who had fled to Memphis and turned him back over to Peacher. Mitchell aptly described Peacher in a press release: "always armed with two guns, Cartridge belt, and blackjack . . . the Arkansas equivalent of a Storm Troop leader in Germany." Other planters also forced families to work on their plantations under the watch of armed guards. Absurdly, Arkansas Governor Futrell sent in 25 National Guardsmen, with the purpose, said its commander, "to guarantee protection against interference to any many who wanted to work." The Guardsmen brandished rifles and even a machine gun and arrested union members for "interfering with labor." A number of unionists ended up on county prison farms to work off their fines at wages of 75 cents a day, well below the union's standard of $1.00 to $1.50 a day.[44]

Violence, imprisonment, and death loomed large but marches and rallies continued. Handcox later told author Greenway how the union broke through the fear:

The laws arrested every man they could get ahold of and took them back to work at the point of guns. They beat up men and women, and they shot some, and tried

to scare us. They ran a lot of folks out. But they couldn't break the strike. We had
marches. We all lined up, sometimes more than a 100 of us on a line, and marched
through the plantations, cross country. In lots of places where we marched the chop-
pers stopped work and went on strike with us. At one plantation the scabs they had
brought from other places dropped their hoes and run like rabbits for cover when
they saw us comin'. As we were marching, we were asking, like somebody asked in the
Bible, "What you mean that you crush my people and grind the face of the poor?"[45]

After a week of repression, the number of people on strike had dropped from
5,000 to 3,000, according to the union. "Day Hand[s] have no crops they have
not crops nothing to eat," a union member wrote. "We who have crops are
Dividing our food with them the best we can the way the thing is now we will
soon Hafter quit." The STFU tried to offset this dire situation by calling for a
"general strike" of all categories of workers, not just day laborers. Bands of workers, sometimes as many as 100 or more, went through the towns, backwoods and
cotton fields of Cross, St. Francis, and Crittenden Counties, urging people to
drop their hoes. The union dropped 2,500 strike leaflets from cars, and workers
spread them from there by hand.[46] Tenants and sharecroppers rallied to support
the day laborers, but police, planters and vigilantes continued to attack strikers,
using the butt end of pistols, axe handles and whips.

Some workers just disappeared. Dave Benson, who had previously been
arrested in Memphis, was arrested again and thrown in the Forrest City, Arkansas,
jail, where authorities repeatedly threatened to lynch him. On June 4, a judge
convicted him on assorted trumped-up charges (including having out of state
license plates!). Clay East came to the courtroom to observe, only to be attacked
by the sheriff and thrown in jail with Benson. A mob then surrounded the jail,
pulled East out and attacked him, shouting "nigger lover" and saying they would
break his neck or hang him. East barely escaped in his souped-up Terraplain as
carloads of vigilantes chased on a wild ride back to Memphis. The badly shaken
Benson and his compatriot Rose Mason got loose from the jail and left town. To
paraphrase John Handcox, the authorities thought black and white all "looked
alike" if they were unionists.[47]

Where is the Man Frank Weems?

On June 8, 1936, sheriff's deputies raided the home of Rev. E. B. McKinney and
arrested five workers hiding there. They sent them all to the county workhouse
on a charge of vagrancy, the same charge so often used after emancipation to
force ex-slaves to work for free. McKinney, out of town on a speaking trip in
Washington, D.C., faced arrest upon his return. Over in Earle near Peacher's
stockade, a black woman union member had been whipped with sticks and a

leather strap, and a white member beaten nearly to death.[48] Sam Bennett, a black laborer who had gone on strike and then hidden in the woods to escape a mob in St. Francis County, ended up on that same day hiding out in Wynne. White men, arriving at two in the morning, beat up a young black man and forced him to tell them where Bennett's brother lived. They invaded his home without a warrant and beat him up too, but found that Sam Bennett had already hopped a freight train to Chicago. Union supporters fought an extended battle to prevent his extradition and, indeed, the Governor of Illinois refused to send Bennett back to Arkansas.[49]

Handcox later described to John Greenway what else happened during that day in Crittenden County. John did not actually participate in this march and uses "we" to explain the experience as he learned it from an eyewitness. His account, while not entirely accurate, conveys the dramatic essence of what occurred:

> On the eighth day of June we had another march. Jim Reese was leadin' it, and Frank Weems, one of the Negro farm hands, was walkin' along next to him. We was singin' union songs when a fellow come up and says the planters was comin'. Frank Weems and Jim Reese said, "Keep marchin' boys, you ain't breakin' no law." Pretty soon a bunch of planters and riders and town bums ride up to us in their automobiles. We stay in line, lookin' at them, wonderin' what they're a-goin' to do. When they git out of their automobiles we see they all got guns and baseball bats. We don't say anything. "Where you goin'?" one of 'em says. "Down the road," says Jim. Then they begin sluggin' us with those guns and bats. A lot of men run for their lives. A lot of us fall down and can't git up again. Then pretty soon they git back in their automobiles an' ride away. Jim Reese, he lays there on the road for maybe four hours. Then he looks around and he sees Frank Weems layin' there beside him. He looks bad. "Are you all right, Frank?" he asks. But Frank Weems doesn't answer him. Then Jim gits worried and gits to go for help. When he comes back Frank Weems is gone. No man in Earle ever saw Frank Weems again. We keep askin' "Where is Frank Weems?" We keep askin' is he in the swamp or in Blackfish Lake or rottin' in a ditch somewhere? We keep askin' it. Where is Frank Weems?

According to other accounts of this incident, Weems, a striking black cotton chopper, and Jim Reese, who was white, had first gone together into Earl, where union activities continued to concentrate, to scout out conditions in advance of an STFU march into town. They discovered a patrol of white men armed with guns, baseball bats, axe handles, and sledge hammers and hurried to warn the marchers to turn back. Before they could reach the marchers five carloads of vigilantes caught up and beat both men senseless. When Reese woke up, Weems had disappeared. Reese thought vigilantes had killed him and thrown his body in the river.[50] Reese proved extraordinarily courageous. He lived to tell the tale, but reportedly later lost his mind from the beating and died an early death. A more immediate martyr was black union member Eliza Nolden, one of the marchers who was attacked by the mob. She escaped to Memphis with permanent brain damage, only to die later from her injuries.[51]

In the midst of this frightening repression, Mitchell called in Rev. Claude Williams to preach a funeral for Frank Weems. Williams, a white firebrand southern preacher who taught the gospel of working-class revolt in his sermons, had organized miners in Arkansas and been widely reviled for supporting racial equality. Williams first checked in with Mitchell at the STFU's headquarters on Broad Street in Memphis. When he did, Willie Sue Blagden, the Socialist daughter of a prominent white Memphis family, asked to go with him into Arkansas. One might have thought that the presence of a prominent white woman would provide protection, but when the pair stopped in a drugstore for sodas in Earle, six white men kidnapped them, took them into the woods and held them long into the night. They beat Williams severely with leather harness straps used on mules in the fields. They pulled up Blagden's skirt and beat her legs, thereafter putting her on a train and sending her marked up body back to Memphis. The others drove Williams around in the backcountry, continuing to beat him and threatening to lynch him. After they finally released him with a warning of death if he returned, he drove back to his home in Little Rock, Arkansas, and collapsed in the arms of his wife, Joyce Williams. It was but one of many violent and fearful incidents Williams suffered that would wreck his peace of mind and his health.[52]

As would later be the case in the civil rights movement, everyone who risked their lives for the cause paid a heavy price, but the terror inflicted on whites got more attention from a national media that largely ignored the terror that blacks faced every day. A photo of Blagden's black and blue thigh circulated in newspapers all across the country and outraged civil liberties supporters. The New York-based national office of the American Civil Liberties Union (ACLU) offered a $1,000 reward to anyone providing information that would lead to the arrest and conviction of anti-union terrorists. "March of Time" film makers came to Arkansas to recreate scenes of marching strikers and the abduction of Williams and Blagden; on August 8, movie houses started to play this newsreel film on screens all across the country. Using union members as a cast, the film portrayed them marching through the streets singing, meeting in church, and getting shot at and pummeled by white police. This and other publicity around the strike, along with the scandalous Peacher peonage case, aroused national concern about the plight of southern agricultural workers that would lead to some victories for the sharecropper movement. However, the commercial mass media largely ignored the assumed murder of Frank Weems, the eventual death of Eliza Nolden, and at least three other black STFU members who died during the strike.[53]

In the 1930s, deadly repression against labor organizers occurred across the country, but eastern Arkansas was in a class unto itself. The body of one anonymous union member was found floating in Coldwater River. [54] Not only Frank Weems, but many other union members took to the creek banks and the woods at night to run for their lives. In an address written to celebrate "Constitution Day," on September 17, 1936, Norman Thomas used the events in Arkansas to illustrate how civil liberties "have steadily lost ground in the United States." He recalled how he himself had been attacked and expelled from Arkansas by the state's supposed "best citizens," and decried the "sadists" who had killed Weems and "the shadow of the plantation and of chattel slavery [that] hangs over us all." Thomas compared the terror in Arkansas to the fascism overseas by Hitler and accused Police Chief Will Lee in Memphis of "playing the role of a small time Mussolini toward the workers." He called on Governor Robinson, President Roosevelt, and the nation, to answer the question, "Where is Frank Weems?"[55]

At this point, John Handcox became a powerful asset to the union movement, putting pen to paper to expose the Weems killing. Its chorus, "where is the man Frank Weems?," became a rallying cry:

> *He was a poor sharecropper*
> *Worked hard every day*
> *To make an honest living*
> *And his multiplied accounts to pay.*
> *REFRAIN:*
> *Now I want somebody to tell me, tell me,*
> *And tell me right;*
> *Yes I want somebody to tell me*
> *Where is the man Frank Weems?*
> *He was a farmer of Crittenden County,*
> *A county just east of Cross,*
> *Where they call them out with farm bells*
> *And work under a riding boss.*
> *Frank heard about the union,*
> *Then he sought to show its aims.*
> *And when he had well understood,*
> *He sure did sign his name.*
> *I'm sure he told his companions*
> *What a grand thing the union would be;*
> *And if we gave it our brave support,*
> *Some day it would make us free.*
> *It was in nineteen hundred and thirty six*
> *And on the ninth of June,*
> *When the STF union pulled a strike*
> *That troubled the planters on their thrones.*
> *The planters they all became troubled,*

Not knowing what 'twas all about;
But they said, "One thing I'm sure we can do,
That's scare the niggers out."
Frank Weems was one among many,
That stood out true and brave;
Although he was taken by cruel hands,
Now he sleeps in an unknown grave.
Sleep on, Frank, if you are sleeping,
Rest in your unknown grave,
Ten thousand union brothers to mourn your loss
And to give your children bread.
REFRAIN:
Now I want somebody to tell me, tell me,
And tell me right;
Yes I want somebody to tell me
Where is the man Frank Weems?[56]

In this song, John sounded themes resonant with other labor protest ballads in similarly repressive places in the southern mines and textile mills. Jim Garland in Kentucky told the story of Harry Sims, a 19-year-old mine union organizer from the North, "the strongest Union Man/That I have ever seen," murdered in 1932 by gun thugs during a strike. Florence Reece in Harlan County sang, "Can you stand it?/Oh tell me how you can?/Will you be a gun thug/Or will you be a man?" Ella May Wiggins, in the 1929 North Carolina textile strike, had intoned, "Now we must stand together, and to the boss reply:/We'll never, no we'll never let our leaders die." Company thugs shot and killed Wiggins at a union rally on September 14, 1929, three days before her 29th birthday. She spoke forthrightly for uniting the African American and white workers in the Communist-affiliated National Textile Workers Union. No one went to jail for her murder. Aunt Molly Jackson in eastern Kentucky wrote of the mining bosses, "Their banner is the dollar sign/And ours is striped in blood." Her half-sister Sara Ogan Gunning offered a solution:

Oh, what can you do about it,
To these men of power and might?
I tell you Mr. Capitalist,
I'm going to fight, fight, fight![57]

Like other labor anthems of the period, the hard-hitting songs and poems written by Handcox accused oppressors and indicted oppression, gave dignity to unheralded organizers like Weems who "stood out true and brave," and promised that someday the union "would make us free." But STFU song leaders added something special to labor protest music when they joined African-American song traditions to the union struggle. Handcox, Brookins, McKinney, and others who worked in the black oral tradition each drew upon a culture they knew by virtue of their family, their religious upbringing, and their own history. An extraordinarily vibrant music of redemption provided backup to their struggle. The despair and anxiety that John and his cohorts lived through in the Delta required not only ballads of martyrdom and freedom, but also the spiritual release of the "sorrow song." Whereas "No More Mourning" had once been thought to voice a certain resignation in the face of life's worst catastrophes, in John's rendition, it became a defiant cry—"Before I'll be a slave, I'll be buried in my grave/ take my place with those who loved and fought before." John had no access to mass media, the halls of government or the sheriff's office, but he could reach other workers by singing a song or publishing a poem which thousands read in *The Sharecroppers' Voice*.

However, no song or poem and no amount of determination could make it possible for rural proletarians to withstand the brutality and toll of hunger sweeping through the Arkansas Delta. The 1936 strike began mainly with day laborers, joined in solidarity by renters and sharecroppers. In 1935, strikers had survived in part by rationing food from their gardens. But by 1936, so many more people had lost their farms that there was little food to be had and strikers could not hold out. Viola Smith, president of her STFU local in Parkin, Arkansas, complained that she had been blacklisted and could get no work, no food, and a planter threatened to put her out of her house. She begged Mitchell for "something to Eat Please Let me no wheather you is goint to help me or not . . . I haven't got any thing to help my self." Such pathetic cries for help rolled in to Mitchell's in Memphis office every day, but he could offer no help.[58] Many struggling agricultural workers thought the union had resources that it did not have.

By the second week of June, almost everyone who could find a job had gone back to work. The union had made no advances, but one would not know it from reading main headline of *The Sharecroppers' Voice* of July, 1936: "UNION CHOPPERS WIN STRIKE." The union executive committee met on July 3 in Muskogee, Oklahoma, and concluded, "The strike had won higher wages and greatly strengthened the solidarity of the union." The committee said wages went up to $1.00 a day for day labor and up to $1.25 for 10-hour days in some areas which, if true, would be about a 25 percent pay increase. It also said membership increased in areas hard hit by planter terror; that "Negro and white workers in the cotton fields have become aware of their common interests," and that this was "only the beginning of the struggle of the disinherited to come into its own."[59] However, Anthony Dunbar, who wrote a careful history of the STFU and southern labor radicalism, concluded that the seven-week strike had not been a victory, but "a disastrous defeat." After the 1936 cotton chopper's strike, wages stagnated, local organization became increasingly isolated, and the union got weaker. H. L. Mitchell's son later wrote that his father had mistakenly counted on publicity to help win the strike, and thus had let the planters know in advance of the strike plans. Mitchell perhaps lacked the tactical and organizational planning skills required for union organizing.[60]

However, much like the civil rights movement in later years, the union's litigation and publicity campaigns did succeed in alerting the nation and political leaders to the terrible economic injustices in the South. The mass media played up the flogging of Blagden and Williams and the black press highlighted the presumed murder of Frank Weems. On September 24, the federal government indicted Peacher on eight counts of "holding and causing to be held certain negroes [sic] as slaves," under post-Civil War anti-slavery statutes. Finally, in federal court, several of the black men Peacher had held in bondage courageously testified against him. The federal judge, a former Governor of Arkansas, instructed 12 white male jurors that "every circumstance points to the guilt of this man" and that the abuses of peonage "ought to be stopped." Peacher boasted, "That jury will turn me loose," but, on November 25, the all-white jury convicted him. The judge fined him $3,500, sentenced him to two year's probation, and barred him from continuing as the deputy sheriff of Crittenden County and the marshal of Earle. Local planters helped him pay the fine, but they did not like the embarrassment of his notoriety. These circumstance forced Peacher to leave the area.[61]

Socialists and liberal allies of the STFU put continuing pressure on President Roosevelt, who was trying to get re-elected in the fall of 1936. A few days before the election, Roosevelt announced he would set up a President's Committee on Farm Tenancy to recommend solutions to the awful conditions that had come to light. In 1937, the federal government created the Farm Security Administration (FSA) to alleviate some of the horrendous conditions suffered by sharecroppers and tenants. The FSA and the Federal Emergency Relief Administration (FERA) created small farming cooperatives that rescued hundreds of refugees from sharecropping, including singer Johnny Cash's family who lived in a "colony" of cotton producers in Dyess, Arkansas. However, the only black man in the colony was a school custodian, and an abusive farm manager expelled the one white man who disregarded white supremacy; when a group met to discuss grievances, the local sheriff broke it up. Such repressive, whites-only policies continued to prevent people from joining the STFU.[62]

"They've Got the Rope and the Limb"

By this time, "Where is the Man Frank Weems?" begged another question: where was the man John Handcox? His participation in the union nearly caused him to "take [his] place with those who loved and fought before" much sooner than he expected. Leading up to the strike of 1936, John had traveled on horseback from plantations, to churches and to union meetings, signing people up in the union. Whatever progress John had made came to a quick end sometime before the strike began on May 18, 1936. If not for the warning he received from a friend, a white man who overheard some threatening comments made at the general store, John would have met the same fate as Frank Weems:

> When I started organizing, I said to my mother and wife, "When a person dies for a good cause, that's a good death. What I'm doing is for a good cause." My mother talked to me about it quite a bit. She knew I was facing danger. A big company [Gennis] owned the plantation I was working on, and the name of the place was Lakeside. It was about 14 miles from Forrest City, Arkansas, on the Saint Francis River. They were the ones who run me out. Them planters had made a threat, they had the rope and the limb, and all they wanted was me. I was lucky enough that a . . . friend of mine…heard 'em talkin' about, "That nigger, John Handcox. We got the rope an' everything, and all we want his him." He come back and told my mother and wife.
>
> I had a high-power rifle, a .303, and I said, "Momma, I ain't goin' nowhere. I'm gonna get my bullets, and get on up side this hill, and the first bunch I see, I'm gonna let 'em have it!" I said "Mama, I aint goin nowhere. I'm gonna shoot it out." sometimes you just do somethin' in the moment. You know, if you'da had enough time or someone woulda stopped ya, you wouldn'ta done it. [So] at first I told my mother and my wife that I wasn't going anywhere.
>
> I wanted to get my rifle and shoot it out. But mama said, "John, you get away from here." She said, "Oh, no, John. If you just injure one of 'em . . . they'll prob'ly kill us all." She was right. They'd do anything to try to get even with me.
>
> Well, I walked about four or five miles to a friend's house that I knew lived on the highway. The Greyhound buses was passin' his house, a two-lane road, one wide enough for you to pass. It was a rock road, wasn't paved. I went over and spent the night with him and then I caught the bus into Memphis, to the STFU headquarters . . . on into Memphis, and I met Clay East and quite a few more of 'em in Memphis.

John recalled, *I imagine I was a lucky man to get away. Some of them didn't get away.* Indeed, the authorities framed up his younger brother Willis (Bill), claiming he had been on a picket line for the union when in fact he had been at home. In the criminal justice system in the Delta, the truth didn't matter: *They caught my brother, and sent him out one of those so-called county reforms [penal farms] and kept him from May up until October. They said he was eight or 10 miles away from home with the pickets, but he wasn't; he was at the house. They was [also] tryin' to get me; they had all the inside on me, but I just got away.*

After John "caught that puppy to Memphis," as he once described his sudden exit on a Greyhound bus, Mitchell sent him from Memphis down to the union refuge in Hill House, Mississippi. John's visit there showed him first-hand some of the cooperative principles of socialism and the Social Gospel in action, deepening his sense that he belonged to a network of people who were going to change the world. While there, Handcox went to a school for labor activists that featured Howard Kester and taught people how to uphold the humanity of the poor and dispossessed on earth through trade unionism. In this unlikely Mississippi setting, John learned more about Socialism than he probably had ever known before, for he could see the principle of sharing in daily operation at the farm.[63] He recalled it briefly,

> *Down in Mississippi we had what is known as summer schools down there. That was Hill House, where some of the Socialist Party people got together and they was trying out cooperative farming. I went down there, I spent a week or a little better down there after I had to leave Arkansas on account of the strike. Mitchell asked me would I like to go down there. When landlords thow'd the people off the land in Arkansas, they made arrangements for some of them to go to Hill House. You see, all the people's find out they belong to the union, they just get that little hay mattress and whatever they had and carry it out and throwed it on the side of the highway. Yeah, they moved them out of their houses. You know, the houses was owned by the company. They made some kind of deal down in Hill House, Mississippi, and they moved the peoples off the road down to Hill House, and they just farmed what was known as "cooperative farming" down there.*

Hill House was one of the interesting offshoots of the STFU, part of its efforts to create a cooperative farming alternative to plantation capitalism. The union had polled its early members in 1934 and learned that most of them wanted government loans to small owner-operated farms; sharecropping with a union contract; or, only as a distant third choice, cooperative farming. Some scholars argue that the Socialists put their ideological commitments above the interests of small farmers by advocating cooperatives, but it seems that the Socialists had a better plan for saving the small farmer than did the capitalist system, which was fast destroying the farmer's way of life. As evictions escalated and cotton mechanization threatened to remove human labor from production, STFU leaders thought cooperative farming provided the only way for the small farmer to continue to exist.[64]

Appalled at what he saw in Arkansas during the 1936 strike, Rev. Sherwood Eddy had gathered money and bought a cheap 2,138 acres in Bolivar County, Mississippi, for people evicted from the Dibble plantation. They began arriving in March, 1936. By August, 12 white and 19 black families lived at Hill House, including the wife of Frank Weems and her eight children. Members of Delta Cooperative Farm belonged to a consumer (buying) and a producer (selling) cooperative, a nonprofit store, and a credit union. They made different hourly wages based on the type of labor they did, working together in jobs not coded by color. A council composed of five members, no more than three of whom could be of the same race, governed the place. So as not to get shut down by the State of Mississippi for violating segregation laws, whites provided most of the day-to-day management, education and medical care. Whites and blacks lived on opposite sides of the road and went to different schools, although blacks got eight rather than the meager four months of school provided by the state. Blacks and whites had equal access to community facilities.[65]

Eddy was so frightened of Arkansas that in a sense he jumped out of the frying pan and into the fire by taking his coop to Mississippi. It prospered but then was sold in 1942 and replaced on larger acreage by Cooperative Farms, Inc., in Holmes County, Mississippi. In 1954, when the White Citizens Council organized to oppose the US Supreme Court school desegregation ruling, *Brown V. Board of Education*, white supremacists attacked the farm as "communist." The economic boycotts and other forms of intimidation that followed eventually shut the farming community down.[66]

Chronicling a Movement in Poetry and Song

By forcing John out of Arkansas, the planters gave him time to write. Returning to Memphis from Hill House, songs and poems poured out of him. Exhorting people to action, painting word pictures of a life that sharecroppers knew all too well, but rarely heard articulated, John clearly contrasted right and wrong, good and evil, simply by telling what he saw. In his poem "King Cotton," he contrasted the bright decorations and flags of the Memphis Cotton Carnival to the shabby conditions of those who did the work, and concluded, "When Cotton is King of any nation/it means wealth to the planter—to the laborer starvation." In "Strike in Arkansas," he wrote out the story of Earle, where planters forced workers into fields at the point of a gun and the "court house ring" convicted unionists with no regard for justice. In "Landlord, What in the Heaven is the Matter with You?" and in "The Planter and the Sharecropper," he described sharecropping as only someone who had lived within it could.

In "Mean Things Happening in This Land," Handcox gave a sharp musical picture of the sharecropper's plight during the strike of 1936. He said it was his favorite composition, and it shows that John did not only draw on church music in writing his songs. He wrote it in a major key but sang it in a haunting blues style, in a minor key. How he came upon the song's melody and structure remains a mystery of some interest. It is similar to "There Are Strange Things Happening in the Land," a broadside that had appeared in the adjacent cotton country of east Texas during World War I. Black song included a genre of disaster songs, as well as songs that pilloried the boss man, low hours, long wages, and bad luck.

The sinking of the Titanic was one such song.[67] This apocalyptic song, written around the same time, spoke of famines, nations fighting nations, and German imperialism: "For the war is going on, causing many hearts to mourn/There are strange things happening in this land." The song condemned war but concluded with a resounding assertion that black soldiers would help to defeat imperialism through their heroic sacrifice, and concluded with a patriotic hope:

> Go tell old Billie Kaiser that Woodrow Wilson said
> He will never quit fighting until he kills him dead.
> There he will ring the Liberty Bell, give old kaiser room in hell,
> There are great things happening in this land.[68]

John recorded (see the next chapter) "Mean Things" in 1937 at the Library of Congress. Unlike his song, "Strange Things" had a commercial life. Folklorist Alan Lomax later came across a blind street singer named Charles Haffer in Mississippi, peddling his own broadside of "Strange Things," concerning World War II. The song concluded, "I say war's goin on, caused our hearts to mourn/ Strange things happening in this land."[69] Sister Rosetta Tharpe, born in Cotton Plant, Arkansas, where one set of John Handcox's grandparents had first settled, recorded yet another version, in 1944, and Johnny Cash said it was his favorite song. Many regard her rhythmic rendition of "There Are Strange Things Happening Every Day," which she accompanied with electric guitar and drums, as the first "rock'n roll" song. John's version of the song later appeared in *Hard-Hitting Songs for Hard-Hit People*, and in other versions with no attribution.[70]

Eastern Arkansas is a long way from east Texas, and John had little if any access to record players, radios, or centers of entertainment. It remains a mystery how or if John ever heard "Strange Things." But the discourse here illustrates, as anyone involved with "folk" or popular music (or any music) already knows, that a song is usually built on something that came before. People borrow from and elaborate on older songs. Like Martin Luther King, Jr., or other ministers, singers and songwriters draw on familiar themes, sounds, and feelings. In the "folk" tradition, the song itself matters more than who wrote it (and knowing who wrote which parts of it mostly interests those who wanted to hold copyrights). As singer and scholar Bernice Johnson Reagon relates, in the southern African American community there was always a model of a leader, a song, a way of being to follow.[71]

In that context, one can appreciate why John's songs had great power. Black theologian Howard Thurman described expressive preaching and singing as "a shaft of light" to people oppressed by slavery and segregation. Black musical scholar Arthur Jones wrote that composers "were simply conduits for the expression of the collective thoughts and feelings of the community."[72] Rev. Brookins may have had a stronger singing voice than John and prided himself on being the

STFU "songster." But after John came to Memphis and started writing, he would increasingly serve as the union's poetic spokesperson. Matching words to tunes, he began to voice both his community's plight and its solidarity.

* * *

John escaped from Arkansas, but his younger brother Willis (Bill) remained trapped on a county penal farm for six months, working for nothing and leaving his family in a starving condition. For a time, no one in his family knew where he was or how to reach him. John saw his brother's arrest as a way to get back at him and, in a similar way, his own absence from Arkansas would leave his wife Ruth and four children without a breadwinner. John thought organizing was worth the risk, as he summarized many years later:

> Back then 'course I knew it was a terrible risk. It's a risk in everything. But if my life is lost tryin' to help someone else, I think that would be a pretty good death, to die knowing you trying to help someone. I go out here and do somethin' crazy and get kilt, that's a life thow'd away. But when you try to work to help the suffering people, the working man, I think that's a life that is not wasted even if you get kilt. You lose your life, you have something to show for it. You'd get recommended or somethin.' Somebody will think of you as bein' one that did this, or one that helped did this.

For Handcox and the thousands of other black and white farmers who joined the STFU, the dream of a different world outweighed the economic and physical risk. Singing songs about their plight helped them to overcome their fears and press on for justice.

CHAPTER 5

Roll the Union On: Interracial Organizing in Missouri

We're goin' to roll, goin' to roll, goin' to roll the union on,
Goin' to roll, goin' to roll, goin' to roll the union on!

—John Handcox

In Memphis, political boss E. H. Crump ruled with a repressive iron hand. Yet the police largely left the Southern Tenant Farmers Union office on Broad Street alone as long as it did not organize in the city (although the police took in H. L. Mitchell for questioning during the 1936 strike). The Hanrahan Bridge across the Mississippi River from Arkansas to Memphis functioned as a gateway to relative safety for many terrorized STFU members. "Union headquarters in Memphis are crowded with refugees from Arkansas," according to the *Sharecroppers' Voice*. Eliza Nolden (who would die from the beating she received in Arkansas) and the wife of Frank Weems and her eight children (who would later take sanctuary in Mississippi) all took refuge in a two-room shotgun shack with Rev. A. B. Brookins and his wife. Writing that he was still a "Socialist From My hart" at age 70, Brookins pleaded with Mitchell to put him back into Arkansas, where officers of the law had beaten and imprisoned him for 45 days and vigilantes had shot bullets through his home, grazing the hair of one of his children. Mitchell wrote to Brookins, "We have to use only the people who can do the work in the field that is needed and younger men who can dodge planters and don't mind going to jail . . . I think too much of you to send you out in bad places."[1]

John Handcox was one of those younger men, but he had no intention of going back to Arkansas to end up at the bottom of the river or in a jail cell, like his brother now on the penal farm. Instead, once back from Hill House in Mississippi, John wrote songs and poems every day, including one of his most famous pieces, "Roll the Union On." He recalled, "I was settin' out in the yard in Memphis, settin' in the sun. They were in the act of marching over in Arkansas when I wrote it."[2] The song, as published in the *Sharecropper's Voice*, went like this:

> *If the planter's in the way, we gonna roll it over them, goin' to roll right it over*
> *them.*
> *If the planter's in the way, we goin' roll it over them,*
> *Goin' to roll it over them, roll the union on.*

It was a classic "zipper" song, similar to many used in the black church and later in the civil rights movement, in which singers changed one or two words to create a new verse. John's verses "zipped in" various people the union would roll over. He, the white singer and writer Lee Hays, and others would "zip" infinite villains into the song: "if the boss is in the way"—"if the merchant's in the way"—"if the banker's in the way"—"if Wall Street's in the way." In John's original version, he targeted some of the persons blocking the sharecroppers' movement: "if Peaches (derogatory for Peacher) in the way"—"if Futrell (the Governor) in the way." The cadence was perfect for hand clapping, marching, standing in unison, or picketing. The format was so simple a child could learn it after hearing the first verse. The "gonna roll" mantra invited a call-and-response ("gonna roll—gonna roll") that created an emotional echo-chamber.

Although not the same, the tune carried elements of a number of other popular songs. When *The Sharecroppers' Voice* published the song, it likened the tune to "Polly-Wolly-Doodle"—an ubiquitous American song copyrighted in 1880 and thought to be derived from an African American or minstrel song familiar to black and white alike.[3] To the same tune, the STFU songbook included "On the Picket Line," a song from the Industrial Workers of the World (IWW):

> On the line, on the line,
> Come and picket on the picket line.
> In one strong union we'll join hands.
> Come and picket on the picket line.[4]

"Roll the Union On" also bore similarities to "Roll de Ole Chariot Along," an old church song that went back to slavery days. As first published in 1927 and sung at the Hampton Institute, a black college founded during Reconstruction, the song was not about rolling over anyone but about rolling together to a better world. (However, verse six the song read, "Ef de precher's in de way/Jus' foll him over/Ef ye don't hang on behin'").[5] Numerous other church songs used the phrase "Roll On" as a metaphor for individuals traveling a righteous path to personal liberation. "I'm a-rollin', I'm a-rollin', I'm a-rollin' through an unfriendly world," went one spiritual.[6] Both the theme and the tune of "Roll the Union On" inspired upbeat, defiant feelings of robust forward movement and heartfelt hopes for change.[7] John's songs proved powerful in part because so many people knew the tunes and the universe of feelings they invoked, but he rightly maintained that they were his own creations.[8] Properly and militantly sung, "Roll the Union" did not sound much like any of its cousins. John estimated that he wrote perhaps as many as 20 such songs and poems while in Memphis in the spring of 1936, but said he lost many of them in his later travels.

Increasingly, people called for John Handcox to sing and recite his works before union meetings and conventions, and some began to refer to him as "sharecropper's troubadour" or the "poet laureate" of the STFU. For a time, he also became one of the union's most effective organizers. H. L. Mitchell *asked me 'bout goin' up in Missoura,"* and without hesitation John said yes. In June, 1936, he began a new odyssey as the only representative of the union in that state. Addressing letters to Mitchell as "dear comrade," or "dear bro," and signing off as "a willing worker," he proved an enthusiastic organizer. One of the STFU's eastern Arkansas locals called itself the "sisters of right," and another the "willing workers local." John displayed the same passionate dedication to the union.[9]

A Willing Worker

We don't exactly know how John Handcox made his way up to Missouri, since he did not have his own car. Most travelers would have gone from east to west over the Mississippi River out of Memphis. Reaching West Memphis, Arkansas, one hits the north-south highway, Route 61. With a right hand turn, one goes north through the eastern Arkansas delta for a few hundred miles, past hellholes of peonage and terror in Crittenden, Poinsett, and Mississippi Counties—traveling past the massive Lee Wilson plantation and the site of the Lowery lynching of 1921. Johnny Cash headed this way en route to an auto factory in Pontiac, Michigan; Muddy Waters passed through moving north to blues clubs in Chicago; and so many others made this journey, that Bob Dylan would sing about a generation later in the song, "Highway 61."[10] This is the journey John Handcox made from Memphis in June, 1936.

Exiting northeast Arkansas, a new territory opens up. Many called it "swampeast" Missouri, also known as the Missouri Bootheel—a heel-shaped piece of rich delta lands wedged up against the Mississippi River opposite from Kentucky and Illinois. One has departed from the states of the old Confederacy: in Missouri, blacks could vote and exercised greater legal rights. But in this isolated, tough, but fertile farming region of "Swampeast" Missouri, the spirit if not the laws of Jim Crow still reigned. White landholders in the early 1920s had recruited thousands of black laborers, tenants, and sharecroppers from the Deep South. They preferred blacks as more experienced and industrious workers, paid at lower wages, and with fewer rights. Whites also flooded into the region, and used violence to drive black labor competitors out, while blacks organized the

Garvey movement in part for self-protection. It was not exactly the Promised Land for uniting black and white workers.[11]

Although now removed from his own kinship networks in Arkansas, John must have easily understood the social and economic terrain in the Missouri Bootheel. Floods, drought, the collapse of cotton prices, and finally the Great Depression had blasted the hopes of blacks and white alike. Both groups of emigrants suffered from disease, poverty, and landlessness.[12] Plantation capitalists, using AAA New Deal funding, were consolidating their hold over the land and pushing out tenants and sharecroppers in favor of paying day laborers. As in Arkansas, African Americans built churches, strong kinship networks, and traditions of solidarity. As in Arkansas, hard-pressed rural people of both races turned to nondenominational, decentralized religion. "Spirit-filled revival," historian Jarrod Roll explains, "whether in Pentecostal-Holiness or independent Baptist churches, offered ordinary people a new source of power in their efforts to confront evil in the world."[13]

John added a union component to this mix by using the same method he had used in Arkansas: going to where people worked, joining with them in the work, and talking union. *I went on up to Memphis, and then started organizin' in Missouri . . . I went 'round to different places organizin' locals. I introduced myself to the different people and chopped a little cotton with 'em, helpin' 'em, to get out there and talk with 'em. I'd get me a sack and pick a day or two with 'em. I set up quite a few locals in Missouri, made a lot of contacts. It was mighty few in Missouri that had their own tools and animals to work with. The biggest half I say was sharecroppers.*

Without a car or a home, John stayed briefly with a black worker named Braxton Taylor in Charleston, contacting workers in and around Missouri's majority-black Mississippi County. Here he met three women who had already asked the STFU for a "women's charter." Within a week, they formed a tiny local of the STFU (with seven founding members), presided over by a black man who had worked in Garvey's Universal Negro Improvement Association (UNIA), on the farm of a white planter named Thad Snow. John wrote to the STFU office, "we will have a good success up here."[14]

Snow enabled that success; he was undoubtedly the most surprising white plantation owner John ever met. A total misfit who detested segregation, Snow had migrated from Indiana in 1910 and pioneered in the budding cotton economy, surviving three major floods, droughts, and then collapsing cotton prices. A well-informed, liberal capitalist with sympathies for both socialism and the New Deal, Snow read works as diverse as Thorsten Veblen and Gandhi. Yet he also owned about 1,000 acres of a cotton plantation, and could get nothing done without the hard work of his black tenants. He believed that his fellow landlords would have a better conscience if they gave agricultural workers better treatment. He invited John and other STFU members onto his land and urged them to organize a union.[15] John even lived on Snow's land for a time and rejoiced at meeting him. He wrote a poem about Snow and sent it to H. L. Mitchell, asking him to "Please fix this up and send Mr. Snow a copy."[16] John's "fix this up" comment suggests the ways that others helped him to edit his diction and punctuation. We don't know if Mitchell sent the poem to Snow, and the union did not publish it in the *Sharecroppers' Voice*. But clearly, Snow's very existence encouraged John's lifelong belief that whites and blacks could work together for a better world:

Missouri's where I met Thad Snow. He was a planter up there, one of the best men in Missouri I know. I wrote a poem about him that's in the recording I did in the Library of Congress . . . "Out on Mr. Snow's Farm, or The Kind of Man We Like to Meet," and it went like this:

> *Early the second Monday in June,*
> *I walked up to Mr. Thad Snow's Home, all alone,*
> *And introduced myself to Mr. Snow,*
> *One of the best men in SE-MO, I know.*
> *He says to me, something for labor ought to be done,*
> *And you are perfectly welcome to go on my farm.*
> *He pointed me out some of the hands in the field,*
> *Told me to talk with them and see how they feel.*
> *Then he asked me what else he could do*
> *To help put our labor movement thru.*
> *I told him his help would be much if he didn't object*
> *For the labor on his farm to join our Union as such.*
> *I walked over Mr. Snow's farm in all ease,*
> *For I knew that Mr. Snow was well pleased.*
> *I sang. I talked and rejoiced as I went,*
> *For I knew I had gotten Mr. Snow's consent.*
> *This is the kind of men we need, you know,*
> *Men that are in sympathy with their labor, like Mr. Snow.*[17]

Snow asked other planters to accept the union on their premises, but his hopes proved to be naive. John thought Missouri planters to be just as nasty as in Arkansas, and in some respects worse. *"The planters up here won't allow the labor to have chicken cow hog or a row of corn,"* he wrote, reporting he was *"really surprise to see the condition like they is up here."* Sharecroppers tried desperately to stay on the land, even as planters filched AAA payments and anticipated replacing most of their labor with the cotton-picking machine already being tested out by the Rust Brothers.[18]

In Missouri, John quickly confronted difficulties. On June 14 he reported to Mitchell, *"The High Sheriff of Mississippi County told some of the union officers that they could not operate until they get legal rights from Jefferson City."* Southern towns often required union organizers to register themselves, like a loaded gun, with authorities. Of course, such a self-revelation could alert employers to get rid of the organizer or intimidate their workers so they wouldn't join. John wrote, *"I know nothing about no law,"* and ignored it. But he also expressed concern that many of the people he met in Missouri were *"afraid to take hold this opportunity."* John felt concerned as well about the reluctance of whites to get involved, and asked the STFU to send a white organizer to help him with recruiting.[19]

On July 23, however, John wrote proudly to J. R. Butler, *"I have succeeded in getting some of the white connected with the S.T.F.U."* He did so by joining forces with a white union man named J. C. Kirkpatrick, who lived in a little town called Deventer. For 16 years, Kirkpatrick had belonged to the United Mine Workers of America (UMWA) and he remained a loyal unionist. His family was *"in a very bad condition having to catch work as he can but he say that he is will to do all he can for the STFU and is willing to give his life for it if necessary,"* John wrote to Butler. *"You can't imagine how proud I'm of him."* The two went to a little place called Pinhook, where they inspired agricultural workers with their words and songs. Together, John wrote enthusiastically, *"we kindled a fire that will burn forever."* The two men planned to spend the next week organizing in various places.[20]

Although blacks constituted the majority of the people the union organized, John experienced greater interracial contact in Missouri than he had in Arkansas. His education, slight as it was, often exceeded that of whites. John, like his father before him, could do figures in his head, and could handle the paperwork of enrolling union members and making field reports to Mitchell and Butler in Memphis. His experiences at all steps up and down the agricultural ladder, and even his knowledge of bootlegging, came in handy. He remembered his entrance into Missouri organizing this way:

> *There were some white. I had just 'bout as good of luck organizin' the whites in Missouri as I did the coloreds. I had the privilege of getting quite a few of the whites into the organization. 'Course, the poor whites didn't know how to read. And in the part of Missouri I was in, those bootleggers went right across the Mississippi River into Kentucky and brought back moonshine to sell in Missouri. I remember one time the FBI's showed up and they was chasing moon shiners around there. And they run up on this preacher with this jug. They say, "what they hell you doin' with that jug." He said "I'm a minister, I'm a minister. I come down here to buy me some fish." "What kind of fish?" He says "I buys eels, I'm gonna put this eel in the jug and ca'y 'em back home." They laughed at that guy about that jug, and they let him go.*

Schooled in the ways of rural people, he knew how to joke and get along, and to address their concerns with a humble demeanor.

> *The way I would approach them about the union, I ask them was they satisfied of being treated like they was, and talk with 'em and reason with them, and tell them*

we can do better. All we got to do is unite and we could demand more from the planter. Makin' a speech, it would run along that line. We could be able to demand more wages, and a better place to stay. White folks and black folks was all in the same boat. If one drowned, the other one would drown. Although, we had discrimination because the landowner taught discrimination.

Although blacks and whites attended separate schools and churches and lived separate lives geographically and politically, they did not find it impossible to meet together. He recalled:

We didn't have segregated locals in Missouri, 'though there wasn't that many whites up there, just cotton pickers. To my knowing, we never did have a discriminatory local. Not where I was. The meetings was mixed, and we enjoyed 'em. The relations between the union members was splendid. They had whites and blacks in the same organizations in Missouri. We'd usually start with a song and then a prayer and then go to general business. We'd sing together, and we'd read the different articles in The Sharecropper's Voice, and sing some more. I usually led all the singing when I was at the meeting. I often read minutes and reports, too.

According to historian Jarod Roll, John had tapped into preexisting networks of religiously committed activists, both black and white, that existed just outside of Charleston and near Henson, Missouri. They opened meetings with prayers and scripture, and many belonged to evangelical Pentecostal and Holiness sects. John remained skeptical of preachers, but he liked the kind of religion that fired up workers to organize, and it fired him up too. *"I have raise my hand to God and I will not turn back,"* he wrote to Mitchell.[21]

John picked up on that feeling of religious inspiration to transform an old black church song, "Lord, I Want to Be a Christian In My Heart." The standard song told of the singer's resolve to "be a Christian," to "be more loving," "to be more holy," and "to be like Jesus . . . in my heart." According to an early black scholar of spirituals, John Wesley Work, slaves often overcame the "stupendous burden of human bondage, with all its inherent sorrows and heart breakings" by adopting a sentiment of love instead of hate. Songs with this point of view did not in any way suggest submission, but rather insisted that, "The world needs to know that love is stronger than hatred."[22] In that vein, John adapted this spiritual.

The spiritual has a line later in the song, "I don't want to be like Judas." John's rendition of "In My Heart" began by enumerating those *"I don't want to be like:"* Governor Futrell and Paul Peacher. These references suggest that he first wrote this song during the 1936 strike and his Memphis exile. The song then went on to pay homage to white Socialist and STFU leaders who *"I want to be like."* His verses listed Mr. Snow, Butler, Mitchell, Norman Thomas, and Howard Kester, who had taught him about the union Social Gospel in Hill House, Mississippi.

It would have made just as much (or more) sense to devote verses to black STFU leaders Brookins or McKinney, but having grown up in the bowels of segregation, John especially appreciated white exemplars of union solidarity and anti-racism. More, he wanted other whites to emulate their behavior.

John sang the chorus, *"In My Heart, In My Heart,"* in an eerie, almost pathetic, falsetto, quite different from his normal speaking and singing voice. Occasionally, as in his version of "Oh Freedom After 'While," John slipped into falsetto, adapting a standard trope of the black song tradition. Throughout black history, singers and poetic spokespersons had served as "conduits for the expression of the collective thoughts and feelings of the community," as one music scholar put it.[23] John increasingly played that role in Missouri, albeit with Socialist politics. He mentioned God only occasionally and Jesus not at all, but his Social Gospel held out hope for a better future through organizing and human solidarity as a means to fulfill God's justice.[24] In Missouri, he found more evidence for his labor protest songs: "I see people daily that was hungry; I see people daily that was raggedy; I see people daily that was homeless."[25]

On a more mundane level, John found a way to exist in Missouri. By the end of the July, 1936, Handcox had found a place to live in Henson, had lined up a union meeting for every night of the week, and was raising money to buy a used car. He had already set up six locals in Mississippi County.[26] His concerns had become those of an organizer: he wrote to "Mr. Butler" at STFU headquarters in Memphis that membership enlistment remained slow because people had no money to pay dues until harvest season; he asked to go to an organizer's training school planned by the union; he wanted to set up a county central council; and he needed membership books and stamps.[27]

John entered into a phase of organizing in Missouri that would far surpass his efforts in Arkansas, which had been cut short by the threat of a hangman's noose. "John L. Handcox evangelized to his listeners that only the land, the Lord, and the union could save them," wrote historian Robert Ferguson. "Handcox's songs demonstrated a belief that a leftist and activist interpretation of the Social Gospel of Jesus, with the help of the Southern Tenant Farmers' Union, would deliver the suffering sharecroppers from the plantation economy into fair labor practices where black and white agrarians could finally scrape out a decent living."[28]

"Join the Union Tonight"

John's ability to recite poetry from memory—he could still remember and recite some of his poems at the drop of a hat even 50 years later—made him a captivating presence. Like rap artists in later years, he could rhythmically recount people's troubles and hopes, without written notes. He could also sing their troubles into action. John put into service in Missouri another song he probably wrote while in

Memphis—the jaunty, "Join the Union Tonight." It did not sound like a "Negro hymn" and could just as easily be fitted to white country music as to black gospel. Like a singing historian, he explained the origins of the sharecropper's struggle that he had witnessed in Arkansas, and used that story to convince people to join the struggle:

> In 1933 we plowed up our crops
> Join the union tonight.
> Oh them planters had such a sop.
> Join the union tonight.
> Refrain:
> Come along, oh workers come along,
> Help the union to grow strong.
> Oh get enrolled, stop toting such a load.
> Join the union tonight.
> One man can't do nothing by hisself
> Join the union tonight.
> But work hard and starve to death.
> Join the union tonight. [Refrain.]
> In the AAA in '34
> Join the union tonight.
> Planters' children labor hours or more
> Join the union tonight. [Refrain.]
> Back a year the union start
> Join the union tonight.
> Sharecroppers did not get that far.
> Join the union tonight. [Refrain]
> When the union first begun
> Join the union tonight.
> Planters laughed and had their fun
> Join the union tonight. [Refrain]
> We're tired of working in the field
> Join the union tonight.
> Plan on standing on our heels.
> Join the union tonight. [Refrain]

Sung in a major key with an upbeat tempo, "Join the Union Tonight," as historian Jarod Roll comments, "evoked the tone and tenor of a revival meeting." The song declared that if listeners wanted justice, it was their responsibility to go out and get it. "Plan on standing on our heels" threatened a strike. "Just as individuals at revival meeting had to accept Christ to achieve salvation, tenants had to choose to join the STFU and if necessary to take action to achieve their common economic goals," Roll explained. And that decision "had to be taken 'tonight,' since tomorrow or next week might be too late." The song announced that, "organized workers were an undeniable force, no matter how strong the opposition might be."[29] Like many of John's songs, "Join the Union" could become an anthem when used in congregational (in unison) singing, accompanied with hand clapping and foot stomping. (One can also imagine it in a country music style accompanied by guitars and drums.)

John's letters from Missouri to STFU headquarters in Memphis reflected his feelings of inspiration that resulted in part from the interracial character of some of the mass meetings he organized in the summer and fall of 1936. He and Kirkpatrick built a mixed-race local in Pinhook, and by August, John was holding meetings of various union locals every Saturday night. He announced that Mitchell himself would turn up at one of these gatherings, and although Mitchell did not make it, John wrote to him, *"all the white members were there to meet you."* These workers got whites in other areas to join, and *"they all seems to have lots of confidence in me and think this [the union] is the thing they need so bad."*[30] But amidst these signs of success, a tendency emerged for whites to want a "white charter" and a "white local." As a lone black organizer, John found himself in a vulnerable position. He told Mitchell as early as June 14, *"I think we need a white organizer up here."*

No one could expect to build a mass movement of white and black around a solitary black organizer. John dreamed of firing up an interracial movement and creating a central labor council to provide a planning mechanism for various locals, but the STFU provided no backup.[31] Snow and white union members urged John to bring in a white STFU "street speaker," and John repeatedly asked Mitchell or Butler to come or to send Claude Williams. Mitchell praised John, writing, "we all think you are doing great work there," and pledged to send someone. By August 17, John and his comrades had organized 15 more whites into another local, but the STFU simply had no money to send someone and more or less left him to his own devices.[32]

Handcox felt inspired by his life of organizing, but he also expressed fears about his wife Ruth and their four children back in Arkansas, wondering how they could survive without him. His move to Missouri may have been the beginning of a long deterioration of his relationship to Ruth, who experienced extreme stress in his absence. John recalled: *"when I left home [Arkansas], I left enough food that if my wife used it properly, it probably would have taken care of her and the kids for a year or more. I had barrels of flour, sacks of sugar, and stuff like that. I had a cow or two."* However, things did not go as planned. *"They moved soon after I left . . . The owner took her crop away from her, and she and the kids went and stayed with her dad."*

John's exit from Arkansas proved disastrous to his family. Authorities had retaliated against John by arresting his brother Bill—for carrying a gun, a strange charge in a rural country where almost every male carried a one. They jailed him in Forrest City, a regional stronghold of the KKK, then put him on a county penal farm, where riding bosses sometimes worked prisoners to death. Folklorist Alan Lomax described such southern prison farms as "a chain of hellholes strung across the land like so many fiery crosses to remind the Southern blacks that chains and armed guards and death awaited them if they rebelled."[33] Of course, John's mother feared what would happen to Bill, and not only had authorities sentenced him to the county work farm for six months, they had also fined him $200. Bill's inability to pay the fine gave the law an excuse to confiscate not only Bill's crop but also John's crop, thus forcing Ruth to go to live with her father. Ruth lost her independence, while the whole family lost its tenuous economic base.

The fate of his brother, his wife, and his extended family worried John for another reason. "The people up here ask me what protection has a union member. I been telling them what strong protection we have," John wrote to Mitchell on June 14. But he feared that the ACLU $1,000 reward to convict anyone of victimizing union members and the union's pledge to defend its workers was only a bluff, and that in fact no one had the ability to protect them.[34] Three months later, John wrote to Mitchell that his brother "never had know pistol and he have enough witness to prove that he was not even at the place they claims he were."[35] Mitchell promised to help but the union could not even locate Bill in the prison farm system and could do nothing about this frame up, among many others.[36]

John's assignment in Missouri also meant increasing financial uncertainty, and John pleaded with Mitchell to send him a paycheck. By October 13, he wrote, he had been reduced to organizing only on Sundays because he had to go out in the fields during the week to make money. *My wife and all my children is sick and I have been picking cotton and sending them some money along. I wish you would please send me some money for I up against a hard point.* He added, "*I have walk a new pair Shoe out since I have been up here . . . I'm walking and talking and doing all I can to establish more locals.*" But, he put in his P.S., "*I'm penny less.*"[37]

A few days later, John wrote sarcastically, "*I do not mind giving my life for the union or the people. But [I] do feel that God would displeaured at me to give my life and family to.*" He added that he had pledged to God not to turn back, and "*I can truly say that I'm willing to do all in my power to promote the best interest of the union.*"[38] Nonetheless, the stress of organizing had become apparent: John now signed his letters not as "a Willing Worker," as previously, but simply as "A Worker."[39]

"One Man Can't Do Nothin' By Hisself"

John's efforts to get a white STFU leader into the state finally succeeded. On September 26, 1936, on a Saturday night, all of the union members got together to hear a rousing speech by Claude Williams, in the Charleston city park—reserved and partially paid for by Mr. Snow (John called him "our secret dective [detective]"). It turned out to be not only a meeting but also a picnic, displaying the "social equality" that racists so abhorred. *"Everybody had a plenty to eat and it were not serve us white and colored but as a big family dinner,"* John wrote, featuring pies, cakes, baloney, pickles, chicken, and other delicacies.[40] By bringing in Claude Williams, John upped the ante in his efforts to create a different kind of world, for reasons that would soon become apparent.

John asked him to come back, and on November 5, 1936, Williams returned, to preach his "gospel of the working class" at a tiny black church in Crosno, Missouri. This mass meeting definitively sharpened the class politics of John's organizing. Rev. E. B. McKinney opened the meeting in his gracious and authoritative way. We can imagine that this black minister made his typically powerful appeal to union members, and especially to African Americans, urging them to have no fear and to lift themselves up through group effort. We have no notes of McKinney's speech, but historians have pieced together a powerful talk made by Claude Williams, who was by now known as a "red" preacher of the Social Gospel.

Williams connected with working-class people through his version of sanctified religion. He viewed Jesus as a revolutionary who sought to build the Kingdom of God on earth by tearing down the wrongs that separated people from each other and replacing them with "an order of justice and brotherhood for everybody." Williams declared that working-class people could bring about the kingdom of heaven on earth. "There is an abundance if we seek this order," Williams asserted, and he urged his listeners to adopt the power of the union as a "new Pentecost." He denounced heartless planters for starving workers and their children and vowed that the power of the people would overcome the power of the planter. He shouted out that unionism was "the most Christian thing in the world" and urged people to "get converted" into the union. His preaching drew black workers, who predominated in the audience, into a call-and-response mode, with shouts of "amen!"—"talk!"—"preach union!"[41]

Williams preached his social justice gospel with a hard-edged take on the labor movement, saying: "What it is not: Santa Claus, relief program, land agency, etc., etc. It is: uniting all workers to make a just world in which all working people will have jobs, security, culture, home, health."[42] And, unlike almost every white person in the South, Williams openly rejected the cardinal principle of white supremacy. He made a point of explaining that, instead of five races of inferior and superior beings, as white supremacists explained race, "there is only one race—the human race." Such words may seem commonplace today, but in 1936, it was unusual for a white southerner to pointedly go against the prevailing racial doctrine. Williams was frankly and refreshingly anti-racist. And though he had been arrested, thrown out of his church, beaten up, and nearly lynched, he remained incorrigibly militant. In coming to Missouri, he had insisted, "I am particularly anxious that a meeting be planned in the town where the mayor denied us permission to speak."[43]

Williams also made singing a cardinal means of group empowerment, and John likely sang at this gathering in the Crosno church. John reported back to the STFU, "I think his speeches meant much to us." He wrote that Claude's preaching brought about an "increase in members and more interest in the old members," who asked for Williams to come back again.[44]

Although he was one of the STFU's most steadfast supporters, Williams posed challenges to other whites. He belonged to both the Socialist Party and the Communist Party, and identified fiercely with the latter's bold anti-racism. Williams condemned racism as a special human evil central to American capitalism and said it could only be eradicated through agitation and special education among whites. Communists in the 1930s constantly pushed for black leadership, whereas, Williams later complained, the SP leadership in the mid-South had always been virtually all white. The SP state platform for Tennessee in 1912 said racism was "injected into the minds of the white wage-worker against the negro and other races is only a tactical method used by the capitalist class to keep the workers divided in the economic field." Many white Socialists continued to see no need for fighting racism as such, thinking that problem would be resolved when workers united to abolish wage slavery. Even in the 1930s, in nearby Memphis older white Socialist Party members eschewed "social equality" and mostly worked through the segregated craft unions of the American Federation of Labor (AFL) or within the confines of the small Jewish community.[45] Williams found the Socialist approach to eradicating racism inadequate.

However, the Socialist Party did have a strong strain of anti-racism. Its early leader Eugene Debs started out in an all-white railway union, but later strongly rejected racism.[46] Revolutionary Socialists like the STFU's Howard Kester and SP leader Norman Thomas took an aggressive stance against racism; Kester repeatedly put himself at risk, investigated lynchings and defying segregation laws and practices.[47] Kester and Williams had gone to Vanderbilt's theology school together, and shared feelings of outrage against both racism and capitalism. Their choice of political parties, nonetheless, would divide them and many others on labor's left. H. L. Mitchell had witnessed a horrendous lynching as a child, in which whites chained a black man to a stake and burned him to death, and he clearly rejected white supremacy. Nonetheless, the issue of what to say and do about racism would become part of a larger conflict between CP and SP supporters inside the STFU.[48]

Both the SP and the CP in the early 1930s had been fiercely sectarian. They only became friendly as part of a "united front" that the CP promoted after 1935 in response to the rise of fascism in Europe, where CP and SP disunity in Germany had paved the way for Hitler's seizure of power. In the US, some 20,000 SP and CP members held a unity conference in New York City in November 1935, creating the Workers Alliance, the organization that sent Dave Benson to help the STFU in its 1936 strike. Williams and Mitchell together issued a letter to "comrades" to also hold a conference to create "a unified socialist movement in the Southern States."[49] CP and SP labor leftists made other efforts to unite as well.[50]

However, CP activists and their allies clearly placed themselves to the left of the SP on racial matters and by doing so made a profound impact on the social movements of the 1930s. The CP explained racism as a human prejudice emanating from workers as well as capitalists, and launched various campaigns to save its various victims. By fighting for the lives of nine young black men framed up and given death sentences on false rape charges in Scottsboro, Alabama, CP activists opened growing collaboration between labor and civil rights organizations.[51] African Americans tended to appreciate the CP's militant approach to fighting racism, and black workers tended to disregard anti-communism, which segregationists and employers constantly used to divide social movements and to frighten white workers away from unions.[52]

Handcox, McKinney, and some other African Americans within the STFU embraced the Communist challenge to the Jim Crow system and challenged their own white allies in the labor movement. McKinney expressed some discomfort with Mitchell and J. R. Butler, who respectfully used the titles "Mr." and "Mrs." and earnestly sought black participation in the union, but also tended to dominate its decision making. They liked Williams's aggressive pursuit of black leadership and "social equality" and thought he was sincerely trying to move the union forward. White Socialists like Mitchell, highly aware of the CP's bad reputation for manipulating and taking over organizations, suspected Williams of raising racial issues merely as a ploy to get black support and to thereby gain personal power within the union. The messianic preacher-organizer was not subtle, polite, or tactful, was often egotistical and self righteous and touched nerves that would later help to blow the STFU apart.

An Interracial United Front

In the fall of 1936, John Handcox developed a powerful synergy with Claude Williams and, more importantly, also became comrades with Owen Whitfield, a "jackleg" (self-ordained, nondenominational) African American preacher. A writer at the time described Whitfield as "a thin, light-skinned man with Indian features"—like John, the product of Native American, white, and black heritages.[53] Whitfield pastored at a number of black churches, including the Crosno church, and was quickly becoming a powerful black working-class leader in Southeast Missouri. Whitfield had lived in the state since 1923 and suffered extreme privation as a sharecropper, tenant, and small farmer. He and his wife Zella had witnessed the premature death of their infants, and by 1936 were almost at the breaking point in having to deal with life's hardships. Zella described their miserable experience in Missouri:

I am the mother of eleven children and during my 26 years of sharecropping and raising my family, I had many hardships. I worked in the cotton fields sick or well. Many is the day when I picked and chopped cotton when I ort to of been in bed. I worked when I was expecting a baby and my feet have swollen so I could not bear any kind of shoe on my feet. But I worked right on. I stopped work long enough for the baby to come and for me to get a little strength back. And that was as soon as the baby was 3 weeks old. I never had a doctor during child birth. Just an old woman who didn't know what she was doing half the time. I had to take my babies to the cotton fields and lay them at the end of the cotton rows and exposed to all kinds of insects. And some time I have went to nurse my baby and there would be a big snake laying close by.

Zella Whitfield went on to describe insect and flea-infested living quarters, steamy hot nights without ventilation, children without milk who were bitten by spiders and rats, and "fat back and bread for breakfast, corn pone and beans for lunch and the same thing for super when we had anything." She recounted, "These things that my family and I have suffered speaks for thousands of other white and Negro families all over the south lands. And this is why I have taken up the work that I am doing or trying to do." Her life demonstrated the maxim that black women typically worked as hard as their husbands or harder, and she helped Owen to build the union.[54] A listing of the STFU in 1937 showed that at least nine of its locals consisted entirely of women.[55]

The Whitfields previously had embraced the organizing efforts of the Universal Negro Improvement Association (UNIA) until the federal government arrested and deported its leader Marcus Garvey. They also had followed the preaching of a Japanese nationalist who called on blacks to join a pan-Asian movement against the dominant white society, until the man was arrested by the federal government. The revolutionary social gospel of Williams now provided another fork in the road, turning the Whitfields toward militant interracial unionism as a vehicle of deliverance.

Whitfield repeatedly told of an epiphany he had one day while working in the fields, in which God told him that He had created an abundance of goods, so there was no reason for people to be poor. "Somebody's getting' it. If you ain't, that's your fault, not Mine." Placing this epiphany into a union framework, Whitfield preached, much like Williams and McKinney, that working-class people of all colors should take it upon themselves to fulfill a Gospel of self-help by organizing.[56]

Following his pro-union sermons in Missouri (he made a number of other speeches after Crosno), Williams returned to his home in Arkansas, but continued to stay in touch with the Missouri organizers. Whitfield and Handcox increasingly worked more or less as a team, with John carrying out the functions of a union organizer and Owen providing evangelical inspiration. Together they created 15 new STFU locals, with Handcox singing and reciting and Whitfield preaching the gospel of unionism. E. B. McKinney also played an increasingly active role as a black leader in the STFU, but was sometimes gone on speaking engagements in the North to raise funds.[57]

Missouri must have been a heady brew for John. In working with Whitfield, he experienced an increasingly powerful sense of black solidarity. On the other hand, he also experienced a greater degree of equality in race relations than he had in Arkansas. More than 50 years later, John recalled with special pleasure the evenings of congregational singing and feelings of group solidarity among both blacks and whites in Missouri. However, he also remembered a sense of disquiet and unease as whites sometimes reacted to him with apathy, skepticism or hostility. He recalled:

> *I remember one night I was in Missouri, we had a moonlight meeting, and most people take and use the cotton sacks and sew 'em together and make beds to sleep on. It was pretty beautiful moonshine, and I was talking 'bout surplus cotton. I says, "I say it's a capitalistic lie talking 'bout a surplus of cotton." I says, "if the poor people was able to buy the amount of material they needed, they could burn up all those old straw mattresses and use cotton mattresses." It was white guys about a 100 yards or more from the big house, listenin' to my speech. I heard one say, "listen to that nigger tell that damn lie!" But I was tellin' the truth! You see, they said there was a surplus of cotton, and that's why we were sufferin' so bad. And I said, "There's no surplus of cotton! If we had the cotton that they say was 'surplus' manufactured into clothes and bedding and stuff, you could get off of these hay mattresses and have some good clothes that wouldn't be wearing patches."*

John's description suggests only part of the difficulty a black man could have in talking when a white man was listening in. Yet in virtually the same breath, John also expressed pride at his role:

> *Well, didn't nobody boo me. I guess when you don't get booed you think you doing pretty good, or you're well accepted. I can truthly say that some was overjoyed, had the same feeling that I had. Because you know after I would make a speech or talk with 'em they would come and shake my hand, and say "that's what we need, and we glad you come," and all that. Which make you feel pretty good if you know the odds against you, you know, that money is against you.*

The New Era School

Life in the union remained dangerous and extremely difficult—particularly for a lone organizer like John Handcox. He had no money and, although oriented to Socialism and the Social Gospel by Howard Kester in Mississippi, he had no training in union organizing. The union had talked of sending him to an orga-nizer's leadership school, but the STFU had so far only sent whites (and only a few of them) to get any training. Rev. Brookins argued with union leaders that for each white member who went to a school a black member should also attend.[58] Plans for a formal school for STFU members finally came to pass, to be held in December, 1936, in Little Rock. But, incredibly, white STFU leaders chose an all-white teaching staff, ignoring warning signs that blacks like Brookins and McKinney were losing patience with the lack of blacks in union leadership. McKinney and H. L. Mitchell had already clashed that summer over whether the union should confront racism as such and bring forward more black lead-ers. Mitchell wrote to McKinney, "you ought to forget the race lines and think of them really important ones—class against class—the solidarity of black and white workers." Claude Williams planned to host the school as part of his grow-ing educational work with Commonwealth College, and now insisted that the school should include an equal number of blacks and whites. He took it upon himself to appoint Handcox to the staff, he wrote to Mitchell, to rectify "the conspicuous absence of Negroes on the teaching staff."[59]

A 10-day session of the New Era School began on December 13 and included 10 black and 8 white STFU students, both men and women. Meeting only two blocks from Little Rock's Central High School, the location of the civil rights movement's great struggle for school desegregation 20 years later, the New Era School utterly defied the white South's rules against "social equality." Myles Horton of Highlander Folk School participated as a teacher at New Era as did rank and file STFU activists like Henrietta McGee. As Williams summarized, students experienced "the opportunity to worship the same God at the same time in the same place. Jim Crow was not present."[60]

At the New Era School, John led singing of "Oh Freedom," "Roll the Union On," and other songs. Lee Hays, who briefly worked as an STFU volunteer orga-nizer early in 1936, had lived at Commonwealth College as a staff member under the tutelage of Claude Williams, who in 1937 would become the college's direc-tor. Hays absorbed music as if it were air; he would later provide the world with some of the great songs and stories of the South, as a member of the Almanac Singers and then the Weavers. Claude Williams, he later wrote, "has dug up folk singers and songwriters and set them to work fashioning songs for particular meetings or causes," often based on songs they already knew. Indeed, Hays later said Williams should have received some credit for parts of John's songs.[61]

In Little Rock, Williams, Hays, and Handcox sang and learned songs from each other and added "zipper" verses to "Roll the Union On." Early printed versions of the song list the authors as Hays (who put the song in the Commonwealth College song book), Hays and Williams, and, later, Hays and Handcox. Hays was adept at revising any song to fit the times; he refashioned the hymn, "I Will Overcome," for example, into a union song at the New Era School long before it became popular. More than anyone, he popularized "Roll the Union On" and added some of its verses. Early published versions of the song listed Hays and Williams as its creator, but not John Handcox. Others listed Handcox and Hays together. Despite the multiple singers involved in creating this song, however, there should be no doubt that John Handcox originally created "Roll the Union On." The varied authorship listed in printed versions of this song reflects the "folk process," in which people inserted phrases and used tunes and words interchangeably, to create powerful group singing. But there is no reason to dispute John's memory of writing the song in Memphis during the 1936 cotton choppers' strike. His version of the song first appeared in *The Sharecropper's Voice* in January, 1937, and he recorded it at the Library of Congress in March. Although he did not claim credit for it during that recording, his verses on "Peachers" and Gov. Futtrell provide internal evidence that the song was written by John at the time of the strike.[62]

The New Era school came at a high time for America's Labor Left, which had shifted from sectarianism and white dominance to a broad united front that took anti-racism seriously. The power of organized labor helped to ree-elect President Roosevelt to a second term and made possible the "second" New Deal's Social Security, Wagner National Labor Relations act, workmen's compensation, Fair Labor Standards, and other laws limiting labor exploitation. Sadly, southern segregationist Democrats—Joe Robinson of Arkansas first among them—and northern Republicans insured that low-wage agricultural and domestic workers remained excluded from most of these protections. Nonetheless, unions were on the move. Sit down strikes by Flint auto workers beginning in December, 1936, as well as the growing role of African American labor activists in the NAACP, the National Negro Congress, and the Southern Negro Youth Congress (SNYC) all promised to create an integrated, activist labor movement. The rise of the Congress of Industrial Organizations (CIO) likewise promised to democratize the economy and improve the lives of millions of workers.[63]

"You Are of the People Who Want the Kingdom of God—Not the Planters"

In this highly politicized period, the STFU met in convention in Muskogee, Oklahoma, from January 14 to 17 of 1937. The meeting began in high spirits, banners hanging from the walls biblically declaring, "What mean you that you crush my people and grind the faces of the poor?" and "Let justice roll down as the waters and righteousness as a mighty stream." The convention began with 126 delegates, most of them white Oklahomans. Many people from eastern Arkansas and Southeast Missouri could not get to Muskogee because of storms causing the Mississippi River to overflow its banks. Blacks from eastern Arkansas drove through mud and raging floods and managed to get there the next day. Rev.

Brookins led the singing of "the official union song," "We Shall Not be Moved," and the Wagoner County Choir sang "Ain't Going Study War No More" and "I'm So Happy That I Can't Sit Down."[64]

Claude Williams declared that "the first general strike was called by God himself" when Moses led the slaves against the Pharoah. He said the Kingdom of God was not for the planters but for the people, who should carry out the will of God through "unity of class." In order to reach that unity, he urged members to reject "the lies that you were taught in school about five races in the world" and to understand "there is one race, and that is the human race." To really grasp that idea, he said, workers must join together not only intellectually. "We must be emotionally convinced before we can work together."[65]

Group singing provided a means to reach that emotional unity. On the second day of the convention, a chorus developed at the New Era School led the audience in singing 15 minutes of John Handcox's songs—"Oh Freedom," "Hungry, Hungry," "Roll the Union On," and "Mean Things." Rev. Brookins concluded the set by leading delegates in singing "We Shall Not Be Moved."[66] Owen Whitfield followed up on this robust opening by blessing the people and reassuring them of heavenly support in his prayer:

> You are a Union God, and we need You because You will lead us out of our troubles . . . We are not asking You to come down here and to think for us. But Almighty Lord, we ask You for your aid.

Although the STFU prioritized class struggle, the tenor of the convention made it very clear that the union opposed racism. It was a practical obstacle to the emotional unity needed for the STFU to succeed. Walter White of the NAACP told the convention how he had barely escaped with his life when he had investigated the Elaine Massacre and said that the STFU was far ahead of earlier efforts because blacks and whites had now joined together. Some 30,000 STFU members among three million sharecroppers might not seem like much, but he said they had brought the sharecroppers' plight to the nation's attention, and reform legislation to alleviate their plight would soon follow.[67]

Convention delegates backed up these comments from the podium with their own emotional testimony from the floor. "I'm just a broken-down cowboy from Texas," said one delegate. His local consisted of 50 whites but he assured the delegates that "the Mexican and the Negroes are okay, and they are organizing with us." John Allen, one of the African Americans from eastern Arkansas who had been forced to flee for his life, preached, "When I get a chance to eat, I find myself saying Union. I begin to pray and I get to say Union. When I set down to eat, I speak about the Union . . . We want our children to enjoy a breath of freedom. If you turn back, woe be unto you." A black woman from Marked Tree recalled how a planter had inadvertently convinced her that the union "was organizing the poor man" when he told her not to pay attention to the "red-neck" organizers. Interracial class solidarity clearly trumped racial division at this convention. A white delegate from Arkansas addressed the convention goers as "fellow slaves," and others recounted how planters forced them to work for next to nothing and to hold union meetings in secret.

Howard Kester called on John Handcox to cement these emotional convictions by closing Saturday night's session with a song. Handcox at this point clearly knew how to assert himself in front of a large audience and how to lead mass singing.[68] On Sunday morning, Rev. McKinney closed the convention by declaring, "We feel that we have a right to live on the farms that we have built. We are going to say that what we want, a better life for ourselves and our children, is going to be ours."[69] The convention not only exemplified a united spirit of struggle, but envisioned radical changes in racial plantation capitalism. Against efforts of planters and the federal government to engross the land into the hands of a few, the STFU revised its union constitution to read, "the earth is the common heritage of all." It called for "wage slavery in all its forms" to be abolished in favor "of a new order of society wherein all who are willing to work shall be given the full products of their toil. We seek to establish a co-operative order of society by legal and peaceable methods."[70]

Despite a powerful level of unity inside the convention, outside the mass media was perpetuating an avalanche of red-baiting. A local newspaper reporter wildly misquoted comments by a fraternal delegate to the convention from Commonwealth College, depicting the convention as a forum for racial equality, communism, and free love. The article opened the way for denunciations of communism by members of the Arkansas state legislature. The Arkansas United Mineworker Union (UMWA) President David Fowler, who was supposed to speak as a representative of the CIO, withdrew. Mitchell only lured him back to the convention by denouncing Commonwealth and passing a resolution disassociating the STFU from all political parties and from all labor schools, particularly Commonwealth and Highlander.[71]

This incident demonstrated the power of the mass media to divide and destroy, but Claude Williams worsened the situation by going on the offensive against the STFU leadership. In a letter to Gardner Jackson, a crucial New Deal supporter of the union, Williams accused the union of seeding ground to the "racketeering, red-baiting and dictatorial Dave Fowler," who he accused (correctly) of helping the Arkansas legislature to pass a law that would imprison anyone teaching "communism" or "overthrow of the government" for up to five years. Williams also accused Mitchell of selling out both the union and Commonwealth College, whose members and leaders could all be arrested under the expansive language of this legislation. He thought there could be no compromise on the principle of the First Amendment: "The only way we can support civil liberties is to support civil liberties," Williams wrote.[72]

The anti-communist legislation failed, but the "unified socialist movement" that Mitchell and Williams had both sought came apart soon after the Muskogee convention. Complicating differing political outlooks on the left, violent factionalism, incompetence and a lack of education, and personal instability all marked the STFU leadership. White union member Walter Moskop at Commonwealth College in the summer of 1936 had pulled a gun and fired several shots at Mitchell, trying to kill him. Mitchell had supported E. B. McKinney for Vice-President of the union, defeating Moskop's bid for that position (as well as Moskop's alliance with W. H Stultz and other whites who wanted to segregate the union). Moskop's motives seem to have been racial and had little if anything to do with the CP, but Mitchell wrote, "this was the beginning of my anti-communist paranoia." Because the incident happened at Commonwealth, where Communists played a large role, because Stalin's purge trials showed communism in the worst possible light, and because of a seemingly odd comment Communist labor leader Donald Henderson later made about Moskop's assassination attempt, Mitchell's distrust of supposed Communists escalated after this incident.[73] In any case, Mitchell must have been something of a nervous wreck at this point. He briefly resigned his position as secretary of the STFU when someone on his executive board questioned his keeping of the books. The board reappointed him, but factionalism and personal conflicts in the union only worsened.[74]

Conflicts among leaders did not make much sense to most members, John Handcox included. John said that socialism was fine and he supported it, but most workers joined the union to achieve more limited goals:

I joined the Socialist Party in '36 or '37. I don't know whether or not the whites knew anything about Mitchell being a Socialist. A lot of 'em I imagine never heard of Norman Thomas. They didn't take no papers and had no radios. Most of 'em all the news they get was at the grocery store from the boss man. He ain't gon' tell them nothing that'll help them. I thought about that many times. Seem to me I heard Norman Thomas speak, but I can't recall where it was. It's been 50 years or so. Well, I don't know, I think I been a socialist all my life, I think as far as politics. But politics to me, it wasn't that much in the organizing of the Southern Tenant Farmers Union. We was organizin' them on the basis of how they were bein' treated by the landlords, and that they were tryin' to get instilled in them they wasn't gettin' their rightful share. They were gettin' overcharged for what they had to eat.

Whitfield, McKinney, and Handcox all played key roles as black activists in the union – and all identified to one extent or another with the anti-racism of Williams and the CP segment of labor's left. Communists had a reputation for manipulation and power plays, using progressive ends to justify bad means, and in his autobiographical writing black novelist Richard Wright later exposed how an unsavory mix of racism and sectarianism could damage people at a personal level.[75] However, John Handcox felt that, even while overstepping the bounds of prudent politics and alienating people who could be allies, Williams remained an important white voice of anti-racism within the STFU. *"Claude Williams was one of the best, that's the way I seen it. We took a linkin' to each other,"* recalled John.

At this same time, Handcox, McKinney, and Whitfield each developed increasingly testy relationships with white union leaders Mitchell and Butler. Their problems had mostly to do with an impoverished union budget, but also with STFU failure to bring blacks fully into leadership. Handcox, however, avoided internal union conflicts and in his memories of that era preferred to focus on the inspirational messages that brought people together:

> *I can't hardly define the difference between Socialists and Communist. I'm for both of them, because I think they're for the workers. I think the poor man should use his time. Politics should be about the way the people have to live . . . I think that's more profitable than fightin' about the difference between Communists and Socialists and Democrats. I've met 'em all, and I've asked what was the difference. I couldn't see that much. Some of 'em would tell me about Lenin. And then they had a split. I don't really care who they are, as long as they're doin' somethin' to help the workin' people. What little I know about the Communists or the Socialists, they're all workin' for the same thing. I haven't attended any meetin's of either one of 'em.*

Fifty years after the STFU's Muskogee convention, what John especially remembered was how he got there:

> *And then when we had the convention of the Southern Tenant Farmers Union in Oklahoma, they rented a railroad passenger coach. Back in Arkansas, in those days, the whites rode in one section of the coach train, and the Negroes rode in the other section. They wouldn't [be] allowed to ride together. But on this train . . . we commenced to one coming in and chatting, but for a while wound up we was in one half of the coach. And the conductor come through there and say, "Y'all can't do that. You have to go back to your coaches." Well, we didn't pay that any attention 'cause mostly it was the white come to our coaches, to our section, and we sang and had a good time, all the way there and all the way back.*
>
> *Singin', to me, I think is the most inspirational thing you can do to organize labor. I don't know, there's something about songs has more effect than makin' a speech to mind. Anyway, if you makin' a speech, that's just you doin' it. But when all of them is singing, they have a different feelin', they have a feelin' they's a part of what's goin' on. Well, I can't tell you too much about white churches because I don't know if I coulda even went to a white church. But they was right with us all the way, singing and talkin'. It just looked like a family reunion, seemed like, way it seemed to me. You know, just like a family reunion. Everybody was enjoying singing. Well, to my knowing, I think after the people listened to the organizers, they had a different view. It*

brought about a different view between 'em. I really didn't see that much segregation among the members of the Southern Tenant Farmers Union.

*   *   *

John's Handcox's organizing in Missouri had progressed throughout 1936 and the STFU's January 1937 Muskogee convention cemented John's belief that workers could dissolve the ages-old prejudices of the Jim Crow South. However, as H.L. Mitchell later described it in his autobiography Mitchell, the STFU was a makeshift, ramshackle affair, always on the verge of collapse. Wracked by internal leadership conflicts and always plagued by vicious external attacks, the union's contradictions intensified. In 1937, events would undermine the optimism and hope John Handcox expressed in "Roll the Union On."

CHAPTER 6

Getting Gone to the Promised Land: California

The man that wears the finest suit
May be the biggest scamp,
An' he whose limbs air clad in rags
That make a mournful sight,
In life's great battle may have proved
A hero in the fight.

—Paul Laurence Dunbar, "My Sort o' Man"[1]

John Handcox always retained some of the optimism and youthful bravado expressed in what he called his ninth-grade "graduation speech": *"The man that persevered must scale the walls of paradise to gain eternal life and glory."* In early 1937, he had good reason for hope. The sit-down strikes that began in Flint, Michigan, were sweeping through the Midwest, forcing companies like General Motors to recognize unions and sign contracts; unions of the Congress of Industrial Organizations (CIO) expanded; black workers activism and civil rights consciousness in the unions grew. The future looked good.

Upon his return to Missouri from the Muskogee convention of the Southern Tenant Farmers Union (STFU), however, events turned in a different direction to test John almost beyond endurance. The year started with a massive flood. After the 1927 Mississippi River flood, the Army Corps of Engineers had created a "spillway" to divert floodwaters that otherwise would inundate Cairo, Illinois, a town of 14,000 souls. On January 16, 1937, the Mississippi and St. Francis rivers began to overflow. On January 25, the Army Corps of Engineers blew up the main levee in Southeast Missouri with 200 pounds of dynamite; the boom echoed for miles, and the water inundated 140,000 acres, killing half the livestock. Icy floodwaters destroyed crops, homes, and livestock in Mississippi County, the union's stronghold, and wiped out Crosno. The Corps saved Cairo, but the flood displaced 7,000 whites and 5,000 blacks, including nearly all of the STFU's 250 paid members in nine Missouri locals. From his home, Thad Snow watched agricultural workers flee to hastily organized camps in and near urban centers like Charleston. He recalled that many animals left behind suffered death "from slow immersion in icy waters and final drowning." In February, a barge carrying 100 levee workers sank and 30 of them drowned. The 1937 flood forced nearly a million people from their homes in 200 US counties.[2]

It seemed like Armageddon, but John believed he saw a silver lining in the storm clouds sweeping through the Delta. As union members filled refugee camps, an organizing situation presented itself, and John began setting up committees to reconstitute their locals. On January 31, he wrote to H. L. Mitchell that a number of white STFU members working to repair levees were openly wearing their STFU buttons and asking for replacements for their lost or waterlogged union cards. However, the plight of the refugees proved overwhelming: they had almost no food, much less money to pay for union dues. John learned that the Mississippi River flood had also engulfed his family members in eastern Arkansas.[3] On February 5, 1937, John reported to Mitchell on the grim and deteriorating conditions in Missouri:

> I have spent two days with the refugees investigating their conditions. Both white and colored are complaining about they are not getting enough to eat. Those that are having to stay in the tents are have a bad time. They floored the tents with rough lumber on top of all that ice an sleet and fill ticks [mattresses] with straw. And the people having to sleep on the straw ticks on the floor. Some have bed but they will not let them use them. Most all of the people lost everything they had but what they had on.

John wrote that he and "Mr. Snow" had met with an agent from the federal Resettlement Administration (RA) to ask the government to do more to help the flood's refugees—whose diet consisted of *"just a spoon full oatmeal a spoon prunes spoon soup or something else 2 or 3 slices of bread a piece of meat sometime."* The government gave refugee families four dollars a week, but they had almost no place to buy goods. John wrote, they made a *"horrible sight,"* and he thought that *"if things don't change we will have to have a hungry march or something."* He urged the union to print placards for merchants in sympathy with the union to put in their windows and asked for money to help people in the "tent colonies."[4]

STFU President J. R. Butler wrote back that "if the organizer wants to give them his fee that we can give them a membership book and one year's dues." This letter suggests that the union paid John for each member he signed up, but it could not have been much, since workers paid as little as ten cents a month in unions dues. Now Butler asked John to give up that pittance, and enclosed five dollars for his survival. He also wrote that Claude Williams "is somewhere in the East, and there is no one else that we can send up there that would be of any help. You will have to take the bull by the tail and look after things for a while."[5]

Writing back on February 19, John joked that Butler's comments reminded him of the story of *"a fellow holding a bull tail and he running away[.] His partner told him to hold the Bull, hold the Bull! He replied how in the hell can I hold him an neither foot touching the ground (smile)."* He also wrote, *"I think that we'll be able to enroll all of the colored refugee at Charleston,"* but he expressed sharp disappointment with the white workers. *"They are dumb they never read no paper or nothing to see what labor is doing But if there is eny way you can get a white man up here to stay a while I certainly would be glad."* He added, *"It seem like all the white members have lost all interest in the union."* Even Kirkpatrick and Frank Riley, enthusiastic white unionists who had gone to the Muskogee STFU convention, promised to hold meetings but never did. It was a turning point for both the union and for John, who concluded, *"The colored people seem to be pushing forward and the white backward."*[6]

The government placed blacks and whites in separate camps, and while virtually all the black refugees John talked to in Charleston wanted to join the union, the whites just kept asking for a white organizer. John told Butler that bringing in him or other white organizers *"would not do eny good if they all set down just as soon as you all leave."* He saw it as a wasted opportunity: *"It mighty discouraging to me for I feel like this is a good time to demand something[.]"* More charitably, John acknowledged, *"I know the hardship that the white people went through."*[7]

With little support from the STFU or from whites, Handcox and Whitfield began relying almost exclusively on blacks. They organized an Official Council of the STFU Refugees, which excoriated the federal government for having caused "the most disastrous flood in the history of our country" and for having "taken from us almost everything we possessed." The Council declared, "We the members of the STFU and refugees" would refuse to go back to the spillway unless the government and planters met their demands. They wanted a better share (half of each) of the corn and cotton they produced and to own their own farm animals for their own use. They demanded that the government replace their wrecked dwellings with homes, including screens in the windows and toilets (inside or outside); they wanted freedom to trade with various merchants, instead of being locked into the company store; cash furnished at fair rates of interest; and modern schools equal to those provided to white students. Handcox and Whitfield spread their demands through flyers to the refugee camps and made the union presence known by passing around copies of *The Sharecropper's Voice.*

Handcox and Whitfield continued to champion demands of the Missouri Council members in meetings with local RA administrators throughout February, while recruiting more spillway refugees into the union without charging membership dues or organizing fees. The union had previously fought to raise farm incomes through strikes that had only momentarily raised wages, but this newest disaster presented an opportunity to press for more systemic changes through federal government action as part of a larger reform agenda.[8]

In sharp contrast to the earlier great Mississippi River floods in which Republican administrations had done little to help, New Deal agencies responded to the crisis. The Resettlement Administration (RA) offered loans, seeds, and coordinated relief; the American Red Cross and the US Public Health Service vaccinated people to protect them against diphtheria, typhoid, and malaria; various government agencies provided food, clothing, and shelter.[9] As the Army Corps diverted rising waters in May, the Red Cross and the RA issued cash subsidies, provided aid to reconstruct homes, garden seeds for food crops, and medical aid.[10]

According to Thad Snow, rural people in this region had regularly recovered from flooding, and knew how to respond. Before the spring of 1937 was over, refugees had returned, planting crops, and cleaning the mud and sewage out of their homes. For Snow himself, it was a time of unmitigated disaster. During the flood, his second wife died (his first wife had also died), leaving him with two young girls. He experienced a total breakdown and left for Mexico, hoping to salvage his health. When he returned in January of 1938, he would find his sharecroppers living on a diet of cornmeal, salt, and water, slowly starving.[11]

In the midst of this chaotic disaster, black women took an especially active role in demanding that government improve the lives of their families. Historian Jarod Roll tabulated forty-one women leaders, at least ten of them black, in the STFU in 1938.[12] Zella and Owen Whitfield increasingly took charge. Using his many contacts among remnants of the Garvey movement, pastoring three or four churches, drawing on the power of evangelical religion and on fire with the gospel of working-class organizing, Whitfield would expand the STFU in Southeast Missouri to some 2,000 members by the fall of 1937 and to over 4,000 members and 29 locals in 4 counties by 1938.[13]

Unhappily for John Handcox, even as blacks rushed into the STFU, whites seemed to become more passive and ambivalent toward the union. The government had organized spillway refugees into segregated camps; Pentecostal and other Protestant churches, along with everything else, remained segregated at a time when John felt everything should be integrated. John had experienced some success in working with whites in Deventer, but even there a white union member wrote to H. L. Mitchell, "The white people of this county is ready to join but they want to be in local to their selves and let the negro be to their selves and all work for the same thing."[14] Segregation blocked John's access to white workers, even as blacks flooded into the union. John's dream of an integrated movement of the agricultural working poor began to die.

Travelling North: The Sharecropper's Troubadour

While tragedy hammered John in Missouri, terror continued to hammer the union's strongholds in Arkansas. In February, an awful story emerged of how whites kidnapped two young black men from a courthouse in Duck Hill, Mississippi, chained them to a tree, and applied a blowtorch before riddling their bodies with bullets.[15] Howard Kester's testimony about this horrific lynching led the US House to pass a federal anti-lynching bill in 1938, but conservatives in the Senate, including Arkansas Senator Joe Robinson, filibustered it to death.[16] Vicious planter campaigns of intimidation forced many union members into silence. In Mississippi County, Arkansas, on the 30,000-acre plantation of Lee Wilson (who, according to the union, received half a billion dollars in government money under the AAA to not grow crops), intimidation reigned. When cotton choppers on that plantation went on strike in the spring of 1937, police arrested black strike organizer Joe Cook for "intimidating labor" and a judge gave him a two-year sentence at the county work farm. Planters and riding bosses here and elsewhere rounded up other strikers and, as they had done in previous strikes, forced them to work at the point of a gun. Mitchell said planters had revived the old slave patrols of the antebellum years.[17]

Conditions did not get any better during the summer. In Forrest City, where John had once organized, a court used the ridiculous "intimidating labor" charges to jail two STFU members for leading a strike of Works Projects Administration (WPA) workers.[18] In October, when the union's attorney appeared in court to defend three union members from bogus charges in John's home turf of St. Francis County, a mob attacked them all.[19] Civil liberties, during the height of the New Deal, still did not exist for union organizers in Arkansas.

In this context, John's writings continued to play an important role in rallying support for the union. His poem, "Hero of the STFU" published in *The Sharecropper's Voice* in February 1937, under his pen name of John Henry, elaborated on the meaning of the death of Frank Weems in the cotton chopper's strike of the previous year. Song writer Earl Robinson later wrote that IWW organizer Joe Hill, executed by the State of Utah in 1915, had "never died" because his spirit went on to organize. John similarly called on people to face sacrifice with courage and even enthusiasm. His poem read, in part:

> *The STFU cannot help but grieve*
> *Over such a hero lost,*
> *A man who fought for the right,*
> *Regardless of the cost.*
> *The STFU needs more Weems who for suffering*

Humanity their lives would give.
Frank Weems' body is dead now,
Yet forever he will live.
The loss of a real union member
Makes all of us feel sad,
But anybody dying for a good cause,
His death is not really bad.[20]

STFU leaders increasingly saw John not as only an organizer but also as a cultural worker and they called on him to go on a tour to raise money and publicity in the North. STFU and Workers Defense League supporters in 1935 had set up "National Sharecroppers Week," with Norman Thomas as its chair. The effort from March 1 to 7, 1937, galvanized various religious leaders and political advisors from Washington, D.C., to Harlem in New York City, to areas of the Midwest. John went north with a delegation of STFU members and they played a particularly important role in getting the black press to take up the sharecropper's cause. In this era, thousands of black people passed newspapers by hand through their communities, with the Chicago *Defender* having its largest circulation outside of Chicago along the railroad lines that ran south through eastern Arkansas. The Baltimore *Afro-American*, the Pittsburgh *Courier*, and the *Amsterdam News* in Harlem, all publicized efforts to aid southern sharecroppers and agricultural workers in their struggle for a better life, highlighting the atrocities committed in the South.[21]

Rev. McKinney had paved the way for the first "Sharecropper's Week" in 1935 by speaking to a Harlem audience about the "dodalum [or doodalum] book," an accounting ledger that planters used to cheat their tenants by charging preposterous rates of interest. The *Amsterdam News,* in a front-page story, labeled sharecroppers the "Worst New Deal Victims" because AAA programs had driven them off the land. Other stories publicized the fatal flogging of Eliza Nolden, the beatings of Willie Sue Blagden and Claude Williams, J. M. Reese, Frank Weems, and other planter terrorism.[22] In 1936, black press publicity helped to spur union supporters in the North and the Midwest to send supplies to the STFU, and two groups in New York City, called Friends of the Sharecroppers and the League for Southern Labor, had held dances at the Savoy Ballroom in Harlem in November (headlined perhaps incongruously as "Dancing Feet Aid Southern Field Slaves).["23]

Northerners sometimes embarrassed southerners by expecting them to go on "stage" with bandanas on their heads and wearing overalls, and Sharecropper's Week of 1937 seemed like an opportunity for such embarrassment. The advance publicity for Sharecropper's Week's "grand finale" featured the wife of Frank Weems, the white worker J. M. Reese who had been brutalized with Weems, and John Handcox, described as a "union poet, [who] will sing sharecropper songs."[24] But John and his delegation, probably prompted by H. L. Mitchell who often dressed in a coat and tie for such events, refused to present themselves as sharecropper caricatures. A photo of the event, held on March 7, showed Reese, Handcox, H. L. Mitchell, J. R. Butler, and the STFU's black activist Marie Pierce, all of them well dressed, with the men wearing suits and ties. Perhaps to add to their credibility as farm workers, the *Amsterdam News* reported they had "the mud of the field still on their boots."

A critical aspect of the STFU remained its interracial character, and in a front-page news story, a black reporter described Reese as a "revelation." Here was a white man who had stood up to white terrorism along with Frank Weems, and (despite injuries that would unbalance him the rest of his life) continued to stand for an interracial union. It also reported that Handcox, the lone black man in the group, had been "chased from Forrest City, Arkansas, for union activities. The most colorful 'cropper of the lot,' he has written twenty poems about the conditions of the sharecroppers."[25]

The presence of Handcox, Reese and other STFU activists prompted northern black newspapers and the Left and labor press to frame the story of the STFU as a fight for labor rights and civil liberties. While John was in New York, actors put on a pro-labor play written by John Wesley, called "Steel," at the Labor Stage Theater on 106 West 39 street. During breaks in the performance, the program featured "John Handcox, sharecropper poet and minstrel." The "minstrel" characterization of John was unfortunate, but as a result of the performance New Yorkers donated more funds for the STFU.[26] Along with the Workers Defense League, the STFU had sponsored a previous play about the sharecroppers, called "Sweet Land." [27] Following Sharecropper's Week, black newspapers continued to cover stories about the STFU.[28]

John and the union entourage went on to Chicago, where he sang and recited his poems at another Sharecropper's Week event. The Chicago *Defender* prominently featured the photo from the New York appearance on the front page, with the headline, "No Color Line Among These People." The STFU members, it said, "have forgotten Race and color and have united to fight their common evils." In breaking the color barrier, the STFU raised hopes that unionization would create a new day and a new way in the South.[29]

To his shock, while in Chicago John discovered that Frank Weems was still alive! Weems met him during Sharecropper's Week and told him how, after thugs had beaten he and Jim Reese into insensibility, he had made his way secretly to Tyronza and then to Chicago. He was so frightened that he did not reveal his existence to the union until John rediscovered him, nearly a year after Weems had fled Arkansas. *The Sharecroppers' Voice*, in June, 1937, announced with a huge headline, "Frank Weems Alive!"[30]

Another discovery occurred during this trip: the discovery of John as a poet and singer. H. L. Mitchell suggested that John go to Washington, D.C., to record. Charles Seeger, a distinguished music scholar and leftist political radical, now ran the Special Skills Division of the federal Resettlement Administration—the very agency helping the sharecroppers in Missouri and Arkansas in the wake of the 1937 flood. The RA decided to preserve and promote people's culture in the resettlement projects, while the Works Progress Administration also took up a campaign to record folk artists. Seeger had barely started his recording project before Congress shut it down for financial and political reasons. But while a small window of opportunity existed, Seeger's Skills division recorded John Handcox, on March 9, 1937.

The Library of Congress card catalogue labeled him as the "singer from Missouri" and the sleeve on his tape recording describes his songs "as sung by John Handcox, formerly of Brinkley, Arkansas, now of Columbia, Missouri" (John did not live in Columbia, but may have been there briefly).[31] Staff member Sydney Robertson recorded John and it does not seem that John met Charles Seeger, but two years later Seeger's son Pete listened to the recordings with rapt attention. As Pete explains in the preface to this book, John's songs and poems helped open him up to a new world of southern labor music. That moment of discovery would immortalize John as the sharecropper's troubadour when, thirty years later, Seeger, Alan Lomax, and Woody Guthrie published John's songs and poems in *Hard-Hitting Songs for Hard-Hit People*.[32]

John's recordings became part of the Library of Congress Archive of American Folk Song. With no accompaniment and in a plaintive and strained voice that reflected the harsh circumstances of his life, John rolled out his songs and poems, one after the next: "Raggedy, Raggedy," "Going to Roll the Union On," "Join the Union Tonight, "In My Heart," "No More Mourning," "There is Mean Things Happening in This Land," "The Planter and the Sharecropper," and "Landlord What in the Heaven is the Matter With You?" John did not know what became of these recordings and they fell into obscurity. Only labor songster Joe Glazer, who tracked these songs down in 1959, seemed aware of them.[33] Why? In the summer of 1937, John left the union and disappeared from history.

A "Disgusted Worker"

After John returned from his journey to the North, he experienced a cruel twist of fate. To save funds, the STFU's National Executive Committee (NEC), decided to revoke the commission of its field organizers. It stipulated that they could reapply for their commissions but it apparently never informed John of this fact. Only McKinney, Mitchell, and Butler now had salaries (forty to sixty dollars per month), but the NEC also decided to add Owen Whitfield to their executive committee. It then hired him as the one paid STFU field staff member in Missouri. Indisputably, he had proved to be an energetic, charismatic organizer with extensive contacts and a wide following.[34] But what this meant for John was that he no longer had funding (pitiful as it was) or authority as an organizer. On April 8, John wrote Butler a furious letter.

> *You and all the rest of the NEC members know of my union activity and you know what sacrifice and what poems and song I have contributed to the union. I had always taken you to be a fair minded man you have saw my family an you know just how long I have been away from them. Then for you to say you see no reason why I should work and you hate to see me quit the work knowing that not a cent were loted [allotted] to help support my family. Of course I now realize that I have been the good thing. I have been think that the union purpose were to see that every one get justice and to abolish the old Plantation system. I know lots of Planter to treat their hand better than I were treated sent back home broke given know kind of consideration whatever.*

John reminded Butler that he had spent his own money to take delegates to the Muskogee convention and had never been paid back by the union. He thought his members would now question the validity of the union. *"As hard as I work trying to build up the union and the sacrifice I made and then you all ignore me like that they dont see where it could ever benefit them."* Someone, he thought, was *"going to tell a lie"* that his trip to New York had personally benefited him, but he said in fact he had made no money. He angrily asked Butler to send back "Roll the Union On" and any of his other songs and poems in the union's files.

In closing, he noted that he had received *"a very sad letter"* from his wife Ruth in Arkansas and that he would leave Missouri within a week to help his family. He added a note of doubt about the effectiveness of Owen Whitfield. *"I really love him but he's writing commission out on tablet paper,"* working without a union stamp or seal, while pastoring three or four churches at once. However, *"I do not mean to knock on him in eny way."* Handcox concluded, *"The NEC know me and know what work I have done. And if they dont think I deserve an org commission and some help I have nothing else to say."* Earlier, he had signed letters as "a willing worker," then as "a worker," and now he signed off as *"A very disgusted worker."*[35]

John was being dumped. On April 5, H.L. Mitchell had written to Sidney Hertzberg, who organized the Sharecropper's Week in New York, that John had been "complaining" of his treatment. "I am afraid that John Handcox['s] usefulness to the Union is about over due to his trip to New York and the exaggerated opinion he has of himself as a result [of] the attention he received."[36] Mitchell, himself under great strain, was prone to snap judgments. Possibly, fame had gone to John's head; but the real problem was that he wanted to get paid and had continued to complain when the union provided no funds for his work.

On April 12, Butler tried to smooth things over. Writing back to John, he said that the NEC would have rehired him except it did not have the money to do so. He wrote that it only hired Whitfield when an NEC officer raised extra funds to pay a small allowance to him and two others. Butler complained about the tone of John's letter: "The opinion that you seem to have of the Union that it is worse than the planters is a pretty bad one and I am surprised that you feel that way about it after helping to build it." He concluded, "Some of your criticisms were well taken but I want to ask you to consider every thing connected with this matter before you begin telling the people that you have been mistreated and asking them to sympathize with you."[37] John's confidence in the union, and its confidence in him, had collapsed.

When interviewed nearly 50 years later, John said nothing about this falling out. He preferred to remember how the STFU gave people like himself hope, brought blacks and whites together to organize and sing, and gave him an opportunity to express himself as a poet and songwriter. The bitterness of this break may have dimmed with the years, but he was infuriated at the time it occurred. In September of 1937, he must have been appalled to see a photo of Owen Whitfield on the front page of *The Sharecropper's Voice*. He was the lone African American, with five white men, representing STFU district four, which included Arkansas and Missouri.[38] Without comment about John's role in the union, the same newspaper also featured another poem by "John Henry" on its editorial page, closing with these lines:

> *Ten little farmer men—all down and out—*
> *Met to try to find what it was all about,*
> *Organized a Union—right there on the spot;*
> *Each took out his card and signed it on the dot.*
> *Enemies now can't get one without getting all;*
> *The enemy therefore never gets any one at all.*
> *In Union bonds they now take up their stand;*
> *All for one and one for all—to a man.*
> *United, one by one their foes they subdue;*
> *What Union did for them it can do for you.*[39]

John's writings by this time had reached a lot of people in the STFU and beyond. The *Southern Farm Leader*, the newspaper of the Alabama-based and Communist-led Sharecropper's Union, had published at least one of John's poems, and they probably appeared in other publications as well.[40] But John had lost his union, his media, and his audience. When he returned to his family in Arkansas, he could find no work; the planters had marked him as a union man, and he could not stay there. North of the Mason-Dixon Line, however, people still wanted him to come and sing the "good old union song."

Wandering Troubadour

Cut loose from his union, John became a wandering singer and poet like troubadours of old. At the request of the Socialist Party, he went to St. Louis (what happened there is unclear) and then to Chicago. That city had a powerful labor movement. In Chicago, black workers played an important role in organizing the United Packinghouse Workers Union, the United Steelworkers Union, and the Brotherhood of Sleeping Car Porters. The CP and the SP both played active roles in organizing labor and community activities. In the view of one scholar, these politicized northern labor leftists viewed John as a "spokesman for proletarian culture," while in contrast "Handcox was expressing his social indignation in a genre endemic and natural to his community."[41] Put more prosaically, John probably saw Chicago as a place where he could do some good while getting paid for it. According to John, he sold copies of his songs, hoping to send some money home to his suffering family:

After Missouri, the Socialist Party brought me up to Waukegan, and then to Chicago. I met a fella in Chicago from Indiana. There were only a few black people in his little town, and he said he would have to protect me if he took me there, so we didn't go. He seemed real nice. The first night in Chicago I appeared on the program, and I stayed at the YMCA. They paid for my room for a week. I got acquainted with one of the Socialist Party members. He was split up from his wife, and he made me welcome to live at his house. He had a typewriter. I hunted and pecked all of my songs and poems off, and took them over to the Socialist Party headquarters, and mimeographed them. After I got them all finished, I stapled 'em like a songbook. Whenever I'd go to a church or a Worker's Alliance, or anywhere, I always took them along to give to the people. Some would give me a quarter or a dime, and sometimes I'd get $15 or $20 dollars a night.

They kept me on the go constantly. The Socialist Party sent me over to the Pullman Porters union. They were having a strike at the time. Philip Randolph was a spokesman, man. He had a heavy voice. I was on the program at their meeting at the Socialist Party [headquarters]. I really never knew how to accept applause, being from the country. I never knew I should have gone back on stage for applause. Anyway, when I was staying at the Socialist Party member's house, I told him I was lookin' for work. He asked me if I'd ever done any painting. I said no, but he brought his paint and everything, and I painted his house. He gave me $50 for about a week, and he said I was doing a good job.

Northern audiences saw John as a representative of the sharecropper movement. They did not know of his divorce from the STFU. The New-York based *Socialist Call* identified him as "the poet Laureate of the Southern Tenant Farmers

Union now visiting Chicago." It reported that John told the story of the STFU "in song and poetry of his own homely composition," at a gathering at the Debs Hall of the Amalgamated Clothing Workers Union. This followed his participation in Chicago's biggest May Day Parade ever, an incredible event on May 1, 1937, in which an estimated 50,000 people marched through the streets.[42] John heard the Socialist and President of the Brotherhood of Sleeping Car Porters, A. Philip Randolph, at a meeting of workers threatening to strke if the Pullman Company did not sign a contract with the union – which it did, in August of 1937. Union recognition transformed Randolph from a marginal outsider into an increasingly influential spokesperson for black equality within the unions and industry.[43]

John might well have stayed in the roiling union world of Chicago. Industrial and service jobs had lured tens of thousands of African Americans as part of the Great Migration out of the South. But now, in the midst of the "Roosevelt Recession" (the President had pulled back on stimulous spending and sent the economy into a tailspin), John's Socialist friends could not turn up any significant employment for him. Jobs for a man who mainly knew how to plant and harvest cotton, catch fish, and brew moonshine were hard to find. Relying again on his public persona as the sharecropper's poet, on his SP connections, and on his family network, he moved to Detroit. He recalled, *My momma's last marriage, he was a Johnson, Leroy Johnson, he lived in Detroit. I left Chicago, and I went to Detroit.* Migrants from the South typically bunked with relatives, and John hoped to stay with his uncle.

Detroit like Chicago was a mecca for many black southern migrants, but it was not one for John. His family in Arkansas had for many years sent hams, pecans, and syrup to his uncle, and John thought he would be welcomed in his home. In his first night in Detroit, John performed at a Socialist Party meeting and felt good about his prospects. But John awoke the next morning to overhear his uncle's wife saying he would have to find another place for his nephew to stay. John did not let on that he had heard the conversation. He stayed on for more than a month, while extending his contacts with the SP. He then stayed at a Party member's house for a short time and paid him rent of 30 dollars a month.[44] John enjoyed a freer racial atmosphere among Socialists and liberals in the North but outside of these circles he found that both Chicago and Detroit remained rigidly segregated.

He decided to leave Detroit, but before doing so he renewed his acquaintance with Walter White, the famous almost-white leader of the National Association for the Advancement of Colored People (NAACP) who John had met earlier and who had spoken at the STFU convention in Muskogee:

They were holding The NAACP National convention at a big church on Birch Street. I'll never forget that. I was dressed as a farmer, I had on my bandana and overalls. They had the spotlight on me, and I recited some of my poems and songs. After it was over, they asked me if I would be on the program the next night. I had made a commitment to my wife that I'd leave the next day for Oklahoma. I'd been in the north for about three or four months. In Detroit I talked with Walter White, who I'd met in Memphis at some meeting. He had blue eyes, and straight hair, and was light-complected. If a person didn't know he was only half white or a mixed breed, they would have thought he was white. He was a reporter at the Elaine Massacre. He told me he was catching the train back to Chicago, and a white fellow come up to him and said, "you know they're going to hang some nigger down here passin' for white." He says, "Sure enough? If I'd known that I'd of stayed here and watched it." He was getting away all the time.

John's siblings and his wife Ruth had moved from Arkansas, and as he migrated west from Detroit to join them Oklahoma, John found that the ideas and practices of Jim Crow remained in force.

So I went from Chicago to Detroit, and then caught the bus to Tulsa, Oklahoma. I had three brothers who were working up there. They were making twenty-five cent an hour, so I went up there. On the road to St. Louis [on the way to Tulsa], there was two white ladies and three or four black men on the bus, and we all got together and we were singin' songs on the bus. I don't know why they liked me, just seemed like some of my relatives or somethin.' When we got to St. Louis, we all sat down at a table together. I was sittin' there, and here come one of the waitresses, and she patted me on the shoulder and pointed, "your table is over there."

John also recalled that on this trip a white woman demanded that he move to the back of the bus, which he refused to do. In contrast to what would have happened in the South, however, the white driver ignored the incident.[45]

John fervently hoped to be rid of the plague of racism that he had experienced in Arkansas. He did not believe in racial difference and did not want to be a part of a society that made such distinctions. In John's quest for a different kind of world, Claude Williams remained one of his closest allies. Like John, Claude had left Arkansas and lived with his wife Joyce in Evansville, Indiana. Claude continued to lead programs on "the gospel of working-class" in St. Louis and elsewhere. On November 30, 1938, John wrote to him from Oklahoma, addressing Claude as "Dear Comrade." John expressed continuing concern for his Socialist friends in Arkansas and asked about Willie Sue Blagden and his Socialist comrade Don Kobler from Commonwealth College. He then launched into new words he had written for an old gospel tune, "The Old Ship of Zion":

Tis the Southern Tenant farmers union
Tis the Southern Tenant farmers union

Why dont you get on roll, hallelula, get on roll.
We can demand our right if we stick together
We can demand our right if we stick together.
Why don't you get on roll, dont be foolish,
Why don't you get on roll.

John "zipped in" these additional verses: *"We all need more for our labor"; "We can destroy the plantation system"; "Everyone should love their Freedom"; "If you dont do something it'll be worser for your children"*—and finished with, *"Why dont you get in roll, Why don't you get in roll"* (get enrolled). John asked Claude to *"look this over,"* perhaps with the hope that Williams might regularize the spelling and wording of the verses and send it back. He closed with a "smile" and sent his love to Claude's family and friends. The letter shows that John still supported the STFU, and also suggests how Williams had influenced John's songwriting ever since they met in Missouri and at the New Era School in Little Rock in 1936. John and Claude had repeatedly discussed songs and sang them together, and Williams undoubt-edly helped to shape some of his compositions.

In another letter to Williams sent from Bartlesville, dated November 3, 1939, John recounted that *"many drop of water have run under the bridge since you heard from me and still more since I heard from you."* He expressed concern that Claude's health was failing and urged Williams to *"come out and spend some time with me"*—adding sarcastically, *"If negroes were allowed in your town I would have been to see you."* John asked again about Joyce Williams and his friend Kobler and closed, *"What is the STFU doing now I can't heard nothing from them eny more."*[46] John later recalled of Claude, *"Last time I seen him . . . he sent my fare to come to St. Louis cause they was havin' a meetin' there. So I went, and I appeared on the program. Some students from the University of Chicago heard me there, and they invited me to be their guest and go back to Chicago with 'em. So I went, and they was real nice and took me all over Chicago. I didn't do no speaking. They just showed me the town."* It is unclear when this occurred, but it was sometime in 1937. John recalled, *"The meeting in St. Louis was about the union, but there was somethin' goin' on between Claude and H.L. Mitchell that I never figured out."* Apparently unknown to John, Williams at this point had both fallen victim to and exacer-bated internal and external conflicts eviscerating the STFU.

The Decline of the STFU

Virtually all labor radicals favored the CIO's "one big union" idea, and its corol-lary principle of equal rights for racial and ethnic minorities and women. But how to make membership in the CIO work for the STFU became a vexed ques-tion. CIO President John L. Lewis, with help from CIO west coast director and longshore leader Harry Bridges, tried to incorporate the STFU into a union covering agriculturally-related industries such as canneries and cotton compressing and seed oil factories. On July 9, 1937, the STFU participated in the founding convention of the CIO's United Cannery, Agricultural, Packing, and Allied Workers of America (UCAPAWA). By September the STFU had formally joined this awkwardly named alliance of different kinds of locals related to agriculture and processing, on the understanding that the STFU would maintain its autonomy. But the cannery union quickly demanded union dues that sharecroppers and tenants could not afford, and paperwork that neither the tiny STFU staff in Memphis nor barely literate workers in STFU locals could fill out.

Political conflict in labor's left also sabotaged the alliance with the CIO. The white Socialist leaders of the STFU, consisting of Mitchell, Butler, and Kester, clashed with the CIO cannery union president Donald Henderson, a Communist Party member who they believed sought to control union members from the top down. Henderson alienated them with the absurd idea that tenants and sharecroppers should be in one union, day laborers in another; in fact, the only times the STFU had success was when they all joined together. "What affects one, affects the other," editorialized *The Sharecroppers' Voice*. "A man who is a tenant today may be a cropper tomorrow and a day laborer the day after." This was exactly the trajectory John Handcox's life had taken. In addition, sectarian divisions increased across the left. Trotskyites who had broken off from the CP now took over the Socialist Party, issuing increasingly radical rhetoric matched by increasingly less effective action. STFU white Socialist leaders, themselves often sectarian, had good reason to be hostile to and suspicious not only of Communists but of others on the left.[47]

Mitchell increasingly associated Communists with Commonwealth College in Arkansas. He supported STFU activist Claude Williams to become its director in 1937 in hopes of making it into a strong trade union school. However, following the tide of increasing civil rights action in the CIO, Claude now pressed to make the STFU into what he felt would be a more racially progressive union. At a conference in Memphis at the end of September 1937 in which the STFU joined the CIO, Williams nominated a young black leader, Leon Turner, to take Mitchell's STFU executive secretary job. He failed to get him elected.[48] Tensions among union leaders simmered. Then, at the STFU's fourth annual convention held in Little Rock, racial conflicts exploded.

On February 26, 1938, the white owner of the Old Community Hall, where the STFU was meeting, evicted the 200 STFU delegates on grounds that "to mix the races for misguided discussion of controversial subjects means trouble." Delegates moved to an African-American lodge.[49] Rev. McKinney, formerly a follower of Marcus Garvey, sought to elect an all-black slate of candidates to take over the STFU leadership. African Americans constituted 90 percent of those attending the convention, yet they did not agree with him and voted down

McKinney's slate.[50] The STFU's continued use of the old "UMWA formula" of whites in top offices and blacks in lower offices no longer sufficed. African Americans had become a larger proportion of the membership than when the union first formed. Furthermore, the National Negro Congress and black workers within and outside the CIO almost everywhere demanded increased black leadership and heightened civil rights campaigns.[51]

In this context, Rev. McKinney, who had been with the STFU since it first organized and was perhaps its most important grassroots leader, allied with Claude Williams and turned against H. L.Mitchell. McKinney wrote to a number of fellow unionists that Mitchell and other whites had used fears of another Elaine riot as a smoke screen to keep themselves in control of the union. He felt the white leaders has become a clique of "czars." Like John Handcox, he had pressed Mitchell for funding for his work in the field, but had received little of it. With his slate of officers defeated, McKinney went back to trying to organize all-black groups through his church and Garveyite network in eastern Arkansas. In a letter in August, 1938, he further complained that the toilets remained segregated at STFU headquarters in Memphis. It was probably true: the Memphis government made segregated facilities mandatory, and toilets in the CIO hall remained segregated well into the 1950s. McKinney described the STFU as "an office full of poor white people." He wrote that blacks had passively let whites run the union and, as a result, "we are just manufacturing some new masters." Meanwhile, although the union called another "sit down" strike of cotton pickers in September of 1938, it had no power to enforce it.[52]

A perfect storm of disunity soon descended on Williams. He and Owen Whitfield had become partners in running religious institutes to spread the gospel of organizing.[53] On his way to see Whitfield in Missouri, in August of 1938, Williams had stopped to visit STFU President J. R. Butler in Memphis. He left behind his coat that contained an unsigned note by someone who proposed that Commonwealth faculty "capture the union for our line at the next convention," raise money, and expand STFU organizing. This kind of inflated rhetoric was not uncommon on the left. But Williams later protested that he had no desire for the Commonwealth faculty to "capture" the STFU and that someone else had written this plan without his knowledge, consent, or participation. CP members of the faculty had at some point planned to send their "takeover" plan to national CP headquarters but when he learned of it Williams refused to approve of it.[54] Satisfied with this explanation, Butler tried to drop the matter but Howard Kester insisted that Williams resign from the union. Claude refused. At the end of September, the union's National Executive Council put Williams on trial and expelled him, along with Rev. McKinney, creating big headlines and anti-communist rhetoric in the anti-union commercial press.[55]

Williams appealed for reinstatement to the Fifth Annual STFU convention at the end of 1938, held in Cotton Plant, Arkansas, where John's ancestors had first started farming, but delegates overwhelmingly reaffirmed Claude's expulsion. Mitchell brought two African Americans, George Stith, and F. R. Betton, into leadership and the convention also reinstated McKinney, who said he was not hostile to H.L. Mitchell and had simply wanted racial equality in union leadership. Speaking of Mitchell, he said, "I wouldn't go follow him anywhere, but I would go with him anywhere." This reorganization of leadership would hold the STFU together for a little while longer, but scholar Donald Grubbs concluded that the convention "threatened to resemble a funeral."[56]

It was a bitter time for people who had put their lives on the line for the union. Demands for a greater degree of black leadership in the STFU were fully justified. Historian Jason Manthorne has tabulated that blacks constituted 70 to 80 percent or more of the union's membership, yet many blacks felt they did not receive commensurate power at top levels in the union. Butler, Kester, and Mitchell had all made great sacrifices and risked their lives, but they tended to dominate union decision-making. The permanent expulsion of Williams, the temporary expulsion of McKinney, and the loss of Handcox all signaled an open racial and sectarian political schism. This all happened during a renewed red scare initiated by the House Committee on Un-American Activities and southern segregationists, who branded all civil rights advocates and labor leftists as Communists. White Socialists sometimes added to this adverse political climate by publicly red-baiting their former allies.[57] The Hitler-Stalin nonaggression pact of August 1939, defended by Communists as a defensive measure by Joseph Stalin, alienated many who had previously defended the CP. Kester and Williams, who had stood shoulder to shoulder in their efforts to desegregate the South, no longer spoke to each other. Years later, when Mitchell tried to heal the rift from that time, he said Claude Williams harshly rejected him.[58]

The unfolding internecine disaster within the STFU also had its collateral damage in Southeast Missouri, where John Handcox and Owen Whitfield had put in heroic efforts to organize.

The Missouri Roadside Demonstration

Even as schisms widened in the STFU, Whitfield continued working with Williams and became a vice-president of the CIO's cannery union, UCAPAWA. He increasingly identified with the CIO left even as he remained an executive board member and an organizer for the STFU. Largely under his leadership, the sharecropper movement would have one more heyday, which John briefly described this way: *"In 1939 when they thow'd people off the land in Missouri, I was clean out of the picture by then . . . Just grabbed their stuff and them and carried them out there and throwed them all up the highway where Norman Thomas and a bunch of them, I was told, got some tents. They had a tent section set up alongside the side of the highway for some time.*

The 1939 Missouri Roadside Demonstration provided the sharecropper's movement with its most famous moment, even though it occurred in a period of decline for the STFU. The sharecropper movement had started back in 1934, near Earle, Arkansas, when a planter named Dibble cancelled his tenant's annual contracts and replaced them with day laborers at absurdly low wages. Deep in Whitfield's organizing terrain in Southeast Missouri, landlords similarly sought to dispose of their tenants and replace them with wage workers. Whitfield kept both the STFU and UCAPAWA out of the picture and secretly planned a counter-attack. Through church networks, Whitfield organized a mass meeting, publicized by a sympathetic journalist. Singing "We Shall Not Be Moved," he charged his followers with confronting the planters and their minions in Swampeast Missouri.

On January 10, 1939, 1,500 homeless agricultural workers planted themselves, freezing and starving in thirteen roadside camps on highly visible thoroughfares, along highways 60 and 61. Thad Snow had recovered his health and recently returned to the Missouri Bootheel, and now marveled at the audacity of the protest. It drew national publicity that brought the sharecropper's plight once again to the federal government's attention. Local plantation owners and the law, Snow wrote, tried to blame the demonstrations on outside agitators and "reds," but they couldn't find any. Lacking an obvious scapegoat, some of the locals even tried to blame Snow for the renewed sharecroppers' movement.[59]

Besieged by death threats, Whitfield and his family took refuge in St. Louis. STFU organizers in Arkansas proved powerless to help the demonstrators, suffering arrest when they tried to enter the zone of the protests. Claiming they were there to help the evicted people, local authorities loaded roadside demonstrators into trucks, but then dumped them off on back roads to starve and freeze where no one would see them. Whitfield, however, artfully took their case to President Roosevelt, who had already been pressing Congress to help agricultural workers through the Farm Settlement Administration (FSA). Under pressure from the President, the demonstrators, and public opinion, the FSA subsequently moved many of the expelled families into government-sponsored experimental farming communities in Missouri and Arkansas. The FSA provided simple homes (most without indoor plumbing), schools, and social services normally lacking in cotton country for hundreds of black and white families.[60]

In the aftermath of the Missouri roadside demonstration, Owen and Zella Whitfield spearheaded the founding of one of these communities, in Poplar Bluff, Missouri. Within a predominantly white region, 95 families, most of them black, established Cropperville. This village of former sharecroppers became a model for cooperative farming, celebrated many years later in the film, "Oh Freedom after Awhile: The Missouri Sharecroppers Strike of 1939." Cooperative "colonies" continued into the 1950s. Johnny Cash, the "man in black," came out of this environment to carry the musical legacy of rural working-class people in the South onto the commercial airwaves.[61]

Whitfield salvaged victory from tragedy, but he also dropped the STFU in favor of working with the CIO. He complained that during the roadside demonstrations STFU white leaders were more concerned about who was a Communist than they were in aiding the demonstrators. "Must I ask every person I meet what his politic are?" he wrote to H. L. Mitchell. "Must I go among my friends and say to them are you a communist" For its part, In April 1939, the STFU executive council withdrew the CIO cannery union, complaining, among other things, that Communists controlled it. Whitfield maintained his own base, and most of his followers stayed in the CIO after the STFU left it. [62]

Whitfield felt the CIO's cannery workers' union had a more visible commitment to black leadership than the STFU. He continued to work with Claude Williams in preaching his gospel of the working class and switched from organizing sharecroppers to organizing in the factories as a paid union staff member of the CIO's cannery workers' union. The National Labor Relations Act protected the right of industrial workers to organize and vote freely for or against a union, and the CIO's cannery union successfully organized many of them during and after World War II. These new unionists challenged Jim Crow practices and provided a working-class base for the NAACP and the civil rights movement. The CIO's strategy of organizing those streaming out of the mechanizing cotton country into jobs in extractive industries made good sense. Whitfield, however, ultimately became dissatisfied with the union's organizing methods and quit. He spent his last years organizing Cropperville and preaching the gospel of working class organizing in cooperation with Claude Williams. The CIO cannery union, renamed the Food, Tobacco and Allied Workers Union of America (FTA), continued on successfully before falling victim to the red scare in the 1950s.

The Missouri Roadside Demonstration had helped to establish agricultural cooperatives and demonstrated once again the power of protest in the cotton fields, but it did not revive the STFU. In 1938, H. L. Mitchell went to work for the National Youth Administration (NYA), leaving the office in Memphis rudderless for months at a time. Norman Thomas at one point suggested that Mitchell was a good publicist and spokesperson, but did not know the fundamentals of union organizing, such as building strong worker collectives in the field. Rather, he relied on workers to organize themselves and largely stayed in Memphis. What he called his "anti-Communist paranoia" did not help to resolve problems within the union's left. [63] In Tryonza, where the union began, after the CIO cannery union and the STFU split, appeals from the two different unions only confused union members. "Our local has split up. We are not sending money nowhere," one of them wrote. Rev. McKinney disappeared from written history; Commonwealth College collapsed in 1940; Kester went on to an academic career; Mitchell merged the STFU into the National Farm Labor Union of the American Federation of Labor (AFL)—an organization primarily of craft unions that traditionally excluded or segregated black workers.[64] When Mitchell asked organizer David Burgess to re-establish ties with former STFU members in 1944, none of them wanted to talk to him. According to Burgess, after Mitchell's expulsion from Tyronza in 1935 he never went back into Arkansas. He tried to organize the union through correspondence issued from an office in Memphis and entirely lost his base in that state. [65]

No union, in any case, could have stopped the onslaught of mechanization, which laid waste to small farmers and day laborers and left mass unemploymenbt and poverty in the Mississippi Delta in its wake. The mechanical cotton picker, produced by the Rust brothers (ironically, strong union supporters), ultimately took over the cotton fields: the percentage of cotton harvested by machines was only five percent in 1950, but 50 percent in 1960 and 90 percent by 1970.[66] Today, driving through the vicinity of Earle and eastern Arkansas, one sees miles of fields but few people. Even the shot gun shacks are gone. The STFU's vision for cooperatives, in the end, provided the only realistic means for small farmers to stay on the land, but this vision required government assistance and ran counter to the surging ideology of "free market" capitalism after World War II. The civil rights movement later challenged the Delta's landed oligarchy and their "plantation mentality," but the planter's system morphed into a corporate business model that continues in power today.[67]

Mitchell in his later years led a crusading effort to get people to remember the powerful days of the STFU, and remained the union's best promoter. He named his 1979 autobiography after John Handcox's song, "Mean Things Happening in This Land." He wrote, "This book is dedicated to John L. Handcox and the hundreds of other black, brown and white sharecroppers and farm workers who laid their lives on the line . . . only to disappear later into the barrios and ghettos of the cities."[68]

The Promised Land

Historical actors often make their cameo appearance and then leave the stage. John Handcox recognized when that moment came for him to leave. Whenever he felt disrespected on a personal basis he would always get going—much as he had done after his father died. Blues songs often celebrated getting gone from a bad situation, and such songs proliferated in the era of the Great Migration during and after the two world wars. John followed that muse and decided to move on. In Oklahoma, John employed all his entrepreneurial skills. He worked as a carpenter and butcher's helper, and, typical of his ability to make something out of almost nothing, gathered rocks and boulders to build four stone houses on a vacant lot on Virginia Street in Bartlesville: one for his mother, one each for his two brothers, and one for himself, Ruth, and their four children. The Handcox clan all lived on the same street in Bartlesville and took in boarders as well. John also worked briefly for a wealthy white woman but quit when she refused to pay him a decent wage. He ran a kind of boarding house in Oklahoma and for two months in the summer of 1942, near an army camp in Salinas, Kansas:[69]

> *I came up to Oklahoma, I got some orange crates, and large frames and mattresses, and I made beds. I went to keepin' and feedin' people who were working out there. I'd feed 'em and sleep 'em for eight dollars a week; two hot meals, one cold. Everybody was satisfied. If they wanted to come back for more, they had as much as they wanted to eat. I made good. I was in with Safeway Stores, I'd pick up bananas and oranges they couldn't sell. They'd give me a break. I had two ladies working for me, my sister-in-law and another lady. We fed about forty a day. First we were in a two-story house, and then I rented another house for them to sleep in. My crowd got so big, around sixty or seventy by the time we finished up. They were building an army camp.*

John seemed to succeed as a proletarian entrepreneur, but he did not like the cold winter in Oklahoma. As a wartime economy perked up during the summer of 1942, California jobs and sunshine beckoned.[70] A worker he knew convinced him to go to San Francisco and, seemingly without a plan, he and his friend drove west until they stopped at a gas station in eastern California. John recalled, *"I had Kansas plates on the car, and a gas station worker noticed. He said if you want to be where the weather's good, go to San Diego . . . I turned that puppy around and headed to San Diego"*

John remembered November 28, 1942, when he arrived in San Diego, as the best day of his life.[71] It was a far better existence than what he had experienced in Arkansas, Missouri, or Oklahoma. Of his move to San Diego, John beamed in 1985 as he told me, "That was forty-three years ago, and I'm still here."

Get on Board That Union Train

After John disappeared from the union movement, the question remained as to what would happen to his songs and poetry. Lee Hays took credit for "Roll the Union On" and even for "Raggedy, Raggedy," sometimes sharing his authorship with Claude Williams. In Lee's autobiography, he credited Williams as playing an important role in refashioning a number of old gospel songs into freedom and labor protest songs. Claude, indeed, had provided the "transmission belt" for a number of important songs. As one example, after his ouster from the STFU, he led an organizing and educational seminar in Memphis in August 1940, at the Inland Boatmen's Union hall, at the beginning of the CIO's efforts to organize southern cotton and cannery workers. A news account in the anti-union *Commercial Appeal*, which H. L. Mitchell had earlier dubbed "the voice of the planters," described how classic black freedom songs became a part of the labor movement: "Williams starts each meeting with a long singing session. At first the negroes sing their own religious songs, then adapt the tune to union words. They clap and stomp ther feet and roll their eyes as they sing and shout in an occasional well timed 'hallejuhah.' [sic] As the tempo of the singing increases, Williams smoothly directs the turn toward union songs."[72]

In a letter to friends, Claude later shed light on what transpired, minus the newspaper's references to "eye rolling," when Hattie Walls, an African American sharecropper who had led one of the STFU locals in Arkansas, originated a new version of "Gospel Train," which itself was a variant of "The Old Ship of Zion." It was not coincidental that this song resembled the reworked version of the "Old Ship of Zion" that John had sent to Claude in 1938. The song stuck in Williams's head, and he brought to the labor school up how "John Handcox and some other persons had translated all the verses of some old songs, and cited one or two as illustrations. As I paused to better formulate what I was trying to say, Hattie broke in," singing the song but adding "CIO, CIO," in place of "get on board, get on board" in the song's chorus. Woody Guthrie, Lee Hays, Sis Cunningham (both of them previously of Commonwealth College) and the ubiquitous Pete Seeger later teamed up in the Almanac Singers to popularize "Union Train" as a powerful anthem to rally CIO workers. People don't always remember how such "zipper songs" originate, but it seems that Walls, Williams, John Handcox, and Pete Seeger all played a role in this one.[73]

This was but one of the songs that emerged from the freedom movement in the cotton fields to migrate into the industrial labor movement. Mitchell believed that "Roll the Union On" was probably third on the list of the most popular union songs of the time, behind "Solidarity Forever" and the STFU's theme song, "We Shall Not Be Moved." The latter showed up again in the Montgomery Bus Boycott and the civil rights movement in later years, as did "Oh Freedom," "Freedom Train," and the union and black church song, "We Shall Overcome."[74] John had helped to transmit and create black freedom and labor protest music, and to build the STFU as an organizer. But when that movement faded away his role as a cultural worker proved to be his most enduring contribution.

Through his recordings at the Library of Congress, John made the struggles of southern tenant farmers, sharecroppers, and day laborers an indelible part of the historical record that would help shape a more diverse and progressive cultural climate through the "folk music revival" of the 1960s.[75] The folk revival went on without him however, until, like a modern Rip Van Winkle, he re-emerged in the 1980s.

12. Pete Seeger introduces a panel of labor and civil rights singers at the Great Labor Arts Exchange in June 1985: (L–R) Seeger, Guy Carawan, Si Khan, James Orange, John Handcox, CandieCarawan, and Ann Romaine. Michael Honey is in the foreground, recording. Photograph by Larry Rubin.

13. John with fellow folk musician Joe Glazer. Photograph by Larry Rubin.

14. John at the 1986 Great Labor Arts Exchange. Photograph by Larry Rubin.

15. John singing with unidentified guitarist at the Southern Tenant Farmers Union reunion, Memphis, Tennessee, 1982. Photograph by Evelyn Smith Munro.

16. John at Evelyn Smith Munro's house in Laguna Beach, California, holding a copy of *Mean Things Happening in This Land* by H. L. Mitchell. Photograph by Evelyn Smith Munro.

17. Passing it on to the younger generation: John with participants in a labor-themed Augusta Heritage folk festival at Davis-Elkins College, West Virginia, August 1985. Author's collection.

18. John with the author Michael Honey and Pat Krueger, who transcribed most of his oral histories, at Stanford University in 1990. Photograph by William Ferris.

19. John Handcox and the author in 1986. Photograph by Larry Rubin.

CHAPTER 7

"I'm So Glad to Be Here Again": The Return of John Handcox

So I say you never know what life holds in store. And the best thing you can try to do is live a life for others that follow you to say that "Someone has been this way before." And I found out early in life that the best we can be is not good enough, so we have to continue to try to do good.

—John Handcox speaking to Rebecca Schroeder, 1989

Anything I can do to make this a better world to live in, I'm willing, waiting, and ready to do it.

—Interview with William Ferris and Michael Honey, January 15, 1990

There are a million different things that people want to be.
But the greatest thing of all, they want to be free.

—"The Difference In People," John Handcox

During the years after John left the Southern Tenant Farmers Union (STFU), America's great folk song revival unfolded. Pete Seeger and friends built a post-war base for the "folk" music revival with an organization called People's Songs. In December, 1946, Seeger, Lee Hays, and other singers released their first People's Songs album, titled "Roll the Union On." Arkansas contributed a number of important musicians who were more or less John Handcox's contemporaries to a post-war upsurge of popular black music: jazz singer Louis Jordan (born in 1908, in Brinkley, John's birth place), gospel singer Rosetta Tharpe (born in 1921 in Cotton Plant, home of John's grandparents), and bluesman Big Bill Broonzy (born in Jefferson County, in 1903). [1] Other black musicians like Huddie Leadbetter (Leadbelly), Paul Robeson, Josh White, Billie Holiday,

Sonny McGee, and Brownie Terry opened the way for acceptance of people's music within the commercial world. So did the wildly popular Weavers, with Seeger and Lee Hays drawing heavily on the music of the South. [2]

Then, in a flash, red-baiting and blacklisting removed the Weavers and practically every progressive person and movement cause from the airwaves. The red scare assigned labor protest music to near oblivion and largely drove the Left out of the labor movement. The craft and industrial unions merged into a Cold War-oriented American Federation of Labor and Congress of Industrial Organizations (AFL-CIO), and the red scare eclipsed Seeger's hopes for a singing, socially progressive labor movement.[3] However, leftist unions and artists who survived the red scare passed on labor songs to the next generation. Some 20 years after the planters ran John Handcox out of Arkansas, the singing-est movement ever appeared: from Montgomery, Alabama, in 1955, to Memphis, Tennessee, in 1968, the black freedom movement burst forth. It revamped labor songs like "Which Side Are You On?," "We Shall Overcome," and "Union Train" into freedom songs. As during the sharecropper's movement, people found that songs helped them to march, picket, rally, prepare for jail, and transcend fear and violence. Activist Bob Zellner recalled an incident in which police threatened to beat students if they did not disperse; they refused, singing to the police, "We Shall Not Be Moved."[4] In tandem with the rise of the black freedom movement, the "power of black music," according to scholar Samuel Floyd, increasingly infused and changed popular American culture with the inheritance of "those who loved and fought before."[5]

Pete Seeger in 1965 linked the labor and civil rights eras, writing, "in the 1930s, as in the 1960s, it was the Negro people of the South, with their traditions of church singing, who provided some of the best songs picked up throughout the country."[6] The student, anti-war, feminist, environmental, and Black, Red, Brown, and Yellow Power movements all drew upon rich streams of people's music, but the popularization of labor protest and freedom music in the 1960s unfolded without John Handcox. Except for a segment in John Greenway's book, *American Songs of Protest* (1952), John's role in shaping music went mostly unacknowledged. In preparing to publish *Hard-Hitting Songs for Hard-Hit People* (1967), as he tells us in the preface to this book, Pete tried in vain to find John, and thought he had died.

John, however, was alive and well. On November 28, 1942, he had arrived in southeast San Diego at age 38, to apply his many survival skills. He first worked as a driver in an aircraft plant, and also peddled, from the back of a truck, fish that he caught and eggs and watermelon that he grew in his yard. John and Ruth established a residence on 230 South 29 street at the corner of Clay, then at 2978 Commercial, and finally at 3993 Florence, in a house that John built himself. His brothers Willis and George also took up carpentry.[7] John and Ruth's one son, John, Jr., and three daughters—Maggie, Vinnia, and Ruth—as well as John's brothers George, Willis and Leo, and numerous others—as John liked to say, "more people than followed the

Pharaoh"—joined them in the Promised Land. Just as they had moved more or less as an extended family to Bartlesville, Oklahoma, the Handcox family moved practically as a unit to San Diego. [8] As part of the black migration to the West, other migrants flooded into San Diego, and a dozen or more of them at a time stayed in the Handcox home, sleeping on couches, on the floor, even in tents in the back yard. It was an expanded version of the hospitality John's parents had practiced back in Arkansas, and now it also helped him and his family to keep body and soul together.[9]

John's grandmother Vinia (Vina) Nunn, the matriarch and still in many ways the boss of the family, promoted the mass migration because she knew jobs were available during World War II. John's brother-in-law Willie Williams recalled that Vina, after her husband's death in 1923, subsequently focused all her attention on making the family a success. In Arkansas, she had whipped the children in line with a strap, and in San Diego, she planted crops and kept the family going until she died in 1969 at age 91.[10] John's sisters all worked—Vinnia as an aircraft assembler for 15 years, Martha in electronics, Eliza as a seamstress, and his brother George's wife Velma worked at aircraft and naval bases. All of these Handcox women had children, were devout Christians, and helped to build church and neighborhood networks.[11]

Around 1945, as the war jobs petered out, John and his brother Willis (Bill) set up a combination grocery store, restaurant, and boarding house at 29th and Clay Streets, and continued their carpentry.[12] The white-run labor markets of San Diego did not welcome black migrants. When a white carpenter employed John as a "helper," with John doing most of the work but at a lower rate of pay, he quit the job and joined the Carpenter's Union. But he found that the union allowed contractors to discriminate in hiring and he struggled to find equal pay and advancement.[13] In an undated, rambling letter to me, he complained, *"In my working days I have been sent out on jobs an when I got to the job an they seen my face they [say] that they did not need no one."* The racism he encountered by white union members made him so angry that he wrote, what workers *"need today is more unity and less union."* After reciting a verse from "Solidarity Forever," however, he confirmed that he still supported unions. *"The workers make everything an get the nasty end of the stick."* He concluded, *"We have come a long ways an still have a long way to go."*[14]

At mid-century, parts of San Diego still had a semi-rural quality that John liked. He and his older brother George and their nephews could fish for mackerel, and family members still planted crops. His entrepreneurial habits expanded his property holdings as he caught and sold fish and crops, rented rooms, sold groceries, and took carpentry jobs.[15] John loved sunny San Diego, but conservative Republicans and the US Navy, the "whitest" of the armed services, dominated the city. John did not lapse into political inactivity. *"There wasn't but two Negroes working on Imperial Avenue, in a grocery store and a drugstore,"* he later told a reporter for the San Diego *Tribune*. Working with civil rights groups, he picketed two other white-owned groceries until they agreed to hire African Americans. He picketed a theater as well but, according to John, the owner told him, "I'll close my show up before I'll hire niggers." The pickets continued and the theater closed.[16]

Not far from downtown, John settled into the heart of Logan Heights, where San Diego's restrictive covenants and rank discrimination forced most African Americans to live. The Norman Baynard Photograph Collection at the San Diego History Center depicts Logan Heights as a vibrant black community populated by Masons, war veterans, church members, workers, and singing groups, with people holding picnics, weddings, and graduations, and organizing in civil rights, the Nation of Islam, and political campaigns.[17] When he joined a small chapter of the Socialist Party, agents of the Federal Bureau of Investigation (FBI) soon came snooping around. If they thought they would scare him, they were wrong, as John told Marjorie Miller, a reporter who interviewed him in 1985 for the *Los Angeles Times*:

> *They come by and I invited them in to my friend's house, but they said, "No, you come out to the car." They was asking did I belong to the Socialist Party. I said, "Yes. I prefer it over the Democrat and Republican 'cause they nothing but rich people's parties and I don't have no money." I tell them, "now you all chasing after me, but you didn't do nothing to these people that kill Emmett Till." He was the Negro 14-years old who they killed in Mississippi (for whistling at a white woman). They say they got to go now, but I say, "You all want to talk to me. Well, I'm going to talk to you."*

John never lost his sharp political edge, even during the era of red-baiting Congressman Joe McCarthy. He used his economic independence to do what he wanted, and he wanted to contribute to the accelerating struggle for equality. He told Miller, "If you've never been black, you can't hardly sympathize with what black people went through. I don't hate white people. I don't have no hatred. We're getting a better break now than we ever did, and we're not getting a fair deal now." His experiences made him skeptical of people talking about how good things were now or talking about "the good old days." Toward the end of his life, he wrote that he had lived for over 80 years "and I haven't seen them yet. The good old days will come when the workers get together and demand them."[18] John still had a skepticism about preachers, despite his close ties to a local church run by a son in law: John often refused to go to weddings or funerals, joking he didn't want to make the preachers rich.[19]

John retained the restless spirit of his youth and stuck to his idea that if things did not go well he should "get going." While his wife Ruth earned money by cleaning houses in the affluent parts of town and he made money through entrepreneurship and carpentry, they drifted apart. According to family stories, Ruth's father in Arkansas had once chased John away with a shotgun, but John finally won her hand. Ruth, a strict Baptist, proved a supportive spouse, highly respected by her family members. The Handcoxes had a strong union and an extensive kinship network. Nonetheless, perhaps partly as the result of their many separations and hard times, John and Ruth divorced after more than 23 years of marriage. They had married in Madison, Arkansas, on November 27, 1922; they divorced on April 27, 1954 in San Diego. [20]

John had remarried on February 12, 1951, even before finalizing his divorce to Ruth. He and his second wife Dolly moved into a white area of the city called Golden Hills, where whites threatened to burn him out. He retorted that they couldn't burn him out, but "you might buy me out if I like your offer." He didn't sell the house, but after a little less than four years the woman he married apparently ditched him for someone else. Between this and another subsequent marriage and divorce, John lost three houses and a restaurant to the women in his life. He told me that what his second wife did to him pained him even more than what the planters had done.[21]

Like most working-class Americans, John lived through a lifetime of ups and downs, personal and otherwise. His divorces undercut his accumulation of assets. He met at least one other woman but whether they married is unclear. At times, he lived close to the bone, given all these disruptions in his personal life. All of this pained his first wife Ruth to no end. Yet, to the end of their lives, John and Ruth maintained a strong working relationship, and she took care of him during some of his last days when he was ill. He made do with whatever was at hand. A photo in the *Los Angeles Times* in 1985 showed him smiling in his garden, in a working man's shirt, with a modest cottage in the background.[22]

The Handcox extended kinship networks created a powerful presence in the community, and many younger people revered John and his brothers. The men and women alike of this generation had taken charge of their families during wretched times in the South and then as southern migrants established more or less self-sufficient lives in San Diego. And they planted a huge family tree. John and Ruth's son, John Handcox, Jr., had three children; their daughter Maggie had six; their daughter Vinia had six; and their other daughter Ruth had 13. The extended family grew exponentially, producing some 200 grandchildren and great-grandchildren, at last count.[23] The Handcox clan was so substantial that they helped to fill the New Creation Church, across the street from one of the Handcox homes. It was pastored by John's sister's son, Amos Johnson.[24]

John's extended family knew that he and his brothers Willis and George had experienced difficult times and stood up for their rights in the South, but only vaguely knew about John being a musician and poet. John mostly filled his life with working-class pursuits having to do with survival. His family learned more about his role as a union organizer and cultural worker when he returned to the music world around 1985. In his last years, he cemented his legacy as the sharecropper's troubadour and poet laureate, and his fame as an elder spread in San Diego and the surrounding community. He told those of us who discovered him late in life that his strongest desire was to get his songs and poems out to the world. *"I'm not out for what I can get out of (life), I'm out for what I can put into it, to make a better world."*[25] He noted that he had never copyrighted his songs or poems, and told reporter Marjorie Miller, *"Life is not a matter of money with me,"* adding, *"If my songs help make this a better world to live in, I think I did a lot."*[26]

"Oh No, We Don't Want Reagan Anymore"

On June 15, 1985, I sat in the front row of an audience of labor and civil rights singers and songwriters, tape recorder in hand, at the Great Labor Song Exchange. Meeting at the AFL-CIO's George Meany Center for Labor Studies, we heard a panel I had helped to organize that included luminaries of labor protest music: Pete Seeger, the Johnny Apple Seed of people's music; Guy Carawan, who had spread "We Shall Overcome" and his wife Candy Carawan, who together had documented the rise of freedom songs in the 1960s; Sparky Rucker, an African-American blues and freedom singer from the Knoxville area; Anne Romaine, one of the leaders of the southern folk music revival; song writer and labor activist Si Kahn; the legendary Birmignham, Alabama, civil rights and labor organizer James Orange; and, not least of all, John Handcox. Panelists gave examples of how the civil rights songs of the 1960s spread and linked together multiple social movements for freedom, labor rights, women's liberation, and peace. Some of these songs originated in slavery times, others in labor movements of the 1930s.

When Pete first introduced John, it was an electrifying moment. John, beginning his talk by addressing the audience as *"ladies and gentlemens,"* had a humble yet charismatic presence; indeed, his very existence energized the labor singers. He almost immediately launched into "Roll the Union On." A powerful chorus joined him after John "zipped" in each new verse. This song from the sharecropper's movement of more than 50 years ago unleashed incredible energy. When he sang, his audience instantly adopted a call-and-response model of singing:

> *We gonna roll—we gonna roll,*
> *We gonna roll—we gonna roll,*
> *We gonna roll the union on* [repeat]

With the voices of passionate labor advocates singing in unison, one could hear the power of this song. It didn't sound like "Polly Wolly Doodle" or "Roll the Chariot On," songs the tune is supposedly based upon. It had its own cadence and energy, powered by mass singing and hand clapping. People in this room felt it was needed now as an expression of the labor movement's attempts to revive itself during the era of President Ronald Reagan, when unions were under severe attack. Nor was it difficult for us to transpose "Mean Things Happening in This Land" to the 1980s counter-revolution against all social reforms we were experiencing in our own times.

John recited "Landlord What in the Heaven is the Mater With You?" and told about "the raggedyist man that ever I seen," who prompted him to write "Raggedy, Raggedy Are We." When asked how songs from the cotton country could apply to workers elsewhere, he responded, *"What's unfair is unfair anywhere."*[27] Throughout the conference, John's humble manner in introducing his songs aroused people's empathy. We felt as if the legendary John Henry—John's pen name in the 1930s—had returned. But the real, live John Handcox had been cooking up more new songs, once again building on traditional tunes. John began a song with the chorus: "Oh no, oh no, oh no, we don't want Reagan anymore." How appropriate, I thought: it resembled the tune of a traditional song that intoned, "Oh death, Oh death/Death please stay your hand awhile." John's verses called out the President for his 1981 firing of the air traffic controllers that set off an anti-union offensive by employers across the country:

> *Workers starving all over this land and he wants to spend for defense,*
> *we don't think Reagan's got good sense.*
> *The President of Mexico gave Reagan a white horse,*
> *now he thinks that makes him the poor folks' riding boss.*

John had no trouble getting us to sing, heartily, his chorus:

> *Oh no, oh no,*
> *Oh no, we don't want Reagan any more!*

John started another song with the chorus, *"Stomp your feet, sing and shout, let's get old Reagan out."* His verses alluded to a cascade of objectionable results of the so-called Reagan Revolution: tax cuts for the rich amid fiscal austerity, a huge recession, an epidemic of homelessness, mass unemployment, massive cuts to social welfare programs, a tripling of military budgets and the national debt, and sordid military interventions in Central America. He sang, *"Black and white sleeping in the street, without shelter or a bite to eat,"* and *"he's sending troops to other lands, to kill the poor working hands."* With enthusiasm, we followed our song leader, *"Let's clap our hands, sing and shout, let's get old Reagan out."* Although now often praised and mythologized, unionists viewed Reagan as the leader of a counter-revolution that created a new era of hunger and homelessness. "Reaganomics" made John's old songs—"Mean Things," "Raggedy, Raggedy," and "Join the Union Tonight"—more relevant than ever.

Throughout the rest of the 1980s, as he sang and recited at various folk gatherings, John combined his outrage with a sense of humor that audiences found appealing. I don't know where John found "The Reagan Psalms," and it was not original, but he became fond of reciting them at labor gatherings: "Reagan is my shepherd, I am in want. He maketh me to lie down on park benches. He leadeth me beside still factories. He destroyeth my paycheck, and he leadeth me in the path of unemployment, for his Party's sake"²⁸ John continued to roll out songs to decry the ruthless assaults on the living standards of working people. Before our next Labor Song Exchange, he sent me a poem he wrote about a force that had wiped out cotton farming and millions of other jobs in his lifetime: mechanization. I typed it up and regularized the verses a bit:

I was talking with a group of people the other day.
They say I'm not working—machines have taken my job away.
One with a machine can do more than a thousand men can do in a day.
What else can you say—machines have taken their jobs away.
　　　Jobless, jobless, in the U. S. A.
Many were born on a farm and thought that they were there to stay,
Machines came along and taken their jobs away.
There are millions of people out of work today,
Because machines have taken their jobs away.
　　　Jobless, jobless in the U. S. A.
Go down town, you see people sleeping on the street
with no home to go to, and nothing to eat.
In this land of plenty and home of the brave
machines are taking jobs every day.
　　　Jobless, jobless in the U. S. A.
We are sleeping on the streets and eating out of garbage cans,
We live our lives from day to day.
You go to the employment office and what do they say?
Sorry, we have no work today . . . Machines have taken our jobs away.
　　　Jobless, jobless in the U. S. A.

I regularized the stanzas, set his words to a tune with a rock and roll beat and added two verses at the end to highlight the hope we still felt for the labor movement, even in hard times. At our next Labor Song Exchange in 1986, we sang it together:

Jobless, jobless in the USA
Millions are searching for work every day
Machines have taken their jobs away—
Jobless, in the USA.
Hunger, hunger in the USA
People without a bite to eat
People without a place to stay
Machines have taken their jobs away—
Hunger, in the USA.
Homeless, homeless in the USA

Millions are searching for work every day
Machines have taken their jobs away—
Homeless, in the USA.
Suffering, suffering in the USA
Not a penny in their pockets not a bite to eat
Machines have taken their jobs away—
Suffering, in the USA.
Working, working in the USA,
Working towar.d a better day
Where bosses won't take our jobs away—
Working, in the USA.
Changing, changing in the USA
Changing things until we have our say
Listen friend, there's gonna be a new day
We're gonna make some changes, in the USA.
We're gonna make some changes, in the USA.

Interviewed by Rebecca Schroeder in 1989, John reflected on the hard times he witnessed at the end of his life: *"What, with all this machinery and mechanism, where one person displace maybe thousands, what's gonna happen? [That's] the thing that's worryin' me today . . . Maybe one of these days poor people will wake up. Of course it may cost thousands and thousands of lives to do it. I think we'll have a revolution. I think it's going to be forced on us. I can't get it figured out. Sometimes I wake up at night and try to figure it out, what's gonna happen."*[29]

Like the rediscovery of blues people from the Delta during the folk music revival of the 1960s—only with a Socialist twist—"John Henry's return" clearly energized audiences of labor musicians. This delighted John, and he expressed his feelings of elation with a hand-clapping, foot-stomping acapella presentation at our 1986 meeting:

Let's all join our hands and sing, I'm so glad to be here again.
I'm so glad to be here again, To meet with new and old friends.
Some of you I've never met and some of you I'll never forget.
If we all get together, Oh yes we can, make this world a better land.
Let's all join our hands and sing, I'm so glad to be here again.

In 1989, the Labor Heritage Foundation gave John its Joe Hill Award as a poet and composer of creative labor music. For four years, the folk music circuit had called John to a new life, in which he gained more attention than he had in the 1930s. He sang at Davis and Elkins College in West Virginia, with Pete Seeger to clean up the Hudson River, at the huge Vancouver, British Columbia, Folk Festival, and as a featured performer at the Western Worker's Heritage festivals in the San Francisco Bay area from 1987 through 1992.[30] The University of Missouri-Columbia created a John Handcox archive and honored him in a 1989 program. Scholar and participant David Roediger recalled, "the large crowd heard wonderful words from the labor lorist Archie Green, the historian Arvarh Strickland and others, but it was Handcox who brought them out and brought down the house." In singing "Solidarity Forever," John substituted "their horrid gold" for the song's reference to the "hoarded gold" of capitalists, and made numerous quips about his life and labors. A beaming Archie Green walked up to the stage and gave him a long and warm embrace. As John always said, singing is often better than speaking.[31]

Local geniuses are often ignored in their own community, but various communities in Southern California honored John in his last years. On May 13, 1989, more than 1,000 people turned out at the Wilshire Ebell Theater in Los Angeles as part of the 25th anniversary of the Southern California Library for Social Studies and Research, a repository for "movement" history, and honored Handcox for his "immeasurable contributions to the betterment of working people's lives." John told a reporter that he remained a socialist and still believed in the power of music, saying, *"some people don't know how bad things really are unless they hear somebody talking or singing about it."* John told researcher Rebecca that he was happy that so many people had rediscovered his work: *"Most everybody—I mean, quite a few— they didn't get no praise while they were livin'. You didn't hear nothin' 'bout 'em until their death. So I got praise whiles I live—and that makes me feel good."*[32]

"Still Kicking, but Not High"

As old age and health problems set in, John kept his sense of humor. He told a reporter for the *San Francisco Chronicle,* "Still got my teeth and my eyes. I think I'm pretty well put together. Only thing, my pocket's kind of empty." The article, titled "Last of the Legendary Labor Poets," included a photo of John with an impish grin, wearing a knitted cap. He sent me letters and evocative poems about getting ill and growing old, signing them, *"still kicking, but not high."* But like anyone, he faced daunting medical challenges. A series of poems about his hospitalization under the care of a specialist included this thought:

> *If there is any word that I really hate, it is the word Isolate.*
> *It makes you feel that you've lost all your friends,*
> *And that the world has come to a sudden end.*

Hospitalization made him feel perhaps more vulnerable than he did as a labor organizer in the 1930s. *"I know that it will be the day we all dread/ when they take my name off the board and the tag off my bed,"* he wrote. He felt the need to pay tribute to his mother Vina, who had in effect saved him from a lynch mob in the 1930s and stayed with him in San Diego into her nineties:

No One has never had a mother any sweeter.
There are many that may equal but none can beat her.
My mother is forever there, although you may not see her.
She is there in mind and prayer.

As he spoke to numerous folklorists and historians, he seemed to want to sum up the meaning of his life, and kept suggesting that someone should write a book about his life in the STFU. He frequently expressed his belief in the Golden Rule: *"If you preach to your fellow man right, that is the thing that counts . . . Try to treasure the best, is the way it works."* He continued to warn against the virus of racism: *"the separations of the races was to the Big Man's advantage . . . to me, it ain't but one race, and that's the human race—and that includes everybody."* He mused, *"we're all human beings, and we come in the world the same way, and we goes out the same way. What makes one any more than another?"* He especially urged union organizing for the progress of working-class people: *"The person doing the right thing, that . . . makes 'em important. The right thing [for me] happened to be to unionize the labor and the people . . . It won't ever do this country any good when you get scared about unionizing. If all the workers unionized it'd be a better place to live."*[33]

The life of John Handcox spanned most of the twentieth century, and he had seen a lot of changes, some for better, some for worse. He maintained a humble sense that what he had not been able to change the world but he felt blessed that he had been able to contribute: *"When I know that I have helped others, I feel good, I really feel good . . . For to try was better than nothing at all. I feel good, I really feel good."* During my last interview with John, conducted jointly with William Ferris at Stanford University in 1990, he had slowed down a great deal, perhaps battling the cancer that would take his life. Still, in his mid-eighties, he insisted, *"I ain't old."* *"I know a little something about this world, but this afterworld they talking about—they say there's a heaven and there's a hell—I ain't never been there and ain't nobody ever been there and told me about it."* He joked:

This guy was in church and somebody got up and told the congregation that they were just ready and willin', waitin' on the good Lord to call 'em home. And this old brother got up behind him and said, "Brothers and sisters, I hope to make heaven my home, but I ain't a damn bit homesick."

Always a bit skeptical about organized religion, John said he hoped there was a heaven, but he was *"not a damn bit anxious to go there."* He saw religion as a practical matter, and gave thanks for his "God-given talent." He emphasized the importance of *"trying to make this world a better world to live in":*

The workers, we are the ones that made this world. And this world can be an enjoy-able place if we get our rightful share of what we produce. You read me? No worker should suffer. If there's anything that the worker needs to have a happy life while he's here on Earth, the working man should have it. That's the way I feel about it. Do unto others as you would others do unto you. We do that and we will have lived a creative life and a life we won't be ashamed of.[34]

"How I Want to Be Remembered"

On January 31, 1992, at the Laborer's International Hall, a three-hour celebration took place, billed as "The San Diego Labor Heritage Tribute to John L. Handcox." Four choirs performed, and Ernie McCray, a local high school principal and actor, read some of John's poems. Pete Seeger and Joe Glazer joined with John, whose voice had weakened, in performing "Roll the Union On." During part of the proceedings Glazer could be heard encouraging John, to "take it easy," and steadying him at the microphone. Seeger told a *Los Angeles Times* reporter that "he's never quit being a very gentle but persistent activist, going around trying to persuade people to get together to do the things that need doing. I'm just one of his biggest fans. There are women and men like John around the world who work hard for good causes without getting much credit. People like that are the hope of the world."[35]

On September 18, 1992, at the age of 87, John Handcox crossed the river to the great beyond. He had left his body to a medical school to be used in research and wrote, "if my heart could be transferred to someone else, it would be full of love for the workers of the world."[36] On September 26, people gathered in a tribute at the New Creation Church (pastored by John's nephew Amos Johnson). They sang "Raggedy, Raggedy, Are We," and "Mean Things Happening in This Land." People sang these songs telling of a heartless world as joyous odes to a man who linked them to past generations, "those who loved and fought before." The program notes included "How I Want to be Remembered," a short essay by John: *"I want to be remembered as one that volunteered to risk my life to make this a better world for the workers to live in . . . as one that was more than glad to lend a helping hand."*

The assembled audience of friends, family and community members finished the service with a recessional and community sing of "Roll the Union On."[37]

* * *

Amongst the songs John left behind, some exuded a spirit of protest and resistance, but in his last years he also wrote about hope, optimism, and good will. "What a Wonderful World It Could Be" is one such song:

*If we all loved each other
What a fine world it would be,*

> *If we acted as sisters and brothers*
> *What a happy world this would be.*
> *If we all would sing together*
> *What a beautiful song that would be,*
> *If we all would unite together*
> *What a strong union that would be.*
> *If we all rejoiced together*
> *What a happy world this would be,*
> *If we all would walk together*
> *What a great walk that would be.*
> *If we all loved each other*
> *What a fine world this would be,*
> *If we acted as sisters and brothers*
> *What a happy world this would be.*[38]

Over his many decades since the 1930s, Handcox had retained the rhythm of poetry and the lilt of music he learned as a child, as well as a great appreciation of the power of group singing. Bernice Johnson Reagon, one of the great scholars and vocalists of the African American song tradition, explains how such group (congregational) singing creates power:

> Singing is an organizing experience . . . you cannot create a song within the Black American cultural experience if you're not an organizer. You cannot create a song if you're not willing to be organized. You have to hear, you have to be willing to lead, you have to be willing to follow, you have to be willing to experiment and move around the basic themes.[39]

Group singing, according to Reagon, helps people to experience the reality that, despite all their conflicts and differences, there is power in union. The lone voice is not enough to carry the day; one's voice may not be strong, and we can't all be good singers. But many voices singing together can make it possible for endangered people to gather the courage to march through the cotton fields of eastern Arkansas of 1936 or through the streets of Birmingham, Alabama, in 1963. The African American song tradition energized and linked generations from slavery onward. Reagon explains: "The singing suspends the confusion and points to a higher order, sometimes long enough for you to execute the next step. Therefore, singing will not set you free, but don't try to get free without it."[40]

*　*　*

Can we recall a time when a white worker in the heart of Ku Klux Klan country might come up to a black worker and offer his hand extended to the full length of his arm, with his thumb in the palm of his hand, saying "I am for a worker's world," as a sign of union solidarity? Can we recall a time when addressing each other as "Mr." or "Mrs." were acts of human decency that could get you killed? Rev. Ed King, an activist in the Student Nonviolent Coordinating Committee (SNCC), said older people in the civil rights movement of the 1960s did remember the sharecroppers' union of the 1930s, and saw it as the beginning of a profound movement for change. "They would say, 'Well, we thought that was going to be the time when it would happen, but then we had to wait.'"[41]

Instead of the Southern Tenant Farmers' Union vision of cooperative farming, the landscapes of Arkansas farming gave way to flat lands and hills denuded of homes and people, with the remains of a discarded laboring population huddled in poverty in places like Earle. "Freedom After 'While" became freedom denied. Nonetheless, as laboring people today fight for some way to make their way in the global economy, it remains useful to remember when evangelicals, labor radicals, "white" folks and people of color, women and men, combined their dreams and mixed their tactics. They used strikes, protest marches, media publicity, singing, and praying and they besieged government to do something for the working poor. The STFU did not have a narrow, self-interest platform; it was both a citizen's movement and a labor-civil rights and civil liberties movement, with a broad, socialist and reform agenda. It sought union rights, but it also sought to change people's consciousness and the "mean things happening in this land." Memories of this past might help people to organize again today and perhaps more successfully.

This book constitutes an act of recovery. Told through the words and life of one man, it honors an activist and artist, respects the power of remembering and reminds us that one need not be wealthy or famous to take up the task of changing society for the better. John Handcox quipped, *"Of course, I was young and probably crazy too"* when he challenged the plantation elite. But he wanted to be remembered as one of the humble people who joined the sharecroppers' revolt. He signed his letters *"yours for a better world,"* and regarded songs and poems as his form of immortality:

> I started out as a sharecropper's son
> But look at me now, I'm a man with a song.[42]

My hope is that the memories, songs, and poems of a sharecropper troubadour, working in tandem with the research of a labor and civil rights historian, might help us to learn from and honor those who loved and fought before. If we don't honor such people, how can we honor the best in our own selves today? John Handcox taught that singing can arouse people to take united action for the betterment of others and change their world.

Writing about John Handcox reminded me that singing the right song at the right time can also provide great solace. While writing this book, within a space of six months, one after the next, my wife's mother, my mother, and then my father died; so did a number of my friends and mentors, including labor historian David Montgomery. In tributes to these remarkable people, I found myself singing John's song, "Hard to Say Good-Bye" and getting others to sing it with me. Doing so became a kind of shelter in the storm. John had sent me a hand-written rough draft and the title for the song. He was not writing about dying, but simply about leaving people he cared for. I changed a few words to put them into the meter of a song and came up with a melody on the guitar. We sang it together for our friends at the Labor Song Exchange in 1986. I now find myself singing it often to feel that sense of hope that John so cheerfully expressed. Writing about John's life helped me to put some perspective on life as a state of being in which we contribute what we can and then pass away:

> It's hard to say good-bye
> So hard to say good-bye
> Sometimes it seems we just have met
> That makes it hard to say good-bye.
> If we ever meet again
> Be it over land or sea
> You know I will remember you
> Won't you remember me?
> It's hard to say good-bye
> To friends you love so dear
> I hope that God will keep us safe
> And always keep us near.
> Some day we'll meet again
> Up in that Glory Land
> Till then I ask you take my hand
> With sincere and honest love.
> It's hard to Say good-bye
> So hard to say good-bye
> Sometimes it seems we just have met
> That makes it hard to say good-bye.[43]

John had a coda to the song that suggests his strong faith in a better world, both here and above:

> But some day we'll meet in heaven
> With the good lord up above

And sing and be delivered
With sincere and honest love.

*　*　*

Probably all of John's 200 and some grandchildren, great-grand-children, and great-great grandchildren have different memories and understandings of the freewheeling patriarch of the family. Some only partially knew that for some reason John had a degree of fame attached to his name. After his passing, however, one day Camelia Cook turned on the television and got a better understanding of her grandfather.

She saw striking grocery workers marching on a picket line, singing, "Roll the Union On."

"Oh!," she exclaimed. "That's our song!" John Handcox had just returned for a visit.

Notes

"He Was an Inspiration to us All"

1. Charles Seeger recorded seven of John Handcox's songs in 1937. They are available from the Office of Folklife at the Library of Congress, as well as in diskette from University of West Virginia Press, *John L. Handcox.*
2. Alan Lomax, Woody Guthrie, and Pete Seeger, *Hard Hitting Songs for Hard-Hit People* (New York: Oak Publications, 1967, reprinted by University of Nebraska Press, 1999).

Introduction. Music, Memory, and History

1. A simple definition of a "folk" song is one that is widely known and sung but for which we don't know the author. "John Henry" is a good example: sung by people from every walk of life and region, with verses added or subtracted as needed, but with no known author. How do such iconic songs come to be? The top hits of folk songs sort themselves out based on how many folks keep singing them. Some of these are "songs of persuasion" that make it into popular commercial culture. John's songs, by contrast, have a known author and drew upon the familiar melodies and song structures of the folks he grew up with and the religious musical culture he inherited. He was not a "folk" musician but he so grounded his music in the heavily religious black song tradition that Serge R. Denisoff thought John was a preacher and raised on a plantation (wrong on both scores); *Sing A Song of Social Significance.* Bowling Green University: Popular Press, 1972, 55; *Great Day Coming: Folk Music and the American Left.* Urbana: University of Illinois Press, 1971, 35.
2. Alan Lomax, Woody Guthrie, and Pete Seeger, *Hard-Hitting Songs for Hard-Hit People* (1967), published "There is Mean Things Happening In This Land," "Raggedy, Raggedy Are We," "The Planter and the Sharecropper," "Roll the Union On," "No More Mournin," and "The Man Frank Weems." The book did not give John Handcox credit for the last three songs.
3. Songs are especially portable vehicles for building group solidarity and people in all sorts of settings have used them to build social movements. John's music very much falls within the singing traditions of the American labor movement, one reason that labor songsters in the 1980s welcomed him with open arms. "It is our ability to inspire that will make the difference," as labor activist Joe Uehlein put it. See Rob Rosenthal and Richard Flacks, *Playing for Change: Music and Musicians in the Service of Social Movements.* Boulder: Paradigm Publishers, 2011, 251.

4. Throughout history, nameless people have passed down "oral poetry" through memorization and improvization. Nameless singers passed down some of most enduring tunes and words to African American music through a similar process. The question about such music, Charles Seeger asked, was not was it "good" music, but what was it "good for"? If it was good for something, it would survive. "And finally the songs which a nation remembers are truly called folksongs, because so many folks have had a hand (or a throat) in shaping them," Pete Seeger writes. However, Seeger gave up on the term "folk music" in favor of the simple term, "people's music." John Handcox fit that framework as a great innovator of new songs who frequently used old tunes to put them across. Pete Seeger, *Where Have All the Flowers Gone: A Singer's Stories, Songs, Seeds, Robberies*, ed. Peter Blood. Bethlehem: Sing Out, 1993, 84, 146. See also Ruth Finnegan, *Oral Poetry: Its nature, significance and social context*. Cambridge: Cambridge University Press, 1977.

5. Eileen Southern's majestic cannon of black music, for example, says almost nothing about African American freedom or labor protest music: Southern, ed., *Readings in Black American Music* (1971, 1999); and Southern, *The Music of Black Americans, A History* (1971, 1983, 1997). *New Perspectives on Music, Essays in Honor of Eileen Southern*, ed. Josephine Wright, with Samuel Floyd Jr. (1992), has an impressive array of articles but none of them about black labor protest or freedom music.

6. Lawrence W. Levine, *Black Culture and Black Consciousness: Afro-American Folk Thought from Slavery to Freedom*. New York: Oxford University Press, 1997, 15.

7. In the days of slavery, southern camp meetings consisted of both blacks and whites. Many whites themselves were "on the social and economic margins of their society and had psychic and emotional needs which, qualitatively, may not have been vastly different from those of black slavers . . . Yes, these whites were musical, and oppressed too," according to Levine, ibid., 22. William Roy, *Reds, Whites and Blues: Social Movements, Folk Music, and Race in the United States*. Princeton: Princeton University Press, 2010, documents and analyzes the many ways people have helped to create social movements by turning music from a noun into a verb; 2, 19, and passim. Roy characterizes movement music as a powerful means of people expressing their needs and desires. Such understandings of black song and social movement music provides a welcome contrast to Denisoff's earlier sociology of narrowing movement music down into different categories, and with people's music supposedly manipulated instrumentally by Communists. Robbie Lieberman in contrast explains that the "the tenacity of movement culture" resulted from Communists and other people in the Labor Left in the 1930s and 1940s whose concerns went far beyond sectarian agendas, and from the power of a people's music that helped to change American culture as a whole. *"My Song is My Weapon": People's Songs, American Communism, and the Politics of Culture, 1930–1950* (1989), quote on 13.

8. Hosea Hudson, *The Narrative of Hosea Hudson: His Life as a Negro Communist in the South*, ed. Nell Irving Painter. Cambridge: Harvard University Press, 1979; Robin D. G. Kelley, *Hammer and Hoe: Alabama Communists During the Great Depression*. Chapel Hill: University of North Carolina Press, 1990;

Michael K. Honey, *Southern Labor and Black Civil Rights: Organizing Memphis Workers*. Urbana: University of Illinois Press, 1993; and Honey, *Black Workers Remember: An Oral History of Segregation, Unionism, and the Freedom Struggle*. Berkeley: University of California Press, 1999.

9. Linda Shopes, "Editing Oral History For Publication," *Oral History Forum d'historie orale* (2011), 1–24.

10. One can also hear John Handcox on tapes that go with Ronald Cohen and Dave Samuelson, eds., *Songs for Political Action: Folk Music, Topical Songs and the American Left, 1926–53* (1996). Mark Jackson writes, "In Handcox's songs and poems, we find both the timeless artistic expression of one man and a documentary history of the major issues that drove the unionization of tenant farmers in the South and Southwest during the 1930s." Liner notes, "John L. Handcox: Songs, Poems and Stories of the Southern Tenant Farmers' Union" (2004).

11. Alessandro Portelli points out that even "wrong" versions of events can tell us a great deal and "allow us to recognize the interests of the tellers, and the dreams and desires beneath them." Portelli, *The Death of Luigi Trastulli and Other Stories: Form and Meaning in Oral History*. Albany: State University of New York Press, 1991, 2. John's positive account of growing up in the Jim Crow South forces us to not over-generalize about how poorly African Americans survived in the era of Jim Crow; his recall of interracial harmony within the STFU likewise suggests that he perhaps chose 50 years later to dwell on the positive aspects of his experiences. Portelli points out that the most important thing for his work as an oral historian is "always doing my honest best to be true to what I take to be the speaker's meaning." I follow this same rule. Portelli, *They Say in Harlan County, An Oral History*. New York: Oxford University Press, 2011, 10.

12. See the Preface to *Black Workers Remember* on oral histories. Also see Michael K. Honey, *Going Down Jericho Road: The Memphis Strike, Martin Luther King's Last Campaign*. New York: W. W. Norton, 2007 on how memory and historical research can work together to provide a more complete history of social change movements.

13. Michael Frisch, in *A Shared Authority: Essays on the Craft and Meaning of Oral and Public History* (1990), asks "Who, really, is the author of an oral history, whether this be a single interview or an edited book-length narrative?" xx. John Handcox and I produced the text for this book through back-and-forth dialogues, his sharing of his poetry, music and memory, and a lot of historical digging and writing on my part. I feel confident that it represents the spirit and intent of John, and tells his story and history in an accurate way. It is an attempt to present working-class history from the bottom up.

14. Shopes, "Editing Oral History For Publication," 5.

15. John Handcox gave Donald Lance and Rebecca Schroeder permission to write a book about him, and commented, "If it don't hep me, mebbe it'll hep somebody else." Notes taken by Susan Hollister, of an interview conducted on October 16, 1989, recorded in Columbia, Missouri, tapes and notes in author's possession. He also gave me permission to publish his songs and poems and oral history, although we worked on a basis of trust as well as signed a permission form.

1 "Freedom After 'While' ": Life and Labor in the Jim Crow South

1. Paul Laurence Dunbar, *Selected Poems,* ed. Herbert Woodward Martin, Charlottesville: University Press of Virginia, 2004, 165.
2. Rebecca B. Schroeder and Donald M. Lance, "John L. Handcox: 'There Is Still Mean Things Happening'." In *Songs About Work: Essas in Occupational Culture for Richard A. Reuss,* ed. Archie Green., Bloomington: Folklore Institute, Indiana University, 1993, 184.
3. According to Levine and many others, slaves drew from Christianity the idea of ultimate transcendence, so that sorrow songs "were overshadowed by a triumphant note of affirmation," *Black Culture and Black Consciousness, 39–40. The Narrative of the Life of Frederick Douglass, An American Slav*e (1845), quotes in Chapter 2; W. E. B. DuBois, *The Souls of Black* Folk (1903), quotes in Chapter 14, "The Sorrow Songs"; and James H. Cone, *The Spirituals and the Blues, An Interpretation* (1972, 1991), 35, 40. For a sampling of these songs and their unique qualities, see R. Nathaniel Dett, ed., *Religious Folk-Songs of the Negro, As Sung at Hampton Institute.* Hampton, Va: Hampton Institute Press, 1927. He notes that accompaniments to many of these songs "can be carried away only in memory as we have no musical characters to represent them." Introduction, V.
4. Lawrence Levine observes that the Civil War "gave rise to" "Oh Freedom," "Many thousand go," and other spirituals of deliverance. *Black Culture and Black Consciousness: Afro-American Folk Thought from Slavery to Freedom* (1977), 5.
5. John Handcox, interview by Joe Glazer and Michael Honey (May 15, 1985), Library of Congress, The American Folklife Center, Archive of Folk Culture. AFS 24111.
6. Claude Williams to Harry and Grace Koger (n.d.), Claude Williams Papers, box 14, folder 6, Wayne State University Labor Archives. Thanks to Jarod Roll for bringing this letter to my attention.
7. John Handcox, interview by William Ferris and Michael Honey, January 15, 1990, first quote; second quote, John Handcox, "A Living Legend"; third quote from "This Is Your World"; fourth quote from "(We Have the Rope and the Limb) All We Want is Him: (Talking about John L. Handcox)," the latter three documents sent by John Handcox in typescript, all in author's possession.
8. Researcher Jessica Auer has traced John's ancestors back through US Census record. Vina wa John's mother; the 1880 Federal Census locates her as three-year-old Viney (her name would later be spelled Vina, Bina, or Vinia) Nunn living in Randolph County, Alabama, with three siblings, her parents, and her paternal grandparents. Her parents were born in Alabama and Georgia respectively; their parents came from South Carolina; and their parents apparently were born in Africa. John's father, George, was the son of Ben, John's grandfather, who was probably born in Mississippi; Ben's parents, and John's great-grandparents, named Nathan and Judy (Judia) Hancock, were born in Kentucky and Tennessee. The 1880 census lists the birthplaces of Judy's parents as Tennessee. US Census Bureau, *Population Census of the United States: Woodruff County Arkansas* (1870, 1880, 1900); US Census Bureau, *Randolph County* (1880); and US Census Bureau, *St. Francis County* (1900).

9. State of Arkansas Certificate of Death, 979 and 0939273, lists John's father's name as George Handcox, age 49, date of birth October 16, 1873, in Woodruff, Arkansas; his mother is listed as Lizzett Hill, also of Woodruff, and his father as Ben or Berm (illegible) Handcox, born in Mississippi, n.d. George's date of death is listed as March 2, 1923, and the cause "accidental runaway team and wagon." According to Jessica Auer's research, the 1920 Federal Census lists John's grandmother as Liznett, at age 63, though her name appears as Lizzeth in 1900. Census records list John's paternal line as Hancock in 1870, 1880, and 1900; John's parents' marriage certificate from 1899 also lists their last name as Hancock. The 1910 and 1920 censuses, however, spell their last name Handcock. The 1930 census records for both Vina and some of her children revert to the spelling Hancock. Census takers interviewed a member of each family and transcribed the oral testimony of their names onto the census record, but the poor penmanship of some census takers makes deciphering the spelling they ascribed difficult. World War I draft cards (1918) for George (John's father) and George Jr. (John's brother) list their last names as Hancock but their signatures suggest that they assumed alternate spellings. George's signature appears as Handcock, while George Jr. clearly signs as Handcox. The names Willis, Eliza, Nathan, George, Ruth, and John appear throughout John's father's and his own generation. US Census Bureau, *Randolph County* (1880); US Census Bureau, *Woodruff County* (1900); US Census Bureau, *Population Census of the United States: Monroe County, Arkansas* (1910, 1920, 1930); US Census Bureau, *St. Francis County* (1930); US Census Bureau, *Population Census of the United States: Washington County, Oklahoma* (1940); "Arkansas, County Marriages, 1837–1957," *Family Search*, Geo Hancock and Bina Nunn, (1899); and "U.S. World War I Draft Regiation Cards, 1917–1918," *FamilySearch*, GS Film Number 1530564.

10. US Census Bureau, *Woodruff County* (1870).

11. W. E. B. DuBois, *Black Reconstruction in America: An Essay Toward a History of the Part Which Black Folk Played in the Attempt to Reconstruct Democracy in America, 1860–1880.* New York: Atheneum, 1983; first published, 1935.

12. Quoted from Handcox, "We Have the Rope and the Limb," typescript in author's possession.

13. In 1880, John's mother and maternal grandparents, the Nunns, lived in Randolph County, Alabama. The family is found in the census again in 1900, living in Wheatley Township in St. Francis County, Arkansas, at which time the family owned their own home and land, and continued to do so until at least 1920. The Nunns had at least ten more children by 1900. Viney was married to George by this time, and living on land in Cotton Plant Township, Woodruff County, not far from Wheatley. By 1910, Vina and George had purchased a plot of land in Monroe County, and George's brother, Nathan, also moved from Cotton Plant in Woodruff county to Monroe County and secured a plot of land. US Census Bureau, *Randolph County* (1880); US Census Bureau, *Woodruff County* (1900, 1910, 1920, 1930, 1940); US Census Bureau, *Monroe County* (1910, 1920, 1930); US Census Bureau, *St. Francis County* (1880, 1920, 1930); and "Arkansas, County Marriages, 1837–1957."

14. Jessica Auer's research documents that Willis Nunn (John's maternal grandfather) outlived his wife Eliza. In 1920, a widowed and 76-year-old Willis lived with three of his younger children, Eliza, Elbert, and Ollie, as well as two grandchildren. Sometime after John's father's death in 1923, John's mother Vina and most of her children returned to St. Francis County, Arkansas, where she and her family had first settled after migrating from Alabama. George Jr. was married the same year of his father's death, and he and his young bride Velma made the move to St. Francis; John's younger brother Willis married Lucille Polk in 1929 in St. Francis, and also settled near his extended family. In 1930, Vina was renting a household and caring for four of her children, including young Leo, born just a year before his father's death. Her father, Willis Nunn, lived with his namesake and grandson, Willis Hancock, nearby until his death in 1933. US Census Bureau, *St. Francis County* (1920, 1930); "Arkansas, County Marriages, 1837–1957," *FamilySearch*, George Hancock and Velma Alexander (1923), GS Film number 2409192; and "Arkansas, County Marriages, 1837–1957," *FamilySearch*, Willis Handcock and Lucille Polk (1929), GS Film number 2404065.

15. US Census Bureau, *Woodruff County* (1900); and US Census Bureau, *Twelfth Population Census of the United States: Monroe County, Arkansas* (1910, 1920).

16. According to John's granddaughter, John's blue or hazel-green eyes made him especially attractive to women. Telephone interviews, Camelia Cook, July 10, 2009, August 24, 2009.

17. John Handcox letter to Michael Honey (ca. 1986), in author's files.

18. Confederates showed no mercy and took no prisoners, murdering 117 members of the First Kansas Colored, in one of the incidents that occurred during the war. Grif Stockley, *Ruled By Race: Black/White Relations in Arkansas from Slavery to the Present.* Fayetteville: University of Arkansas Press, 2009, 25, 27, 40, 80.

19. Mark Fannin, in *Labor's Promised Land: Radical Visions of Gender, Race, and Religion in the South.* Knoxville: University of Tennessee Press, 2003, emphasizes the continuity of lower-class labor and social movements in the South as a basis for the STFU. See also James D. Ross, Jr., "'I ain't got no home in this world': The Rise and Fall of the Southern Tenant Farmers' Union in Arkansas" (PhD diss., Auburn University, 2004), 53–55; and James R. Green, *Grass-Roots Socialism: Radical Movements in the Southwest, 1895–1943.* Baton Rouge: Louisiana State University Press, 1978, on the links between Populism and other radical and reform traditions. For a detailed account of the hopes and failures of black homesteaders, see Kenneth C. Barnes, *Journey of Hope: The Back-to-Africa Movement in Arkansas in the Late 1800s.* Chapel Hill: University of North Carolina Press, 2004; Stockley, *Ruled by Race*, 103–106.

20. A number of racial massacres occurred when rural blacks tried to form unions or cooperatives. For one example of the grisly white racial violence that gripped the South in this era, see Charles Lane, *The Day Freedom Died: The Colfax Massacre, the Supreme Court, and the Betrayal of Reconstruction.* New York: Henry Holt and Company, 2009.

21. Stockley, *Ruled by Race*, 94, 113–118, passim.

22. Quoted in Stockley, *Ruled By Race*, 135. The 1891 election law more than any other measure established one-party rule in Arkansas, ibid., 125.

23. Steven Hahn, *A Nation Under Our Fee: Black Political Struggles in the Rural South from Slavery to the Great Migration.* Cambridge: Harvard University Press, 2003, 7.

24. Alan Lomax, *The Land Where the Blues Began.* New York: New Press, 2002, 142.

25. Nearly 12,000 African Americans, most of them in the South, owned all or most of their land in 1900. Hahn, *A Nation Under Our Feet.,* 457, 460–63, passim.

26. Ibid, 69.

27. Vina's long life would take her back to St. Francis County, Arkansas after her husband died in 1923, and then to Oklahoma with John, George Jr. and Willis, where she worked as a housekeeper to support herself and her teenaged children still living with her, Martha and Lee (sometimes spelled Leo). Vina would follow John and his wife Ruth to San Diego, California soon after, where she died in 1970. US Census Bureau, *St. Francis County* (1930); US Census Bureau, *Washington County* (1940); and "United States Social Security Death Index," *FamilySearch*, Vinia Handcox, August 1970.

28. "Arkansas, County Marriages, 1837–1957," *FamilySearch*, Geo Hancock and Bina Nunn (1899).

29. Jarod Roll, *Spirit of Rebellion: Labor and Religion in the New Cotton South.* Urbana: University of Illinois Press, 2010, 3.

30. Jeannie Whayne, *Delta Empire: Lee Wilson and the Transformation of Agriculture in the New South.* Baton Rouge: Louisiana State University Press, 2011.

31. Nan Elizabeth Woodruff, *American Congo: The African American Freedom Struggle in the Delta.* Cambridge: Harvard University Press, 2003, 2.

32. Handcox, interview by Ferris and Honey; and John Handcox, no title (n.d.) and "(We Have the Rope and the Limb)," both in author's possession; Lomax, *The Land Where the Blues Began,* vx.

33. Pete Daniel, *The Shadow of Slavery: Peonage in the South.* Champaign: University of Illinois Press *1901–1969* (1972).

34. See Jonathan Wiener, *Social Origins of the New South: Alabama, 1860–1885.* Baton Rouge: Louisiana State University Press, 1978; Gavin Wright, *Old South, New South: Revolutions in the Southern Economy Since the Civil War.* Baton Rouge: Louisiana State University Press, 1996; Roger Ransom and Richard Sutch, *One Kind of Freedom: The Economic Consequences of Emancipation.* London: Cambridge University Press, 1977.

35. Jacquelyn Jones, *Labor of Love, Labor of Sorrow: Black Women, Work, and the Family from Slavery to the Present.* New York: Basic Books, 1986.

36. Alexander Yard, "'They don't regard my Rights at all': Arkansas Farm Workers, Economic Modernization, and the Southern Tenant Farmers Union," *The Arkansas Historical Quarterly* (1988).

37. Michael Honey and William Ferris interview with John Handcox, January 15, 1990, as highlighted in Robert Hunt Ferguson, "The Land, the Lord, and the Union: Earthly and Spiritual Salvation in the Protest Songs of John L. Handcox," *Arkansas Review*, 75–82, 77.

38. In 1921, Arkansas spent $17.06 for each white child and $5.61 for each black child in school. Stockley, *Ruled By Race*, 98, 151.

39. Lisa Clayton Robinson, "Dunbar, Paul Laurence," in Kwame Anthony Appiah and Henry Louis Gates, eds., *Africana: The Encyclopedia of the African and African American Experience*. New York: Basic Civitas Books, 1999, 639–640.

40. Paul Laurence Dunbar, *The Collected Poetry of Paul Laurence Dunbar*, ed. Joanne Braxton, Charlottesville: University Press of Virginia, 1993. Of special note are "When Malindy Sings," 82, "We Wear the Mask," 71, "Sympathy," 102, "Harriet Beecher Stowe," 119, and "Frederick Douglass," 6. Thanks to Elizabeth Stevens for bringing these poems to my attention.

41. Honey and Ferris interview, and Ferguson, "The Land, the Lord, and the Union," 77. George Stith, interview by Kate Born (April 26, 1973), and by Leah Wise (September 29, 1973 and April 25, 1974), selected reprinting in *Working Lives: The Southern Exposure History of Labor in the South*, ed. Marc Miller. New York: Pantheon Books, 1980, 123–124, 128–134, 137–142.

42. John Handcox, phone interview by Donald Lance (July 26, 1989), notes in author's possession.

43. Honey and Ferris interview, January 15, 1990, and see Ferguson, "The Land, the Lord, and the Union," 76–77.

44. John Handcox, "A Living Legend," typescript in author's possession.

45. John Handcox to author (ca. 1986), in author's possession.

46. On Bond, see Woodruff, *American Congo*, 12–13; Dan Rudd and Theo Bond, *From Slavery to Wealth: The Life of Scot Bond: The Rewards of Honesty, Industry, Economy and Perseverance*. Chapel Hill: Academic Affairs Library, University of North Carolina at Chapel Hill, Electronic edition, 2000. On land value, see Stockley, *Ruled by Race*, 83–84; Fon Louise Gordon, "Scott Winfield Bond" in *The Encyclopedia of Arkansas History & Culture*, www.encyclopediaofarkansas.net; Ulysses S. Bond, "Highlights in the Life of Scott Bond," *The Arkansas Historical Quarterly* (Summer 1962).

47. *From Slavery to Wealth*, written by Bond's relatives Dan Rudd and Theo. Bond, built Scott Bond up to be a self-made man in the image that white capitalists held of themselves. Bond apparently applied to start a branch of the National Association for the Advancement of Colored People (NAACP). Bond thought he could recruit 700 to 1,000 NAACP members in the county. Scott Bond to John Shillady (June 4, 1919), NAACP Papers, Library of Congress, Part I, 1919–1939, Series G—Branches, Container 12,F, Madison, Arkansas, 1919. Thanks for this document to Jarod Roll, who notes "I'm not sure Bond was as bad as Handcox made out." Roll, email to author (January 14, 2010).

2 Raggedy, Raggedy Are We: Sharecropping and Survival

1. "Farmer's Memory Sings 'Raggedy' Tune," originally published in *The Commercial Appeal* (April 17, 1982), reprinted in *The Black Worker from the Founding of the CIO to the AFL-CIO Merger, 1936–1955*, vol. 7 of *The Black Worker: A Documentary History From Colonial Times to the Present*, eds. Philip S. Foner and Ronald L. Lewis (1983), 192.

2. Johnny Cash, *The Autobiography.* San Francisco: Harper, 1997. "Raggedy Raggedy Are We" in Alan Lomax, Woody Guthrie, and Pete Seeger, *Hard Hitting Songs for Hard-Hit People.* New York: Oak Publications, 1967, 265. The authors identified the tune to this song as "How Beautiful Heaven Would Be."

3. US Census Bureau, *Population Census of the United States: Brinkley Township, Arkansas* (1920).

4. The family name appears as Handcox on the death certificate of John's father George in 1923. Family members thought John might have changed the spelling of his last name to Handcox to avoid persecution as a union organizer in the 1930s, but the name change had occurred earlier. Camelia Cook, phone interview by author (August 24, 2009; July 22, 2012).

5. Robert E. Lee Wilson drew on Progressive Era business ideas of rationalization and mass organization but with feudal labor arrangements. In 1913, he owned 65,000 acres in Mississippi County, Arkansas, much of it purchased from settlers who sold their lumber rights and their land rights at a pittance, not realizing its potential value. Jeannie Whayne, *Delta Empire: Lee Wilson and the Transformation of Agriculture in the New South.* Baton Rouge: Louisiana State University Press, 2011, 125; Nan Elizabeth Woodruff, *American Congo: The African American Freedom Struggle in the Delta.* Cambridge, MA: Harvard University Press, 2003, 11; and Whayne, "'I Have Been through Fire': Black Agricultural Extension Agents and the Politics of Negotiation," in *African American Life in the Rural South, 1900–1950,* ed. Douglas Hurt. Columbia: University of Missouri Press, 2003. Clyde Woods, *Development Arrested: The Blues and Plantation Power in the Mississippi Delta.* London: Verson, 1998, explains how this racial-economic system took hold. Laurie Beth Green traces the effects of the "plantation mentality" long into the civil rights era, in *Battling the Plantation Mentality: Memphis and the Black Freedom Struggle.* Chapel Hill: University of North Carolina Press, 2007.

6. James Ross Jr., "'I ain't got no home in this world': The Rise and Fall of the Southern Tenant Farmers' Union in Arkansas" (PhD diss., Auburn University, 2004), 22.

7. For accounts of the race riots, see Joe William Trotter, *The Great Migration in Historical Perspective: New Dimensions of Race, Class, and Gender.* Bloomington: Indiana University Press, 1991; and as depicted in the motion picture *The Killing Floor,* directed by Bill Duke (1984).

8. Jeannie Whayne, *A New Plantation South: Land, Labor, and Federal Favor in Twentieth-Century Arkansas.* Charlottesville: University Press of Virginia, 1996, 29–53, for details on the shift from small landholders to renters and sharecroppers, the increasing concentration of African Americans in the latter category, and the refusal of the courts to protect black rights. See Grif Stockley, *Ruled By Race: Black/White Relations in Arkansas from Slavery to the Present.* Fayetteville: University of Arkansas Press, 2009, for chapter and verse of racial violence in Arkansas.

9. Richard Wright, *12 Million Black Voices: A Folk History of the Negro in the United States.* New York: Viking Press, 1941, 46, quoted in John Herbert Hayes, "Hard, Hard Religion: Faith and Class in the New South," (Ph.D. dissertation, University of Georgia, 2007), 313–4.

10. Woodruff, *American Congo*, 78–91, quote on 84; Kieran Taylor, "'We Have Just Begun': Black Organizing and White Response in the Arkansas Delta, 1919," *The Arkansas Historical Quarterly* 58:3 (1999), 264-284. Taylor points out that whites and blacks had two opposing views of the future: blacks looked toward greater freedom, while most whites wanted to maintain the racial status quo.

11. Ibid., 74–83. See also Robert Whitaker, *On the Laps of Gods: The Red Summer of 1919 and the Struggle for Justice That Remade a Nation*. New York: Three Rivers Press, 2009, and Grif Stockley, *Blood in Their Eyes: The Elaine Race Massacres of 1919*. Fayetteville: University of Arkansas Press, 2001.

12. All secondary accounts give different numbers on the casualties of the Elaine riot. See James Green, *The World of the Worker: Labor in Twentieth-Century America*. New York: Hill and Wang, 1980, 149; estimate of 25–100 offered by Anthony Dunbar, *Against the Grain: Southern Radicals and Prophets, 1929–1959*. Charlottesville: University Press of Virginia, 1981, 88; Leah Wise, "The Elaine Massacre," in *Southern Exposure* (1974), 9–10; Woodruff, *American Congo*, 84–93. See also coverage in the NAACP magazine *The Crisis* (December 1919.

13. Ibid.

14. Woodruff, *American Congo*, 92–105.

15. Ibid., 132, 136, lynching statistics on 110–112, 136.

16. Erskine Caldwell and Margaret Bourke-White, *You Have Seen Their Faces*. Athens: University of Georgia Press, 1995, 6.

17. Pete Daniel, *The Shadow of Slavery: Peonage in the South, 1901–1969*. Champaign: University of Illinois Press, 1972; Douglas A. Blackmon, *Slavery by Another Name: The Re-Enslavement of Black Americans from the Civil War to World War II*. New York: Anchor Books, 2009.

18. Surprisingly, perhaps, John misremembered the date of his father's death. He told me his father died in 1921 and in a written account he said 1913. According to the death certificate (previously cited), his father died in 1923.

19. John Handcox, interview by Rebecca Schroeder (October 16, 1989).

20. Woodruff, *American Congo*, 72–73. Five men were lynched in Arkansas in 1919, and at least 18 around the Delta, a number of them military veterans.

21. Howard Kester, *Revolt Among the Sharecroppers*, with an introduction by Alex Lichtenstein. Knoxville: University of Tennessee Press, 1997; Norman Thomas and William R. Amberson, *The Plight of the Share-Cropper*. New York: League for Industrial Democracy, 1934; George Brown Tindall, *The Emergence of the New South, 1913–1945*. Baton Rouge: Louisiana State University Press, 1967, 409–15; and Donald Grubbs, *Cry From the Cotton: The Southern Tenant Farmers' Union and the New Deal*. Chapel Hill: University of North Carolina Press, 1971.

22. Quoted in Woods, *Development Arrested*, 111.

23. Ibid, 118, 119.

24. See Pete Daniel, *Deep'n as It Come: The 1927 Mississippi River Flood*. Fayetteville: University of Arkansas Press, 1977; and John Barry, *Rising Tide: The Great Mississippi Flood of 1927 and How it Changed America*. New York: Simon & Schuster, 1997.

25. Thanks to Jessica Auer for finding these names and birth dates in the 1940 Census.

26. John Handcox, "King Cotton," poem (1936), Southern Tenant Farmers Union Papers (STFU) microfilm edition, Reel 3, Southern Historical Collection, University of North Carolina at Chapel Hill; the poem is republished in Philip S. Foner and Roland Lewis, eds, *The Black Worker from the Founding of the CIO to the AFL-CIO Merger, 1936–1955.* Philadelphia: Temple University Press, 1983, 192.

27. Donald Lance, Interview notes (July 26, 1989), Donald Lance Papers, Western Historical Manuscript Collection, University of Missouri-Columbia.

3 The Planter and the Sharecropper: The Southern Tenant Farmers' Union

1. John Handcox, "A Living Legend" (n.d.), typescript in author's possession.

2. William Manchester, "The Cruelest Year," in *From Reconstruction to the Present*, vol. 2 of *Portrait of America,* ed. Stephen Oates (1983), 198; and see Irving Bernstein, *The Lean Years; A History of the American Worker, 1920–1933.* Boston, Houghton Mifflin, 1960.

3. Ned Cobb and Theodore Rosengarten, *All God's Dangers: The Life of Nate Shaw* (1974, 1984), 264; Woody Guthrie, "Pretty Boy Floyd," in Guthrie, Alan Lomax, and Pete Seeger, *Hard Hitting Songs for Hard-Hit People.* New York: Oak Publications, 1967, 115. .

4. James R. Green, *Grass-Roots Socialism: Radical Movements in the Southwest, 1895–1943.* Baton Rouge: Louisiana State University Press, 1978.

5. Glenda Elizabeth Gilmore, *Defying Dixie: The Radical Roots of Civil Rights, 1919–1950.* New York: W.W. Norton & Co., 2008. Anthony Dunbar provides a collective portrait in *Against The Grain: Southern Radicals and Prophets, 1929–1959.* Charlottesville: University Press of Virginia, 1981. Erik S. Gellman and Jarod Roll parallel the lives of Claude Williams and Owen Whitfield, both of whom worked closely with the STFU. *The Gospel of the Working Class, Labor's Southern Prophets in New Deal America.* Urbana: University of Illinois Press, 2011.

6. Quoted in Manchester, "The Cruelest Year," 198.

7. Harvey Klehr, *The Heyday of American Communism: The Depression Decade.* New York: Basic Books, 1984, 33–4, 51–4, 57, 59, 60–2, 65, 67; Robin D. G. Kelley, *Hammer and Hoe: Alabama Communists During the Great Depression.* Chapel Hill: University of North Carolina Press, 1990; Hosea Hudson, *The Narrative of Hosea Hudson: His Life as a Negro Communist in the South*, ed. Nell Irving Painter. Cambridge, MA: Harvard University Press, 1979; Progress Publishers, *Recent History of the Labor Movement, 1918–1939.* Moscow: Progress Publishers, 1977, 192–202.

8. Ronald Cohen, *Work and Sing: A History of Occupational and Labor Union Songs in the United States.* Crockett, CA: Carquinez Press, 2010, 70–3; and John A. Salmond, *Gastonia 1929, The Story of the Loray Mill Strike.* Chapel Hill: University of North Carolina Press, 1995, on textile strikes and ballads. A photo of Ella Mae Wiggins is on the inside cover of Salmond's book. On the Reeltown shootout and related issues, see *The Narrative of Hosea Hudson*, chapter six; and Cobb and Rosengarten, *All God's Dangers;* Klehr, *The Heyday of*

American Communism, 334; John Beecher, "In Egypt Land," in *Working Lives: the Southern Exposure History of Labor in the South*, ed. Marc Miller (1980), 143–54; Harvard Sitkoff, *A New Deal for Blacks: The Emergence of Civil Rights as a National Issue.* New York: Oxford University Press, 1978, 147–52.

9. Broadus Mitchell, *Depression Decade: From New Era Through New Deal, 1929–1941.* New York: Rinehart, 1947, 179. The New Deal provided a bonanza in cash subsidies for planters as federal programs attempted to restore farm prices to the pre-World War I level, when they were at their highest point in the twentieth century. Norman Thomas to Henry Wallace (April 16, 1935), Southern Tenant Farmers Union Papers [STFU] microfilm edition, Reel 1, Southern Historical Collection, University of North Carolina at Chapel Hill; H. L. Mitchell, *Mean Things Happening in This Land: The Life and Times of H.L. Mitchell, Co-Founder of the Southern Tenant Farmers Union.* Montclair, NJ: Allanheld, Osmun, 1979, 188.

10. Pete Daniel, "The Crossroads of Change: Cotton, Tobacco, and Rice Cultures in the Twentieth–Century South," *Journal of Southern History* (1984), 445. For a discussion of the role of southern congressmen from the cotton states in the establishment of the AAA, and of large planters in running the program, see George Brown Tindall, *The Emergence of the New South, 1913–1945.* Louisiana State University Press, 1967, 392–3.

11. James D. Ross, Jr., "'I ain't got no home in this world': The Rise and Fall of the Southern Tenant Farmers' Union in Arkansas," (PhD dissertation, Auburn University, 2004), 23. Per capita income in the South dropped over 50 percent between 1929 and 1932 and one-fourth of the state of Mississippi went up for sale in bankruptcy proceedings. Tindall, *The Emergence of the New South,* 354–5, 360.

12. Donald Grubbs, *Cry From the Cotton: The Southern Tenant Farmers' Union and the New Deal,* Chapel Hill, University of North Carolina Press, 1971, 19–25, 43–57, and chapter five; Mitchell, *Mean Things,* 102; Erskine Caldwell and Margaret Bourke-White, *You Have Seen Their Faces.* Athens: University of Georgia Press, 1995, 11; Ralph McGill, *The South and the Southerner* (1959). Some of the statistics and stories are recounted in *Our Land Too: The Legacy of the Southern Tenant Farmers' Union*, a film produced by Landon McCray, Kudzu Productions. Clyde Woods, *Development Arrested*, traces how plantation capitalism captured the political and economic power of the Mississippi Delta. Memphis was its base, 125.

13. John Egerton, *Speak Now Against the Day: The Generation Before the Civil Rights Movement in the South.* New York: Alfred A. Knopf, 1994, 154–6; Mitchell, *Mean Things,* chs. 1–3.

14. For the relationship of the Socialists to the sharecroppers and STFU origins, see Dunbar, *Against the Grain,* 83–86; Green, *Grass-Roots Socialism*; James D. Ross provides a detailed account of STFU and sharecropper values and politics in "'I Ain't got no home in this world;" Howard Kester, *Revolt Among the Sharecroppers.* Knoxville: University of Tennessee Press, 1936, 54–9; Tindall, *The Emergence of the New South,* 417; Mitchell, *Mean Things,* 41–59; Grubbs, *Cry From the Cotton,* 27–8; and see the chapter on the STFU in Robert F. Martin, *Howard Kester and the Struggle for Social Justice in the South, 1904–77.* Charlottesville: University Press of Virginia, 1991.

15. Jason Manthorne, "The View from the Cotton: Reconsidering the Southern Tenant Farmers' Union," *Agricultural History* 84 (2010) argues that H. L. Mitchell may have created Isaac Shaw out of a composite of several blacks who helped form the union, but H. L. Mitchell's *Roll the Union On, A Pictorial History of the Southern Tenant Farmers' Union.* Chicago: C. H. Kerr Pub. Co., 1987 offers a picture of Shaw, 25, and at least three photos identify Shaw in the papers of the STFU. No one will know if this quote is completely accurate, as Mitchell was the only one there who wrote it down.

16. Robert F Martin, *Howard Kester and the Struggle for Social Justice in the South, 1904–77.* Charlottesville: University Press of Virginia, 1991, chs. 1–4.

17. Beecher, "In Egypt Land," in *Working Lives*, 1443–54.

18. James Ross depicts conflict between Socialist leaders who wanted a cooperative economy and the members of the union, who mostly wanted their own land and freedom to farm in decent conditions, based on a survey the STFU did in 1935. "I Ain't got no home in this world," 109–21.

19. Jarod Roll, *Spirit of Rebellion: Labor and Religion in the New Cotton South.* Urbana: University of Illinois Press, 2010.

20. "The Reds in Dixie," CP pamphlet (ca. 1934), in Library of Congress; "full equality" quote in Klehr, *The Heyday of American Communism*, 324. The US Supreme Court in the Loving vs. Virginia case overthrew miscegenation laws in 1967.

21. David R. Roediger and Elizabeth Esch, *The Production of Difference: Race and the Management of Labor in U.S. History.* New York: Oxford University Press, 2011.

22. The United Mine Workers had a powerful history of black-white collaboration even within the confines of the Jim Crow South. Daniel Letwin, *The Challenge of Interracial Unionism: Alabama Coal Miners, 1878–1921.* Chapel Hill: University of North Carolina Press, 1998. Even so, whites still pushed blacks into the worst and most dangerous jobs and controlled top positions in the union. Joe William Trotter, *Coal, Class, and Color: Blacks in Southern West Virginia, 1915–1932.* Urbana: University of Illinois Press, 1990.

23. Stith quoted in Leah Wise and Sue Thrasher, "The Southern Tenant Farmers' Union," in *Working Lives*, ed. Miller, 139.

24. Butler quoted in Ibid. Wise and Thrasher, "The Southern Tenant Farmers' Union," in *Working lives: The Southern Exposure History of Labor in the South* Marc S. Miller, ed. (1980), 128.

25. See Michael K. Honey, *Southern Labor and Black Civil Rights: Organizing Memphis Workers.* Urbana: University of Illinois Press, 1993.

26. Mitchell, *Mean Things*, 61, 71, 72.

27. Butler quoted in Wise and Thrasher, "The Southern Tenant Farmers' Union," in *Working Lives*, ed. Miller, 128.

28. Ibid., 131.

29. This account is taken from Howard Kester, *Revolt Among the Sharecroppers.* Knoxville: University of Tennessee Press, 1997, 60–61. Kester's account was originally published in pamphlet form in 1936 and is available in the STFU records, Reel 1.

30. Mitchell, *Mean Things*, 53–4, 59, 71, 72, passim.
31. Dunbar, *Against The Grain*, 90–1; Mitchell, *Mean Things*, 53–4, 59, 71, 72, passim.
32. H. L. Mitchell quoted in Wise and Thrasher, "The Southern Tenant Farmers' Union," in *Working Lives*, ed. Miller, 133–4.
33. Clay East, quoted in ibid., 134; "it was a church" quote from Myrtle Moskop, in Grubbs, *Cry From the Cotton*, 64.
34. Attacks on Brookins are detailed in Howard Kester, "Acts of Tyranny and Terror Committed Against Innocent Men, Women and Children of the Southern Tenant Farmers' Union in Northeast Arkansas," STFU, Reel 1.
35. Washington's letter as an example of religious fervor in STFU meetings is recounted in Ross "I Ain't got no home in this world," 121–4.
36. Bernice Johnson Reagon, *If You Don't Go Don't Hinder Me: The African American Sacred Song Tradition.* Lincoln: University of Nebraska Press, 2001.
37. Music and preaching always played a role at STFU National Conventions; see notes and programs of conventions in STFU Papers.
38. "Southern Tenant Farmers Unon Ritual," February 28, 1938, signals and signs, Reel 7, STFU Papers. Gregory John Hall, "Rituals and Secrecy in the Southern Tenant Farmers' Union," *Australian Journal of American Studies* 21:2 (December 2002), 1–14; "The Disinherited Speak," back cover of the pamphlet.
39. Stith quoted in Wise and Thrasher, "The Southern Tenant Farmers' Union," in *Working Lives*, ed. Miller, 129; Grubs, *Cry From the Cotton*, 66–7.
40. Statistics in Manthorne, "The View from the Cotton," 44–5; M. Fannin, *Labor's Promised Land : Radical Visions of Gender, Race, and Religion* in the South. Knoxville: University of Tennessee Press, 2003, 249.
41. Dunbar, *Against the Grain*, 90–91; Grubbs, *Cry From the Cotton*, 67.
42. Mary G. Rolinson, *Grassroots Garveyism: The Universal Negro Improvement Association in the Rural South, 1920–1927.* Chapel Hill: University of North Carolina Press, 2007, on McKinney, 184–8. She reports 395 members in Arkansas in 1927–8, past the peak of the Garvey movement, but indicates nearly 30,000 sympathizers in the state, based on petition campaigns in support of Garvey, who was imprisoned and then deported by the US government, 200–1.
43. Grubbs, *Cry From the Cotton*, 27–8.
44. Ibid., 68. H. L. Mitchell felt that the unwillingness of the Communists in the Alabama Sharecroppers Union to make concessions to the racial system kept them from organizing whites. Dunbar, *Against The Grain*, 39.
45. H. L. Mitchell, quoted in Dunbar, *Against The Grain*, 107.
46. Grubbs, *Cry From the Cotton*, 68.
47. Ibid., 66.
48. For examples of how these racial difficulties played out in the urban areas where the CIO organized, see Honey, *Southern Labor and Black Civil Rights*.
49. East quoted in Wise and Thrasher, "The Southern Tenant Farmers' Union," in *Working Lives*, ed. Miller, 134; Grubbs, *Cry From the Cotton*, 67–9.
50. Stith interviewed in "The Southern Tenant Farmers' Union," *Southern Exposure*, 1:3 and 4 (Winter, 1974), 6–32. Marc Miller draws upon portions of this special issue in *Working Lives*.
51. Mitchell, *Mean Things*, 117, 119

52. Robert Hunt Ferguson, "The Land, the Lord, and the Union: Earthly and Spiritual Salvation in the Protest Songs of John L. Handcox," *Arkansas Review*, 43: 2 (Summer/August 2012), 75–82.

53. *Southern Exposure* interviews, 29.

54. Elizabeth Anne Payne and Louise Boyle, "The Lady Was a Sharecropper: Myrtle Lawrence and the Southern Tenant Farmers' Union," *Southern Cultures* 4:2 (1998), 5–27.

55. *Southern Exposure* interview of J. R. Butler, 29.

56. Stith quoted in Wise and Thrasher, "The Southern Tenant Farmers' Union," in *Working Lives*, ed. Miller, 134.

57. Kester, *Revolt Among the Sharecroppers*. Also see Robert F. Martin, *Howard Kester and the Struggle for Social Justice in the South*.

58. Kester, "Acts of Tyranny and Terror."

59. Dunbar, *Against the Grain*, 98–9; Marked Tree Mayor J. E. Fox's statement quoted in Fannin, *Labor's Promised Land*, 302.

60. Ward Rogers to Howard Kester (March 29, 1935), STFU, Reel 1.

61. Minutes of the Meeting of the Special Committee of the STFU Held at Marked Tyree (March 7, 1935), STFU, Reel 1.

62. Robert Reid reported 17 blacks arrested for "vagrancy" and wrote that he decided not to hitchhike into England, Arkansas, from Little Rock for fear he would be kidnapped; three letters from Reid to H. L. Mitchell (March and April, 1935), STFU, Reel 1. Reid was severely beaten in another incident.

63. The power of Norman Thomas to articulate the issues in the sharecropper revolt can be seen in his letters to *The Commercial Appeal* (February 1, 1935), and to Secretary of Agriculture Henry Wallace (April 16, 1935), both in STFU, Reel 1.

64. Dunbar, *Against the Grain*, 90–1.

65. Kester, *Revolt Among the Sharecroppers*, 61–3.

66. Stith quoted in Wise and Thrasher, "The Southern Tenant Farmers' Union," in *Working Lives*, ed. Miller, 132. Albert Jackson, Secretary of the ASC in Montgomery, to Comrade Butler (July 4, 1935), STFU, Reel 1.

67. Albert Jackson to Comrade Butler (July 4, 1935), STFU, Reel 1.

68. Robert Wood, *"To Live and Die in Dixie"* (New York: Southern Workers Defense Committee, 1936) the Library of Congress, details some of the repression in this period; see also, Tindall, *The Emergence of the New South*, 506–11, and Honey, *Southern Labor and Black Civil Rights*, chapter two and passim.

69. Letter of repudiation from National Office (n.d.), STFU, Reel 1, and Fannin, *Labor's Promised Land*, 110–11.

70. Minutes STFU National Executive Council, Memphis (June 23, 1935, and September 1, 1935), STFU, Reel 1.

71. Dunbar, *Against the Grain*, 104–5.

72. Dilworth quoted in Wise and Thrasher, "The Southern Tenant Farmers' Union," in *Working Lives*, ed. Miller, 137.

73. Dunbar, *Against the Grain*, 107.

74. Ibid., 107; Mitchell, *Mean Things*, 53–4, 59, 71, 72, passim.

75. Norman Thomas to H. L. Mitchell (December 23, 1935); and Financial Report signed by H. L. Mitchell, both in STFU, Reel 1. See Mitchell, *Mean Things*, 82.

76. Dunbar, *Against the Grain,* 109–10; and Little Rock convention notes (January 1–5, 1936), STFU, Reel 1.
77. This and the following paragraph are based on "You May Ask Me," a written memo by John Handcox, sent to author (n.d.), in author's files.
78. John Handcox to H. L. Mitchell (February 19, 1936); Mitchell to Hancock (sic), February 26, 1936, asking for reports, STFU reel 1.
79. John Henry to some degree defeated white society on its own terms, based perhaps on a real incident in building the Big Bend tunnel in West Virginia, completed in June 1872, in which over 1,000 blacks "labored in inferno-like conditios," according to Levine. By the 1960s, more than 50 recorded versions of the song existed and over a hundred songs about John Henry had been copyrighted. *Black Culture and Black Consciousness,* 421. See Scott Nelson, *Steel Drivin' Man: John Henry, the Untold Story of an American Legend.* London: Oxford University Press, 2006.
80. Mitchell to Handcox, February 22, 1936, on revision of the poem; Henderson to H. L. Mitchell (n.d.,), all in STFU, reel 1.

4 There Is Mean Things Happening in This Land: Terror in Arkansas

1. In January 1937 St. Francis County had 4,457 members and 51 locals, almost twice the number of the next biggest area for STFU, Crittenden, which had 2,487 members in 30 locals, according to Alexander Yard, "'They don't regard my Rights at all': Arkansas Farm Workers, Economic Modernization, and the Southern Tenant Farmers Union," *The Arkansas Historical Quarterly* (1988), 204. Black women played leading roles in the area John Handcox lived. One extraordinary white woman named Myrtle Lawrence came to St. Francis County after being dispossessed of her land, with six children and only two weeks of first-grade education. She was a militant supporter of black–white equality and, like John Handcox, reworked old tunes into union songs. Fannin, Mark. *Labor's Promised Land: Radical Visions of Gender, Race, and Religion in the South.* Knoxville: University of Tennessee Press, 2003, 171; and Elizabeth Anne Payne and Louis Boyle, "The Lady Was a Sharecropper: Myrtle Lawrence and the Southern Tenant Farmers' Union," *Southern Cultures* 4(2) (1998), 5–27.
2. Yard, "'They don't regard my Rights at all' Arkansas Farm Workers, Economic Modernization, and the Southern Tenant Farmers Union." *Arkansas Historical Quarterly* 47(3), (October 1, 1988): 209, 226.
3. H. L. Mitchell on contracts, in Leah Wise and Sue Thrasher, "The Southern Tenant Farmers' Union," in *Working Lives,* ed. Marc Miller, 137–8; and see Yard on the model contract, "'They don't regard my Rights at all'," 226.
4. Donald H. Grubbs, *Cry From the Cotton: The Southern Tenant Farmers' Union and the New Deal,.* Chapel Hill, University of North Carolina Press, 1971, 90; A. Dunbar, *Against The Grain: Southern Radicals and Prophets, 1929–1959.* Charlottesville: University Press of Virginia, 1981, 111; and "Union Men Shot in Back By Officers," *The Sharecroppers' Voice* (February 1, 1936), 3.
5. Dunbar, *Against the Grain,* 112–113; Hood quoted in Grubbs, *Cry From the Cotton,* 91; H. L. Mitchell, *Mean Things Happening in This Land: The Life*

and Times of H. L. Mitchell, Cofounder of the Southern Tenant Farmers' Union. Montclair, NJ: Allanheld, Osmun, 1979, 144. Fearing for their own lives, Goldberger and Smith had driven back to Memphis and set off alarm bells about Kester's presumed murder.

6. Grubbs, *Cry From the Cotton*, 91; H. L. Mitchell to Aaron Gilmartin, March 18, Southern Tenant Farmers Union Papers [STFU], Southern Historical Collection, University of North Carolina at Chapel Hill; and "Jim Ball Framed Up By Officers," *The Sharecroppers' Voice* (March 1936), 2.

7. Not until 1938 did the federal government crack down and make landlords truly responsible for dividing the subsidies with their tenants. By that time, the damage was already done. Yard, "'They don't regard my Rights at all'," 215–224.

8. Dunbar, *Against the Grain*; Mitchell, *Mean Things*, 61–74; and chapter four in Grubbs, *Cry From the Cotton*.

9. Grubbs, *Cry From the Cotton*, 92.

10. "Heroic Earle Local Carries On," "Evictions Continue," and "America Awake," *The Sharecroppers' Voice* (February 1, 1936), 3–4. H. L. Mitchell to Franklin Roosevelt, March 18, 1936; Mary Fox, League for Industrial Democracy, New York, to H. L. Mitchell, March 11, 1936; and Norman Thomas NBC address, "President Roosevelt and the Share Croppers," all in STFU microfilm edition, Reel 1.

11. Thomas to Henry Wallace, April 16, 1935, STFU, Reel 1.

12. Robert Wood, *"To Live and Die in Dixie,"* Southern Workers Defense Committee, 1936, NYC," Library of Congress. See also George Tindall, *The Emergence of the New South, 1913–1945*. Louisiana State University Press, 1967, 506–511; and Michael K. Honey, *Southern Labor and Black Civil Rights: Organizing Memphis Workers*. Urbana: University of Illinois Press, 1993, chapter two and passim on anti-union repression.

13. Gardner Jackson said, "The LaFollette Civil Liberties Committee derived directly out of the STFU," quoted in Grubbs, *Cry From the Cotton*, 97; and Jerold S. Auerbach, "Southern Tenant Farmers: Socialist Critics of the New Deal," *The Arkansas Historical Quarterly* (1968), 127.

14. Grubbs, *Cry From the Cotton*, 99.

15. Ibid., 106–107.

16. Howard Kester, "Acts of Tyranny and Terror Committed Against Innocent Men, Women and Children of the Southern Tenant Farmers' Union in Northeast Arkansas," STFU, Reel 1.

17. The Miami Valley Socialist League in Ohio and church organizations in various cities collected a ton of food and clothing but "to feed several hundred families who have been evicted . . . is an impossible task," wrote H. L. Mitchell to Ernest Morgan, February 15. Two young activists from Montana [names indecipherable] applied to the union but it had no positions. Morgan to H. L. Mitchell, February 15; H. L. Mitchell to Morgan, February 18; Morgan to H. L. Mitchell, March 2, 1936, all in STFU, Reel 1. See Auerbach on Mitchell's salary, "Southern Tenant Farmers," 122.

18. The spelling of John's named remained uncertain: H. L. Mitchell to John Hancox, February 22, and to John Hancock, February 26, 1936, STFU Papers, 92-b.

19. Isaac Shaw to H. L. Mitchell, n.d., in Southern Tenant Farmers Union, *The Disinherited Speak: Letters from Sharecroppers* (ca. 1936), 3, American Radicalism Collection, Michigan State University Library.

20. George Handcox to H. L. Mitchell, February 22, 1936; and H. L. Mitchell to Handcox, March 31, 1936, both in STFU, Reel 1. Mitchell advised the local should put the man on trial and, if found, guilty expel him.

21. H. L. Mitchell on McGhee, *Mean Things*, 128. Southern Tenant Farmers' Union, *The Disinherited*, 20–27. "Anniversary Number" editorial says *The Disinherited Speak* came out "a few months ago," with a circulation of 5,000 copies, *The Sharecroppers' Voice* (May 1, 1936). The letter by Handcox reprinted in this pamphlet came from his time in Missouri (see the next chapter).

22. Letters quoted are from *The Disinherited Speak*; Mitchell, *Mean Things*, 115.

23. John Greenway, *American Folksongs of Protest*. New York: A. S. Barnes, 1960, 217.

24. Robert F. Thompson III, "The Strange Case of Paul D. Peacher, Twentieth-Century Slaveholder," *The Arkansas Historical Quarterly* (1993), 428.

25. Lowell K. Dyson, "The Southern Tenant Farmers Union and Depression Politics," *Political Science Quarterly* (1973), 235–236; Fannin suggests that the CP line about black "nationhood" at a time when agricultural workers were trying to organize a bi-racial union only made it easier for anti-unionists to split white workers away. That would have been disastrous for the STFU. In fact, few whites belonged to the Alabama Sharecroppers Union. Fannin, *Labor's Promised Land*, 114, 232–233

26. J.J. Lynn, from Truman, Ark., to H. L. Mitchell, March 11, 1936, said workers were afraid to act and were not strong enough to win; S. G. Brown, the secretary of a local in Sherrill, warned "better not to ask for a strike until we are stronger," March 9, 1936, STFU Papers.

27. Yard, "'They don't regard my Rights at all'," 202–203.

28. J. J. Lynn to H. L. Mitchell, March 11, 1936, STFU, 104-d.

29. Dunbar, *Against the Grain*, 122.

30. H. L. Mitchell quoted in Wise and Thrasher, "The Southern Tenant Farmers' Union," in *Working Lives*, ed. Miller, 140.

31. Irving Bernstein, *Turbulent Years: A History of the American Worker, 1933–1941*. Chicago, Ill. : Haymarket Books, 2010, and Robert H. Zieger, *The CIO: 1935–1955*. Chapel Hill: University of North Carolina Press, 1997.

32. Dunbar, *Against the Grain*, 122.

33. Letter to H. L. Mitchell, no name, from Heth, Arkansas, February 20, 1936, STFU, Reel 1.

34. Newspaper quote reproduced in Grubbs, *Cry From the Cotton*, 93; and John Handcox, "Landlord What in the Heaven is the Matter with You?," *The Sharecroppers' Voice* (May 1, 1936).

35. H. L. Mitchell To Officers and Members of All Locals, March 4, 1936; J.J. Lynne to H. L. Mitchell, from Truman, Ark., March 11, 1936; S.J. Brown from Sherrill, Ark., March 9, 1936; and H. L. Mitchell "To be read only to closed meeting," March 19, 1936, all in STFU, Reel 1.

36. "Sharecroppers May Strike in Arkansas," *New York Amsterdam News* (March 7, 1936).

37. Robert F. III. Thompson, "The Strange Case of Paul D. Peacher, Twentieth-Century Slaveholder." *Arkansas Historical Quarterly* 52(4) (December 1, 1993), 428.

38. Dunbar, *Against the Grain*, 124.

39. Thompson, "The Strange Case of Paul Peacher," 432–433.

40. Ibid., 433–439.

41. Ibid., 441–442.

42. Dunbar, *Against the Grain*, 124–125.

43. Stith quoted in Wise and Thrasher, "The Southern Tenant Farmers' Union," in *Working Lives*, ed. Miller, 124.

44. STFU Press release, June 2, 1936, STFU, Reel 1; and Grubbs, *Cry From the Cotton*, 102–103.

45. Quoted in Greenway, *American Folksongs of Protest*, 218.

46. Quoted in Dunbar, *Against the Grain,* 125.

47. Dunbar, *Against the Grain*, 125–127; East quoted in Wise and Thrasher, "The Southern Tenant Farmers' Union," in *Working Lives*, ed. Miller, 136; and Grubbs, *Cry From the Cotton*, 104.

48. Dunbar, *Against the Grain*, 125–127; *Baltimore Afro-American* (June 20, 1936), 5; and STFU Press release, June 2, 1936, STFU, Reel 1.

49. Grubbs, *Cry From the Cotton*, 106.

50. Ibid., 109–110.

51. On Eliza Nolden, see Grubbs, *Cry From the Cotton*, 113–114; and *The Sharecroppers' Voice* (July 1936), cited in Fannin, *Labor's Promised Land*, 181.

52. On Claude Williams, see Erik Gellman and Jarod Roll, *The Gospel of the Working Class: Labor's Southern Prophets in New Deal America*. Urbana: University of Illinois Press, 2011; and Cedric Belfrage, who wrote an early versio of the trials and tribulations of Claude Williams, *A Faith to Free the People* (1944).

53. Grubbs, *Cry From the Cotton*, 112–113; "Offer of Reward," New York City ACLU Office, June 3, 1936, STFU, Reel 1; Dunbar, *Against the Grain*, 128; and Grubbs, *Cry From the Cotton*, 111–112.

54. Auerbach, "Southern Tenant Farmers," 124.

55. "Arkansas' Shame," Address Delivered by Norman Thomas, September 17, 1936, STFU, Reel 1. Thomas wrote in the NAACP's *Crisis* that the name of Frank Weems "deserves to be made a symbol like John Brown's in the struggle for emancipation." Reprinted in *The Black Worker from the Founding of the CIO to the AFL-CIO Merger, 1936–1955*, vol. 7 of *The Black Worker: A Documentary History From Colonial Times to the Present*, eds. Philip S. Foner and Ronald L. Lewis. Philadelphia: Temple University Press, 1983, 177.

56. The text of this song is reprinted in Greenway, *American Folksongs of Protest*, 221, and published with tablature in Lomax, Seeger, and Guthrie, *Hard Hitting Songs for Hard-Hit People*, ed. Pete Seeger, with notes by Woody Guthrie. New York: Oak Publications, 1967, 276–277. In Woody Guthrie's introduction to the song it is difficult to know if Woody is quoting John, someone else, or speaking for himself.

57. See John Salmond, *Gastonia, 1929: The Story of the Loray Mill Strike*. Chapel Hill: University of North Carolina Press, 1995; and "The Murder of Harry Sims," 170–171, "The Man Frank Weems," 276–277, "I Am A Union Woman,"

142–143. "I Hate the Capitalist System," 164–165, in Lomax, Seeger, and Guthrie, *Hard-Hitting Songs for Hard-Hit People*.

58. Viola Smith to Mr. Mitchell, June 13, 1936, STFU, Reel 3; Grubbs, *Cry From the Cotton*, 104–113; Mitchell, *Mean Things*, 88–89.
59. *The Sharecroppers' Voice* (July 1936), 1–2.
60. Dunbar, *Against the Grain*, 129; Samuel Howard Mitchell, *A Leader Among Sharecroppers, Migrants, and Farm Workers*. Canada: self published, 2007, 179–181.
61. Thompson, "The Strange Case of Paul D. Preacher," 447–449.
62. Dunbar, *Against the Grain*, 130. See also the extended discussion in chapter six, "The Rediscovery of Slavery," in Grubbs, *Cry From the Cotton*. The Cash family lived at the Dyess Colony in Mississippi County, not far from the STFU centers of strength. Michael Streissguth, *Johnny Cash, The Biography*. Cambridge, MA: Da Capo Press, 2006, 8–14, 23.
63. Ferguson, "The Land, The Lord, and the Union: Earthly and Spiritual Salvation in the Protest Songs of John L. Handcox." *Arkansas Review*, 79.
64. See the discussion by Mitchell, *Mean Things*, 138–143. James D. Ross, Jr., "'I ain't got no home in this world': The Rise and Fall of the Southern Tenant Farmers' Union in Arkansas," (PhD dissertation, Auburn University, 2004).
65. Jerry W. Dallas, "The Delta and Providence Farms: A Mississippi Experiment in Cooperative Farming and Racial Cooperation, 1936–1956," *Mississippi Quarterly* (1987); Mitchell, *Mean Things*, 146–149.
66. Dallas, "The Delta and Providence Farms: A Mississippi Experiment in Cooperative Farming and Racial Cooperation, 1936–1956." *Mississippi Quarterly* 40 (Summer 1987).
67. According to Levine, African Americans had "a strong tradition of disaster songs," which became especially popular in the great depression. The Titanic drew attention in part because it killed whites only, many of them rich folk, and it became a dramatic story popular in the 1920s. So did songs about the Mississippi River floods of 1927 and the 1930 drought. Levine, Lawrence. *Black Culture and Black Consciousness: Afro-American Folk Thought From Slavery to Freedom. Readings in Black American*, New York: Oxford University Press,1977, 257–259.
68. "There Are Strange Things Happening," in *Songs That Changed The World*, ed. Wanda Willson Whitman, 1969, 206.
69. Alan Lomax, *The Land Where the Blues Began*. New York: New Press, 1993, 56–57.
70. In 1948, "Strange Things Are Happening in This Land" appeared in one songbook, n.d., n.p., with no attribution, except as a "Sharecropper Song (Source Unknown)." Sis Cunningham, later of the Almanac Singers, recalled that she heard John sing this song at the STFU national convention in Muskogee in 1937. She and her father later published "Strange Things" with some additional verses they wrote. When the editors of *Hard Hitting Songs for Hard-Hit People* published John's version, "Mean Things Happening in This Land," they added in some of the Cunningham's verses at the end of the song. See Sister Rosetta Tharpe, *"There Are Strange Things Happening Every Day,"* www.youtube.com/watch?v=aLFRxfMoOJY. Roseanne Cash commented about her father, who also recorded the song. Thanks to Ron Cohen for details on Sis

Cunningham. According to Cohen, a version of "Strange Things" appeared in People's Songs, bullcting 1:8 and he reprints a version of the song in Ronald Cohen, *Work and Sing: A History of Occupational and Labor Union Songs in the United States* (2010), 178; see also Cunningham and Gordon Friesen, *Red Dust and Broadsides*, ed. Ronald Cohen, 1999, 158, 160.

71. Martin Luther King, Jr. often echoed themes of previous sermons or even lifted parts of them wholesale, working like a jazz musician rather than a completely original thinker. He also drew on spirituals, as in the phrase "free at last!" at his March on Washigton for Jobs and Freeddom speech on August 28, 1963. Bernice Johnson Reagon, *If You Don't Go, Don't Hinder Me: The African American Sacred Song Tradition* (2001), presents a powerful narrative of intergenerational uplift and struggle, with songs as a vital component.

72. Arthur C. Jones, *Wade in the Water: The Wisdom of the Spirituals*. Maryknoll, NY: Orbis Books, 1993), 23.

5 Roll the Union On: Interracial Organizing in Missouri

1. *The Sharecroppers' Voice*, July, 1936. Brookins to Mitchell, September 7, 1936, Southern Tenant Farmers' Union Papers [STFU] microfilm edition, Reel 3, Southern Historical Collection, University of North Carolina at Chapel Hill. Brookins identified Norman Thomas as "my Socialist Brother and Friend" and repeatedly voiced regret at his inability to go back to Arkansas. On May 24, 1937, he made a general appeal to STFU members to fund him so he could go back out into the field, Reel 4. Mitchell wrote back to Brookins on August 20, 1936, STFU, Reel 1, as quoted here.

2. John Handcox, telephone interview by Donald M. Lance (September 30, 1990, and August 1, 1989), notes sent from Donald Lance to author.

3. James J. Fuld, *The Book of World-Famous Music, Classical, Popular and Folk*. New York: Crown Publishers, 1966, 435.

4. "On the Picket Line" is in an undated, mimeographed collection hand-labeled, "IWW Songs," STFU, Reel 9. The STFU had its own song book, put together by Evelyn Smith. H. L. Mitchell, *Mean Things Happening in This Land: The Life and Times of H. L. Mitchell, Co-Founder of the Southern Tenant Farmers Union*. Montclair, NJ: Allanheld, Osmun, 1979, 128.

5. *Religious Folk-Songs of the Negro, As Sung at Hampton Institute*, Nathaniel Dett., ed. (1927), 192–93.

6. Various books of "Negro spirituals" included some of these "rolling" songs. The Dr. Isaac Watts hymnal was probably the most utilized in the Deep South. See Isaac Watts's *Hymns and Spiritual Songs (1707): A Publishing History and A Bibliography*, ed. Selma L. Bishop (1974).

7. "Roll On," "Roll, Jordan, Roll," "Let the Church Roll On," in John W. Work, *American Negro Songs and Spirituals, A Comprehensive Collection of 230 Folk Songs, Religious and Secular* (1940), 80, 199, 249; and "Roll de Ole Chariot Along," in R. Nathaniel Dett, *Religious Folk-Songs of the Negro, Sung at Hampton Institute* (1927), 192–193, provide examples of the righteous joyfully rolling

along to liberation; see also, "I'm a-rollin," in James Weldon Johnson, *The Book of American Negro Spirituals* (1925), 145. However, none of these songs have the same tune as John Handcox's "Roll the Union On," which comes closer to the tune "Polly Wolly Doodle." Modern gospel choirs sing "Roll the Chariot Along," but their tunes bear only a partial resemblance to John's song. John told me he did not think he got his tune from a church song.

8. Tom Glazer writes, "The melody is based on a gospel hymn, 'Roll the Chariot on,' and is one of the most popular of all union songs. It was written in 1936 at a labor school in Arkansas; an organizer named John Handcox wrote the first verse, while others were written by Lee Hays, then of the Almanac Singer and later of the Weavers." Glazer, *Songs of Peace, Freedom, and* Protest (1970), 281. Pete Seeger said he took the word of Lee Hays and gave him credit for originating the song but now credits the song to John Handcox. Seeger speaking at the Labor Song Exchange, Maryland, May 13, 1985, tape in author's possession.

9. Mark Fannin, *Labor's Promised Land: Radical Visions of Gender, Race, and Religion in the South.* Knoxville: University of Tennessee Press, 2003, 175; Rebecca B. Schroeder and Donald M. Lance, "John L. Handcox- 'There Is Still Mean Things Happening'," in *Songs About Work: Essays in Occupational Culture for Richard A. Reuss,* ed. Archie Green (1993), 184–208, 188.

10. Michael Streissguth, *Johnny Cash: The Biography.* Cambridge, MA: Da Capo Press, 2006, 36–38.

11. Over 9,000 African Americans moved to the Bootheel between fall harvest and spring planting, 1922–23, 57–58; violent attacks followed, as white landlords tried to replace white workers with blacks. Jarod Roll, *Spirit of Rebellion: Labor and Religion in the New Cotton South.* Urbana: University of Illinois Press, 2010, 57–58, 60–61; on Garveyism, 62–75.

12. Ibid., 59, 72–73, 81.

13. Ibid., 88.

14. Ibid., 97–99.

15. Bonnie Stepenoff, *Thad Snow: A Life of Social Reform in the Missouri Bootheel.* Columbia: University of Missouri Press, 2003; and Thad Snow, *From Missouri: An American Farmer Looks Back,* ed. Bonnie Stepenoff. MO: University of Missouri Press, 2012.

16. Quoted in Schroeder and Lance, "John L. Handcox," in *Songs about Work,* ed. Green, 188.

17. This poem is available as part of John Handcox's Library of Congress recordings, *John L. Handcox, Songs,* compiled and introduced by Mark Alan Jackson.

18. Roll, *Spirit of Rebellion,* 96–97. The Rust Brothers were New Deal liberals and labor supporters, but their machinery would ultimately wipe out the sharecroppers.

19. Handcox to Mitchell, June 14, 1936, from the home of Braxton Taylor in Charleston, STFU, Reel 1.

20. Handcox to J. R. Butler, (Dear Bro), July 23, 1936, from Henderson, MO, STFU, Reel 1. Handcox first mis-identified Kirkpatrick as Patrick. And see Roll, *Spirit of Rebellion,* 99.

21. Roll, *Spirit of Rebellion,* 97.

22. John Wesley Work, *Folk Song of the American Negro*. Nashville: Fisk University Press, 1915, 23, 131.
23. Arthur Jones, *Wade in the Water: The Wisdom of the Spirituals*. Maryknoll, NY: Orbis Books, 1993, 23.
24. Understood in their historical context, spirituals provided hope in an otherwise hopeless world. "No more sorrow" could mean God was on the side of the poor and that slaves would eventually transcend their oppressed existence: the spirit of the sharecropper movement among African Americans was not so different from this. James Cone, *The Spirituals and the Blues, An Interpretation*. Maryknoll, NY: Orbis Books, 1972, 1991, 90–96. Mark Fannin, *Labor's Promised Land: Radical Visions of Gender, Race, and Religion in the South*. Knoxville: University of Tennessee Press, 2003, emphasizes how a grass-roots, radical Christianity gave the sharecroppers' movement redemptive power that made it a profound social movement, chapter eight.
25. Honey and Ferris interview with John Handcox, quoted in Feguson, "The Land, the Lord, and the Union," 80.
26. Handcox to Butler, July 23, 1936, signed "a willing worker," from Henson, MO, STFU, Reel 1. Roll, *Spirit of Rebellion*, 97 on the six locals.
27. "A willing worker" in Handcox to Mr. JR Butler, July 26, 1936, STFU, Reel 1.
28. Ferguson, "The Land, the Lord, and the Union," 80.
29. Roll, *Spirit of Rebellion*, 98.
30. A Willing Worker to Mr. H. L. Mitchel [sic], June 20, August 4, and August 7, 1936, STFU, Reel 1.
31. Handcox to Mitchell, September 16, 1936, STFU, Reel 1.
32. Mitchell to Handcox, August 11, 1936, and Handcox to Mitchel [sic], August 17, 1936, STFU, Reel 1. John habitually misspelled Mitchell's last name, while Mitchell sometimes misspelled John's last name as well. Unlike his relationship with Claude Williams, John did not know Mitchell well.
33. Alan Lomax, *The Land Where the Blues Began*. New York: New Press, 2002, 286.
34. A Willing Worker to Mr. H. L. Mitchel [sic], June 14, 1936, STFU, Reel 1.
35. To H. L. Mitchell, Dear Comrade, from a Worker, October 13, 1936, STFU, Reel 3.
36. Mitchell to Handcox, October 17, 1936, in Henson, MO, STFU, Reel 3.
37. To H. L. Mitchell, Dear Comrade, from a Worker, October 13, 1936, STFU, Reel 3, and reprinted in Southern Tenant Farmers Union, *The Disinherited Speak: Letters from Sharecroppers* (ca. 1936), 16, American Radicalism Collection, Michigan State University Library.
38. *The Disinherited Speak*, 16.
39. Mitchell to Handcox, October 17, 1936, in Henson, MO, STFU, Reel 3.
40. A Willing Worker to "Dear Comrade" Mitchell, September 18, 1936, from Charleston, STFU, Reel 1.
41. Gellman, Erik S. and Jarod Roll, *The Gospel of the Working Class: Labor's Southern Prophets in New Deal America*. Urbana: University of Illinois Press, 2011, 70–72. This book documents the rising consciousness of both Williams and Whitfield of the interconnection between racism and class exploitation, and their joint efforts to develop a religion that would help workers cross the racial divide to take charge of their lives and join in a common cause.

42. The phrase that unions are "not Santa Clause," belonged to Claude Williams and got picked up by Whitfield. "Notes to Cotton Workers School of UCAPAWA,"at the Inland Boarmen's Union Hall in Memphis, August 5 through August 18, 1940, in the Claude Williams Collection, Box 17 folder 28, Reuther Library of Labor and Urban Affairs, Detroit. "The Gospel of the Kingdom" and "All Inspired Scripture," of the People's Institute of Applied Religion, reproduced in Gellman and Roll, *The Gospel of the Working Class*, 109.
43. Williams to C. C. Kirkpatrick of Deventer local, October 16, 1936, STFU, Reel 3.
44. Roll, *Spirit of Rebellion*, 100; Gellman and Roll, *The Gospel of the Working Class*, 70.
45. Williams in a letter to Bob Reed, n.d., wrote that the Socialist Party of Arkansas never advanced black leaders in his experience of over 10 years there. This letter came from papers in Bob Reid's collection, now in author's collection. "The Socialist Party and the Negro," Socialist Party Papers, Ser. II, General Correspondence, Tennessee, in microfilm, cited in Honey, *Southern Labor and Black Civil Rights: Organizing Memphis Workers*. Urbana: University of Illinois Press, 1993, 56–57.
46. Eugene Debs, the key founder and leader of the SP, took the position that the class struggle would resolve racism, but he also took a strong stand against racism, saying "the history of the Negro in the United States is a history of crime without parallel." William P. Jones, "'Nothing Special to Offer the Negro': Revisiting the 'Debsian View' of the Negro Question," *International Labor and Working-Class History* (Fall 2008), 217.
47. My characterization scarcely does justice to Kester's varied career as a prophet for change. See Robert F. Martin, *Howard Kester and the Struggle for Social Justice in the South*, especially chapter four, "Race and Radicalism."
48. Gellman and Roll, *The Gospel of the Working Class*, 74–76. Mitchell starts his autobiography with a grisly lynching scene in which he witnessed the dead bodies of blacks murdered by whites: "I could never forget these killings, the violence between blacks and whites, the savagery of mob spirit. Certainly these early impressions helped to determine the course my life was to take." Mitchell, *Mean Things*, 1–2.
49. Dear Comrades, n.d. but seems to be 1936, from Memphis, Tennessee, STFU, Reel 3. A hand written note says the proposed meeting was "held late 1936 Hillhouse Miss."
50. They joined forces at the All-Southern Conference for Civil and Trade Union Rights in Chattanooga, but police raided the meeting and forced participants to retire to the Highlander School. A. Dunbar, *Against the Grain: Southern Radicals and Prophets, 1929–1959*. Charlottesville: University Press of Virginia, 1991, 137–138.
51. See Glenda Gilmore on Communist Party anti-racism in the South, *Defying Dixie: The Radical Roots of Civil Rights, 1919–1950*. New York: W.W. Norton & Co., 2008.
52. "We learned to love the people you white folks hate," is how one black worker explained his rejection of anti-communism. President Roosevelt asked Owen Whitfield whether he was a communist, defining a communist as someone who

stole someone else's property. Whitfield joked that if that were the case, whites must be the real communists, since they had stolen the land from the Indians. Gellman and Roll, *The Gospel of the Working Class,* 98

53. Journalist Mildred G. Freed described Whitfield in 1939, in "Ten Million Sharecroppers," *The Crisis* (1939), reprinted in *The Black Worker,* vol. 7, Foner and Lewis, eds., 193–196.

54. "I was a Sharecropper," Zella Whitfield, attached to a series of documents from Claude Williams titled "The Vicious Circle," in the Claude Williams Collection, Box 17 folder 28, Reuther Library of Labor and Urban Affairs, Detroit.

55. Locals of the Southern Tenant Farmers Union, 1937, STFU, Reel 7.

56. Erik S. Gellman and Jarod H. Roll, "Owen Whitfield and the Gospel of the Working Class in New Deal America, 1936–1946," *The Journal of Southern History* (May 2006), quote on 311.

57. Roll, *Spirit of Rebellion,* 100.

58. Brookins to the executive council, August 18, 1936, STFU, Reel 1; and Jason Manthorne, "The View from the Cotton," 36.

59. Mitchell to McKinney, July 31, 1936, in STFU, Reel 2, republished in *The Black Worker,* V. VII, Foner and Lewis, eds., 178–79. Williams to H. L. Mitchell, November 19, 1936, STFU, Reel 3.

60. Gellman and Roll, *The Gospel of the Working Class,* 75–76.

61. Robert Koppelman, *Sing Out, Warning! Sing Out, Love!: The Writings of Lee Hays* (2003), 70. Thanks to Ronald Cohen for this citation.

62. Gellman and Roll, *The Gospel of the Working Class,* 75–76; "Roll the Union On," in *The Sharecroppers' Voice* (January 1937). Serge Denisoff wrote that Handcox was "following in the footsteps of Claude Williams," probably a complete reversal of the reality in which Handcox spread the songs of his culture to Williams and Hays. *Great Day Coming,* 34. In *Sing a Song of Social Significance,* Denisoff writes that people associated with Commonwealth College, including Alan Lomax, "collected" John's songs, which is closer to the truth, 55.

63. For the labor-civil rights context for this period, see Erik S. Gellman, *Death Blow to Jim Crow: The National Negro Congress and the Rise of Militant Civil Rights.* Chapel Hill: University of North Carolina Press, 2012.

64. "Tenant Farmers Convention Asks Land Ownership," in the *Socialist Call* (January 23, 1937), estimated that 150 people attended the Muscogee convention.

65. Southern Tenant Farmers' Union Proceedings of the Third Annual Convention, 2–3, 15–16, STFU, Reel 4.

66. "Program" Third Annual Convention Southern Tenant Farmers Union, STFU, Reel 4, quotes on 16, 17, 18 and 19.

67. Ibid., quotes on 17, 18–19.

68. Ibid., and 45–49.

69. Ibid., 54.

70. Dunbar, *Against the* Grain, 154; and Howard Kester, *Revolt Among the Sharecroppers.* Knoxville: University of Tennessee Press, 1997, 50.

71. Dunbar, *Against the Grain,* 153–155; and Gellman and Roll, *The Gospel of the Working Class,* 77–79.

72. Williams to Gardner Jackson, January 23, 1937, STFU, Reel 4.

73. H. L. Mitchell, *Mean Things* , 104–105; Moskop had apparently tried to kill Mitchell earlier and Howard Kester stopped him. Martin, *Howard Kester and the Struggle for Social Justice in the South*, 104.

74. Ibid., 102–103; Mitchell to Executive Committee of the STFU, Oct. 3, 1936, STFU, Reel 3; and A. Dunbar, *Against the Grain*, 130–133.

75. Richard Wright, *American Hunger*. New York: Harper & Row, 1977; Fannin, *Labor's Promised Land : Radical Visions of Gender, Race, and Religion in the South*. Knoxville: University of Tennessee Press, 2003, 116–117.

6 Getting Gone to the Promised Land: California

1. Paul Laurence Dunbar, *Selected Poems*, ed. Herbert Woodward Martin (2004), 13.

2. Jarod Roll, *Spirit of Rebellion: Labor and Religion in the New Cotton South*. Urbana: University of Illinois Press, 2010, 106–107; and Erik S. Gellman and Jarod H. Roll, "Owen Whitfield and the Gospel of the Working Class in New Deal America, 1936–1946," *The Journal of Southern History* (May 2006), 304–348. Bonnie Stepenoff, *Thad Snow: A Life of Social Reform in the Missouri Bootheel*. Columbia: University of Missouri Press, 2003, 46–49; Thad Snow, *From Missouri: An American Farmer Looks Back*, ed. Bonnie Stepenoff. MO: University of Missouri Press, 2012, 171.

3. Roll, *Spirit of Rebellion*, 107; Handcox to Mitchell, January 31, 1937, from Charleston, MO, Southern Tenant Farmers' Union Papers [STFU] microfilm edition, Reel 4.

4. John Handcox to H. L. Mitchell, February 5, 1937, STFU, Reel 4.

5. J. R. Butler to John Handcox, February 14, 1937, STFU, Reel 4.

6. Handcox to Butler, February 19, 1937, STFU, Reel 4.

7. Ibid.

8. Roll, *Spirit of Rebellion*, 108–109; "Super-Flood Drives Thousands of Union Members From Homes," *The Sharecropper's Voice* (February 1937).

9. Gellman and Roll, "Owen Whitfield," 312–313.

10. Roll, *Spirit of Rebellion*, 109–111, 112–131.

11. Stepenoff, *Thad Snow*, 50, 68.

12. Roll, *Spirit of Rebellion*, 109.

13. Gellman and Roll, "Owen Whitfield," lists 4,600 members in 1938 with 29 locals, 314, 316.

14. Roll, *Spirit of Rebellion*, 113.

15. "The Duck Hill Outrage," *The Sharecroppers Voice* (February 1937).

16. Anthony P. Dunbar, *Against the Grain: Southern Radicals and Prophets, 1929–1959*. Charlottesville: University Press of Virginia, 1981, 158.

17. "Planters Revive Slave Patrol," endorsed as a written by H. L. Mitchell, 1937, STFU, Reel 6.

18. "Union Organizers Are Arrested While Defending Rights of Labor," *The Sharecropper's Voice* (June 1937).

19. "Mob Attacks," *Amsterdam News* (October 16, 1937), 23.

20. "Hero of the STFU," *The Sharecroppers Voice* (February 1937).

21. "Share Cropper Talks, NAACP Weeps," publicized a black woman who told of "Living Death in Dixie" at an NAACP conference in St. Louis in 1935. "Mobs Go on Rampage," *Amsterdam News* (April 30, 1930), 3. Talks, NAACP Weeps," (July 6, 1935), 1. "Sharecroppers Burdens Will Be Aired," *Amsterdam News* (February 6, 1937), 3.

22. "Tenant Farmers' Problems Have Airing Before NAACP," *Amsterdam News* (July 6, 1935), 7; "The Sharecroppers, Worst New Deal Victims, Appeal to Workers Here for Aid in Arkansas," *Amsterdam News* (March 2, 1935), 1.

23. "Dancing Feet Aid Southern Field Slaves," *Amsterdam News* (November 28, 1936), 4.

24. "Harlem to Celebrate Sharecroppers' Week," *Amsterdam News* (February 27, 1937), 24.

25. "Color Line Bunk to Dixie Farm Slaves," *Amsterdam News* (March 6, 1937), 1, for the above two paragraphs.

26. "Sharecroppers in New York," *Socialist Call* (February 20, 1937), 3.

27. "Plight of Sharecroppers is Told in 'Sweet Land,'" *Socialist Call* (February 6, 1937), 11.

28. Reese lived in exile at Hill House, Mississippi, while Marie Pierce, an African American, and others lived in exile in Memphis. Kester later said more than 40 families "have been driven from Arkansas and adjoining states because of union activities." "Croppers Head Near Lynched For Activities," *Amsterdam News* (December 4, 1937), 10.

29. "No Color Line", *Chicago Defender* (March 13, 1937), 1.

30. "Frank Weems Alive!," *Sharecroppers' Voice* (June 1937).

31. How the recordings were made is a little uncertain. The Library of Congress in Washington, D. C., apparently did not have a recording lab at that time so most recordings were done in the field by Robertson, Margaret Valiant, and other collectors. However, it appears the recordings occurred in Washington, D. C. Archie Green, "A Resettlement Administration Song Sheet," 81–83, in the records of the Resettlement Administration, Recordings Collection, box 1 of 1, Archive of Folk Culture, Library of Congress, 1939/016. And Charles Seeger and Margaret Valiant, "Journal of a Field Representative," Introduction by Jannelle Warren-Findley, *Ethnomusicology* (May 1980), 169, in the same files.

32. The LC Card catalogue lists the recording as 3237A1 and numbers on the sleeves of the John Handcox recordings are 3237, 3238, and 3239. These recordings and more are available on Mark Jackson's compact disc titled, "John Handcox: Songs, Poems, and Stories of the Southern Tenant Farmers Union" (2004). David King Dunaway confirms Pete working at the Library of Congress in the fall of 1939, *How Can I Keep From Singing? The Ballad of Pete Seeger* (2008), 64.

33. The first edition of People's Songs after World War II published "Roll the Union On," as a product of Commonwealth College; it later listed Williams and Hays, in that order, as the song's authors. Thanks to Ron Cohen for these details. The latter version of the song, n.d., is in author's collection. Joe Glazer inquired with Mitchell about John's songs and obtained a listing of them from the Library of Congress. Mitchell to Glazer, October 23, 1959, Archie Green

Collection, Original Deposit 1, Folder 150, Southern Folklife Collection, University of North Carolina at Chapel Hill. Thanks to Jessica Auer for finding these documents.

34. J. R. Butler to Handcox, April 12, 1937, STFU, Reel 2. Thanks to Jarrod Roll for copies of this and other Handcox correspondence. Gellman and Roll, "Owen Whitfield," paraphrase of Whitfield, 311 and 304.

35. Handcox to Butler, April 8, 1937, STFU Papers, File 52. Thanks to Jarrod Roll for sending me this manuscript copy.

36. Quoted in Jason Manthorne, "The View from the Cotton: Reconsidering the Southern Tenant Farmers' Union." *Agricultural History* 84 (2010): 38; Mitchell to Hertzberg, STFU, Reel 4.

37. Butler to Handcox, April 12, 1937, STFU Reel 4.

38. *The Sharecroppers' Voice* (September, 1937), 1. The Board members were Odis Sweeden, Oklahoma, a Cherokee Indian, James Sager, Texas, Whitfield, Missouri, Walker Martin, Alabama, J. R. Butler, Arkansas, and H. L. Mitchell, Tennessee.

39. *The Sharecropper's Voice* (September, 1937), 1; "Poem," editorial page.

40. "The Planter and the Sharecropper," *Southern Farm Leader*, New Orleans (July 1936). This newspaper can be found on the microfilm version of *The Sharecropper's Voice*.

41. According to Denisoff, labor songsters like Handcox and Jim Garland, once conscious of their role as a spokesperson for their people and their region, took on a new role as "folk entrepreneur." Denisoff sees the Labor Left as manipulative instrumentalists fitting such people into their Marxist framework. However, the most ardent supporters of southern music, especially labor protest music, such as Pete Seeger primarily appreciated its inherent performative and historic meaning, as well as its political meaning. Denisoff, *Great Day Coming: Folk Music and the American Left*. Urbana: University of Illinois Press, 1971, quote on 36.

42. "50,000 March in Chicago's Biggest May Day Parade," *Socialist Call* (May 8, 1937), 3. Thanks to Jessica Auer for digging this story out of the records in Davis Library at the University of North Carolina-Chapel Hill.

43. The Court upheld the amended Railway Labor Act on April 1 and Pullman signed a contract on August 25, 1937. Jervis Anderson, *A. Philip Randolph, A Biographical Portrait*. [First edition]. Harcourt Brace Jovanovich, 1972, 224–225. Randolph fought long and hard within the AFL and then the AFL-CIO for equal rights.

44. Summaries of telephone interviews with John Handcox by Donald Lance (July 26, and August 9, 1989), in author's possession. John told me this story as well.

45. Lance telephone interview with Handcox summary (August 1, 1989), in author's collection.

46. Handcox to Williams, November 30, 1938 and November 3, 1939, both in the Claude Williams Papers, Reuther Library of Labor and Urban Affairs, Wayne State University, Detroit. Thanks to Erik Gellman and Jarod Roll for sending me copies of this correspondence. See Honey, *Southern Labor and Black Civil Rights*, 138–139.

47. Editorial quotes in *The Sharecroppers' Voice*, July 1936. The Trotskyist movement entered the SP as a bloc in 1936 and bitter factional fighting in the next two years, destroying the party as a viable entity. Under their leadership, the *Socialist Call* in 1937 displayed increasingly revolutionary rhetoric but documented less and less action. Repression in the Soviet Union and the Hitler-Stalin nonaggression pact would also place the CP in an untenable position, as collaboration between the two parties collapsed. Mari Jo Buhle, Paul Buhle, and Dan Georgakas, eds, *Encyclopedia of the American Left*. New York: Garland Pub., 1990, 720–721, 152–153.
48. On the UCAPAWA convention and the political conflicts on labor's left, see Dunbar, *Against the Grain* 156–161.
49. "Oust Sharecroppers From Arkansas Hall, Southern Folk Say Nix After Crowd Comes," *Amsterdam News* (March 5, 1938), 5, reproduced by ProQuest Historical Newspapers.
50. Dunbar, *Against the Grain,* 164–170.
51. See Gellman, *Death Blow to Jim Crow*.
52. McKinney to J. R. Butler, August 31, 1938, in *The Black Worker*, vol. 7, Foner and Lewis, eds., 185; McKinney to Wiley Harris, July 29 and August 11, 1938, and to H. L. Mitchell, April 28, 1937, both quoted in Mark Naison, "Black Agrarian Radicalism in the Great Depression: The Threads of a Lost Tradition" *Journal of Ethnic Studies* (Fall 1973), 59–60. Naison provided one of the earliest and most prescient analyses of the politics of the STFU. White Communists and black union activists protested segregation in the Memphis CIO hall, and left unionists got run out by the CIO's emerging Cold War leadership for doing so. Honey, *Southern Labor and Black Civil Rights: Organizing Memphis Workers,* chapter nine, and 219, 233, 256, 276. H.L. Mitchell to all Locals, September 19, 1938, called for another cotton pickers strike but there is no evidence that it was effective. Reel 9, STFU papers.
53. Williams taught at a Commonwealth College "Cotton Preachers' Institute" in Little Rock, which held that unionization was the key to progress in the South. "Preachers Back Move To Organize Tenants," *Amsterdam News* (September 17, 1938), A3, ProQuest Historical Newspapers. Gellman and Roll, *The Gospel of the Working Class*, 92–93.
54. J. R. Butler to Claude Williams, August 22, 1938, with enclosure, and Williams to Butler, August 15, 1938, in *The Black Worker*, vol. 7, Foner and Lewis, eds., 181–184. William H. Cobb and Donald H. Grubbs, "Arkansas' Commonwealth College and the Southern Tenant Farmers' Union," in *The Arkansas Historical Quarterly* (Winter 1966), 306–311.
55. Cobb and Grubbs, ibid.; "Remove 2 Heads of C.I.O. Union, Rev. Claude Williams Ordered Ousted," New York City *Amsterdam News* (October 1, 1938), 12, ProQuest Historical Newspapers.
56. Donald Grubbs, *Cry From the Cotton: the Southern Tenant Farmers' Union and the New Deal*. Chapel Hill, University of North Carolina Press, 2000, 178–179.
57. "Breach in Ranks of Tenant Farm Union Widens as Charges Fly," *Amsterdam News* (April 29, 1939), 15, ProQuest Historical Newspapers.
58. Mitchell was bitter as well, calling Williams a "pathetic figure" who "followed the Communist Party line all the days of his life, because he knew of no other line to

follow." Mitchell, *Mean Things,* 174. A photo of a Fellowship of Reconciliation Interracial Student Conference held at Le Moyne College in Memphis in 1932, sadly, shows Kester and Williams side by side, as revolutionary Socialists. The personal relationships between the three men ended abruptly. Martin, *Howard Kester,* 60.

59. Gellman and Roll, "Owen Whitfield," 321; Snow, *From Missouri,* 192–207.
60. Gellman and Roll, "Owen Whitfield," 321–326.
61. Stephanie A. Carpenter, review of *Oh Freedom after Awhile,* a PBS film by Steven Ross et Al., *Agricultural History* (Winter, 2001), 119–22; John Herbert Hayes, "Hard, Hard Religion: Faith and Class in the New South" (PhD dissertation, University of Georgia, 2007).
62. Whitfield to H. L. Mitchell, February 28, 1939, quoted Naison, "Black Agrarian Radicalism," 61.
63. Grubbs, *Cry From the Cotton,* 189. "All his life he fought against the Communist demons in the labor movement and was haunted by them," believing Harry Bridges and Donald Henderson were "agents for the Soviet Union," according to Mitchell's son. Samuel Howard Mitchell, *A Leader Among Sharecroppers, Migrants, and Farm Workers: H.L. Mitchell and Friends,* n.p., n.p., printed in Canada (2007), 223, 224.
64. Dunbar, *Against the Grain,* 180–181; Mitchell, *Mean Thing,* chapters 14–15, 191–192.
65. H. L. Mitchell had not been back in Arkansas to organize since 1934, and blacks and whites remained divided and demoralized, according to David S. Burgess, *Fighting for Social Justice, The Life Story of David Burgess.* Detroit: Wayne State University Press, 2000, 56–60. Burgess worked with Mitchell in a successful battle to save the Delmo Homes cooperative living project, 61–71.
66. Gavin Wright, *Old South, New South: Revolutions in the Southern Economy Since the Civil War.* Baton Rouge: Louisiana State University Press, 1996, statistics on 243.
67. See Whayne, *Delta Empire: Lee Wilson and the Transformation of Agriculture in the New South.* Baton Rouge: Louisiana State University Press, 2011, and Clyde Woods, *Development Arrested: Race, Power, and the Blues in the Mississippi Delta.* New York: Verso, 1998.
68. Mitchell, *Mean Things,* dedication to John Handcox quote on cover page. An appendix in Samuel Mitchell, *A Leader Among Sharecroppers, Migrants, and Farm Workers,* provides an amazing list of the many places his father went to promote the history of the STFU.
69. Jessica Auer's research on 1940 Census records and city directories found many of the Handcox clan living in close proximity. Notes from John Handcox telephone interviews by Donald Lance (July 26, 1989 and August 1, 1989), in author's possession; and Rebecca B. Schroeder and Donald M. Lance, "John L. Handcox- 'There Is Still Mean Things Happening'," in *Songs About Work: Essays in Occupational Culture for Richard A. Reuss,* ed. Archie Green (1993), 201.
70. Notes from John Handcox telephone interview by Donald Lance (July 26, 1989), in author's possession.

71. Handcox interview by Lance (July 26, 1989); and quote, Handcox interview by Lance (August 1, 1989).

72. "C.I.O Brings Negroes Here To Get Instructions for Unionizing Farm Workers; Williams, Ousted From Tenant Union For Red Connections, Leads 'Classes' At Illinois Avenue School; Yough Congress Sends Helper," *Commercial Appeal*, (August 16, 1940).

73. Claude Williams to Harry and Grace Koger, n.d., Claude Williams Papers, Folder 6, Box 15, recalling the 1940 UCAPAWA school in Memphis. Pete Seeger recalled traveling through Memphis and he probably heard this song at the time or from Claude Williams shortly thereafter. Personal interview (January 19, 1986), Washington, D. C. See, Honey, *Southern Labor and Black Civil Rights*, 138–139.

74. See the discussion in Roy, *Reds, Whites and Blues: Social Movements, Folk Music, and Race in the United States*. Princeton: Princeton University Press, 2010, 163, 195–196.

75. Writers who explain this period of transition from the 1930s to the 1960s, and take John Handcox into account, include Dick Weisman, *Which Side Are You On? An Inside History of the Folk Music Revival in America*. New York: Continuum, 2005; Ronald D. Cohen, *Rainbow Quest: The Folk Music Revival and American Society, 1940–1970*. Amherst: Amherst University Press, 2002; Ronald Cohen and Dave Samuelson, eds., *Songs for Political Action: Folk Music, Topical Songs and the American Left, 1926–53*. Battle Ground, Indiana: Bear Family Records, *1996;* Joe Glazer, *Labor's Troubadour*. Urbana: University of Illinois Press, 2001; Rosenthal and Flacks, *Playing for Change: Music and Musicians in the Service of Social Movements*. Boulder, Colo.: Paradigm Publishers, 2011; Roy, *Reds, Whites, and Blues*; and Denisoff, *Great Day Coming*. There are many more books about the so-called folk music revival but—like the work by Eileen Southern and others on the history of African American music—not many of them look seriously at the political role of labor protest music or John Handcox.

7 "I'm So Glad to Be Here Again": The Return of John Handcox

1. Broonzy claimed to Mississippi as his birthplace, but much of what he claimed was not true. Bob Reisman, *I Feel So Good: The Life and Times of Big Bill Broonzy* (2011), 7. Eileen Southern, *Biographical Dictionary of Afro-American and African Musicians* (1982), gives details on Broonzy, 49, Jordan, 222, and Tharpe, 372–373.

2. Thanks to Ron Cohen for his notes on the People's Songs 1946 album, *"Roll the Union On,"* Ash Records, from Cohen email, April 23, 2013. Numerous studies of folk music and the left have been done and are cited elsewhere. See particularly Roy, *Reds, Whites, and Blues,* and a short book, Alan M. Winkler, *"To Everything There is a Season": Pete Seeger and the Power of Song*. London: Oxford University Press, 2009.

3. For a recent adept treatment of how labor's red scare evolved, see Jennifer Luff, *Commonsense Anticommunsm: Labor and Civil Liberties Between the World Wars.* Chapel Hill: University of North Carolian Press, 2012.

4. Moe Foner, *Not For Bread Alone: A Memoir.* Ithaca: Cornell University Press, 2002; Kerran L. Sanger, *"When the Spirit Says Sing!": The Role of Freedom Songs in the Civil Rights Movement.* New York: Garland, 1995, chapter five and 151–152, on "We Shall Not Be Moved" and other songs. For an overview of the People's Song movement and the folk music revival, see Ronald Cohen, *Rainbow Quest: Folk Music Revival and American Society, 1940–1970.* Amherst: Amherst University Press, 2002; Josh Dunson, *Freedom in the Air: Song Movements of the Sixties.* Westport, CT: Greenwood Press, 1965; David King Dunaway and Molly Beer, *Singing Out: An Oral History of America's Folk Music Revivals.* New York: Oxford University Press, 2010.

5. Samuel A. Floyd, *The Power of Black Music: Interpreting Its History from Africa to the Unitd States.* New York: Oxford University Press, 1995.

6. Pete Seeger, *Pete Seeger: In His Own Words*, eds. Rob Rosenthal and Sam Rosenthal. Boulder, CO: Paradigm Publishers, 2012, 88.

7. Researcher Jessica Auer located John's brother George and sister-in-law Velma living close by to John in a 1947 City Directory that listed John's occupation ad "driver" and George's as "carpenter." By 1959, she found John's younger brother Leo, listed as a carpenter, and his wife Cath, at 3960 Florence, and John's brother Willis and Lucille living on 2884 Clay Street. In 1959 Ruth was listed as a domestic worker at 3140 K. Street, and in 1969 she lived at 3160 K. Street, along with George's son George, Jr. San Diego City Directories, 1943, 1947, 1959, 1969, listed under "U.S. City Directories, 1821–1989," database online, Provo, UT, USA: Ancestry.com Operations, Inc., 2011; and *Polk's San Diego City Directory* (Los Angeles: R. L Polk and Co. Publishers, 1959)

8. Ibid.

9. Researcher Jessica Auer traced the Handcox family through the US City Directories, 1821–1989, database online, Provo, UT, USA: Ancestry.com Operations, Inc., 2011, and Polk's San Diego City Directory (R. L Polk and Co. Publishers, Los Angeles, 1959). Telephone interview with Camelia Cook, July 22, 2012.

10. Willie Williams, telephone interview by author (September 2, 2010).

11. Profiles of Handcox family members sent by Camelia Cook, in author's possession.

12. "U.S. City Directories, 1821–1989"; and *Polk's San Diego City Directory*; John D'Agostino, "Labors of Love Honoree," *Los Angeles Times* (January 31, 1992), based on an interview with John Handcox. His granddaughter Camelia Cook confirmed and elaborated on the details, telephone interview by author (August 22, 2012).

13. Handcox interview by Donald Lance (July 26, 1989), notes in author's possession.

14. John Handcox, undated letter, in author's possession.

15. John McLaren, "Labor troubadour still inspires," *San Diego Tribune* (January 2, 1989), recalls the Carpenter's union discrimination; Rolla Williams, "Fat bass

found on opening day at Otay Lake," *San Diego Union* (January 24, 1991), quotes George Handcox, almost surely John's older brother.

16. Handcox quote on Imperial Avenue, McLaren, "Labor troubadour"; quote on the theater owner, in Marjorie Miller, "Socialist Gains Belated Recognition; Efforts to Organize Poor Farmers Led to Inspirational Music," *Los Angeles Times* (April 14, 1985).

17. The San Diego History Center has a photographic exhibit of Logan Heights from 1939–45, portraits of a proud community taken over many years by Norman Baynard. There are at least two Handcox family photos among the 500 that have been inventoried. They include a number of Nation of Islam photos and a Hancock Advanced Lubrication service station, which could be related to John's family as well. One photo shows John with his mother and several grand children (91:18476–163), and another shows a large gathering of the Handcox grandchildren with John under a tree in a park on Clay Avenue in 1969 (91:18476–164). See the San Diego History online photographic finding aid. Granddaughter Camelia Cook looked through 500 of the photos, telephone interview by author (July 22, 2012).

18. Ibid., and John Handcox, "To Those That Are Concerned," typescript, n.d., in author's collection.

19. Camelia Cook, telephone interview by author (August 22, 2012).

20. Jessica Auer located their marriage and divorce records.

21. Willie Williams, telephone interview by author (September 2, 2010); Camelia Cook, telephone interview by author (September 12, 2010); and Michael Honey conversation with John Handcox, 1985. Jessica Auer was able to trace some of these marriages and divorces through census and city records. "California, Marriage Index, 1960–1985," and "California, Divorce Index, 1966–1984," database online, Provo, UT, USA: Ancestry.com Operations, Inc., 2011.

22. Camelia Cook, telephone interview by author (July 10, 2009).

23. Ibid.

24. Ibid. (August 22, 2012).

25. John McLaren, "Labor troubadour still inspires," *San Diego Tribune*, January 2, 1989.

26. Ibid.

27. Tape recording at the Labor Arts Exchange, May 13, 1985, in author's possession.

28. The "Reagan Psalms" concluded: "Five thousand years ago, a man named Moses said: 'Pick up your shovel and mount your camel or ass, and I will lead you to the Promised Land.' Five thousand years later, a man named Roosevelt said: 'Lay down your shovel, light up a Camel, and sit on your ass, for this is the Promised Land.' Now watch Reagan, for he will take your shovel, sell your camel, kick your ass, and tell you: 'There is no Promised Land.'"

29. The song lyrics and the Handcox quote are reproduced in Rebecca B. Schroeder and Donald M. Lance, "John L. Handcox—'There Is Still Mean Things Happening'," in *Songs About Work: Essays in Occupational Culture for Richard A. Reuss*, ed. Archie Green. Bloomington: Folklore Institute, Indiana University, 1993, 184–207, 202–203.

30. Young people loved Handcox and his music, as I witnessed when he sang his songs before a packed auditorium at Elkins College in West Virginia in August of 1985. He sang at a Midwest labor song exchange in Chicago and performed at the Western Worker's Heritage festival just months before his death. Documents and audio tapes in author's files.

31. A John L. Handcox collection exists at the Western Historical Manuscript Collection, University of Missouri-Columbia, and see also the Donald M. Lance Papers. David Roediger, "'Their Horrid Gold': John Handcox and the Uncopyrighted Red Songbook," in *The Big Red Songbook*, eds. Archie Green, David Roediger, Franklin Rosemont, and Salvatore Salerno (2007), 23–24.

32. John also recalled to a reporter the "Sundown towns" with signs that said, "nigger, don't let the sun set on you in this town," the lynching that his father witnessed in Arkansas, as well as his grand-father telling him that "old marse" had forced his slaves to eat from a horse trough. He remembered walking four miles one way to school, and how his grandmother would zealously spank the children to get them to work long hours in the fields. He recalled the day he went to find United Farm Workers Union leader Caesar Chavez at his Bakersfield office, but he wasn't there. McLaren, "Labor troubadour." Rebecca Schroeder interview with John Handcox, October 16, 1989, transcribed by Susan Hollister.

33. Quote Rick Delvecchio, "Socialist Gains Belated Recognition," *San Francisco Chronicle*, February 5, 1988, B5. "We come in the world the same way," in Rebecca Schroeder interview, October 16, 1989.

34. Thanks to Robert Ferguson for his prescient interpretation and for his transcript and interview notes of John L. Handcox, interview by Michael Honey and William Ferris (January 15, 1990), William R. Ferris Collection (#20367), Southern Folklife Collection, Wilson Library, University of North Carolina at Chapel Hill.

35. "San Diego Salutes! John L. Handcox," Friday, January 31, 1992, sponsored by Grass Roots Events, at the Laborers International Hall, 4161 Home Avenue. Flyer in author's collection. John D'Agostino, LAT, ibid. Frank Green, "Seeger's is still one of the more forceful voices that's left," *San Diego Union* (January 31, 1992).

36. John's typescript, quoted in Schroeder and Lance, "John L. Handcox," 204–205.

37. Tape recording in author's possession; program, "Legendary Labor Poet John L. Handcox, February 5, 1904–September 18, 1992, Memorial Service," New Creation Church, 7830 Carlisle Drive, Lemon Grove, California, Rev. Amos Johnson, Jr., officiating; Frank Green, "John L. Handcox dies at 87; an early labor organizer, writer of folk music," *San Diego Union*, September 25, 1992; Camelia Cook, telephone interview by author (August 22, 2012).

38. Melody and arrangement by Michael Honey.

39. Bernice Johnson Reagon, quoted in *A Circle of Trust: Remembering SNCC*, ed. Cheryl Lynn Greenberg. New Brunswick, N.J.: Rutgers University Press, 1998, 112.

40. Ibid., 119.

41. An example of not forgetting the past is the Southern Tenant Farmers Museum, opened on October 6, 2006, in Tyronza, Arkansas, with an opening event titled "Raggedy, Raggedy Are We," Highlighted by scholars Orville Vernon Burton,

Mark Allan Jackson, Nan Woodruff, and Jeannie Whayne. The Ed King quote is in Elizabeth Anne Payne and Louis Boyle, "The Lady Was a Sharecropper: Myrtle Lawrence and the Southern Tenant Farmers' Union," *Southern Cultures* (1998), 24.

42. Quip from Honey and Ferris interview; "sharecropper's son" quote in typescript, n.d., in author's possession.

43. John's original rough draft with Sheila Stewart is not the same as the way I have reproduced it here, which is the way John and I sang "Hard to Say Good-Bye" together and the way the song has appeared in labor music circles. John sang it that way, and Pete Seeger transcribed the music the way he heard John sing it. The last verse of John's original rough draft was left out, however, and in a sense it might be the strongest conclusion to the song.

Bibliography

John Handcox Songs and Poems

"Raggedy, Raggedy Are We"
"Roll the Union On"
"Join the Union Tonight"
"In My Heart"
"No More Mourning"
"There is Mean Things Happening in This Land"
"The Planter and the Sharecropper"
"Landlord, What in the Heaven is the Matter With You?"
"The Man Frank Weems"
Lyrics by John Handcox, music and arrangement by Michael Honey, in author's possession:
"Hard to Say Good-Bye"
"Jobless in the USA"
"What A Great World It Could Be"

"John L. Handcox: Songs, Poems and Stories of the Southern Tenant Farmers' Union." Edited by Mark Alan Jackson, University of West Virginia Press, cd, 2004. Recorded by John Handcox at the Library of Congress on March 9, 1937, with interviews by Michael Honey and Joe Glazer.
To hear other songs of John Handcox, go to; http; //faculty.washington.edu /mhoney/.

Oral History Interviews

Camelia Cook. Interviews with Michael Honey. July 10, 2009, August 24, 2009, July 22, 2012, August 22, 2012, telephone.
John Handcox. Interview with Michael Honey. May 16, 1985, Silver Spring, Md., transcribed by Patti J. Krueger.
John Handcox. Interview with Michael Honey and Joe Glazer. May 15, 1985, Washington, D.C. transcribed by Patti J. Krueger; audio copies available in the American Folklife Collection, Archive of Folk Culture, Library of Congress, and on "John L. Handcox," University of West Virginia Press compact disc.
John Handcox. Interview with Joe Riggs, notes, in author's possession.

John Handcox. Interview audio tape with Rebecca Schroeder, October 16, 1989, Columbia, MO. CD 2, track 2, transcribed by Susan Hollister, in author's possession.

John Handcox. Interview with Donald Lance. July 26, 1989, September 30, 1990, August 1, 1989, telephone notes, in author's possession.

John Handcox. Interview with William Ferris and Michael Honey. January 15, 1990, audio tape, transcribed by Robert Hunt Ferguson.

Pete Seeger, personal interview with Michael Honey, notes, January 19, 1986, Washington, D.C.

Willie Williams. Interview with Michael Honey. September 2, 2010, telephone.

Manuscripts and Archives

Archie Green Collection. Southern Folklife Collection, University of North Carolina at Chapel Hill.

"Arkansas, County Marriages, 1837–1957." Index. *FamilySearch.com.*

American Radicalism Collection. Michigan State University Library, East Lansing, MI.

Claude Williams Papers. Walter P. Reuther Archive of Urban Affairs, Wayne State University, Detroit, MI.

Department of Labor, Washington, D.C.

Donald M. Lance Papers, 1938–2002. Western Historical Manuscript Collection, The State Historical Society of Missouri, Columbia, MO.

John L. Handcox letters and poems, hand-written and in typescript, in author's possession.

National Association for the Advancement of Colored People Papers. Library of Congress, Washington D.C.

Logan Heights photo collection. San Diego History Center. San Diego, CA.

Resettlement Administration Records. Archive of Folk Culture, Library of Congress, Washington D.C.

Southern Tenant Farmers Union, manuscript collection and microfilm. Southern Historical Collection, University of North Carolina at Chapel Hill, Chapel Hill, NC.

"United States Social Security Death Index." *FamilySearch.com.*

US Census Bureau. *Population Census of the United States: Randolph County, Alabama.* 1880. Retrieved via ancestry.com.

US Census Bureau. *Population Census of the United States: Woodruff County Arkansas.* 1870, 1880, 1900, 1910, 1920, 1930, 1940. Retrieved via ancestry.com

US Census Bureau. *Population Census of the United States: Monroe County, Arkansas.* 1910, 1920, 1930. Retrieved via ancestry.com.

US Census Bureau. *Population Census of the United States: St. Francis County, Arkansas.* 1900, 1920, 1930. Retrieved via ancestry.com.

US Census Bureau. *Population Census of the United States: Washington County, Oklahoma.* 1940. Retrieved via ancestry.com

"US City Directories, 1821–1989." Database online, Provo, UT. *Ancestry.com*

"US World War I Draft Registration Cards, 1917–1918." *FamilySearch.com.*

William R. Ferris Collection. Southern Folklife Collection, Wilson Library, University of North Carolina at Chapel Hill.

Periodicals

Baltimore Afro-American
Chicago Defender
Commercial Appeal (Memphis)
The Crisis
Los Angeles Times
New York Amsterdam News
San Diego Tribune
San Diego Union
The Sharecropper's Voice
Socialist Call
Southern Exposure

Secondary Sources

Allen, William Francis, Charles Pickard Ware, and Lucy McKin Garrison, comp. *Slave Songs of the United States.* New York: Oak Publications, 1965.

Anderson, Jervis. *A. Philip Randolph: A Biographical Portrait.* [First edition]. New York: Harcourt Brace Jovanovich, 1973.

Auerbach, Jerold S. "Southern Tenant Farmers: Socialist Critics of the New Deal." *Arkansas Historical Quarterly* 27(2) (July 1, 1968): 113–131.

Barnes, Kenneth C. *Journey of Hope: The Back-to-Africa Movement in Arkansas in the Late 1800s.* Chapel Hill: University of North Carolina Press, 2004.

Barry, John. *Rising Tide : The Great Mississippi Flood of 1927 and How It Changed America.* New York: Simon & Schuster, 1997.

Beecher, John. "In Egypt Land." In *Working Lives: the Southern Exposure History of Labor in the South*, ed. Marc Miller (1980), 143–154.

Belfrage, Cedric. *A Faith to Free the People.* New York: The Dryden Press, 1944.

Bernstein, Irving. *The Lean Years; A History of the American worker, 1920–1933.* Boston: Houghton Mifflin, 1960.

———. *The Turbulent Years: A History of the American worker, 1933–1941.* Boston: Houghton Mifflin, 1970.

Bishop, Selma L. *Isaac Watts's Hymns and Spiritual Songs, 1707: A Publishing History and a Bibliography.* Ann Arbor: Pierian Press, 1974.

Blackmon, Douglas A. *Slavery by Another Name: The Re-Enslavement of Black Americans from the Civil War to World War II.* New York: Anchor Books, 2009.

Bond, Ulysses S. "Highlights in the Life of Scott Bond." *The Arkansas Historical Quarterly* 21(2) (July 1, 1962): 146–152.

Buhle, Mary Jo, Paul Buhle, and Dan Georgakas, eds. *Encyclopedia of the American Left.* New York: Garland Pub., 1990.

Burgess, David. *Fighting for Social Justice: The Life Story of David Burgess.* Detroit: Wayne State University Press, 2000.

Caldwell, Erskine and Margaret Bourke-White. *You Have Seen Their Faces*. Athens: University of Georgia Press, 1995.

Carpenter, Stephanie. Review of *Oh Freedom after Awhile*, a PBS film by Steven Ross, et. al. *Agricultural History* 75(1) (Winter 2001): 119–122.

Cash, Johnny. *The Autobiography*. San Francisco: Harper, 1997.

Cobb, William H. and Donald H. Grubbs. "Arkansas' Commonwealth College and the Southern Tenant Farmers' Union." *The Arkansas Historical Quarterly* 25(4) (December 1, 1966): 293–311.

Cohen, Ronald D. *Rainbow Quest, The Folk Music Revival and American Society, 1940– 1970*. Amherst: Amherst University Press, 2002.

———. *Work and Sing: A History of Occupational and Labor Union Songs in the United States*. Crockett: Carquinez Press, 2010

Cohen, Ronald and Dave Samuelson, comp. *Songs for Political Action: Folk Music, Topical Songs and the American Left, 1926–53*. Battle Ground: Bear Family Records, 1996.

Cone, James H. *The Spirituals and the Blues, An Interpretation*. Maryknoll: Orbis Books, 1972, 1991.

Cunningham, Sis and Gordon Friesen. *Red Dust and Broadsides: A Joint Autobiography*, ed. Ronald Cohen. Amherst: University of Massachusetts Press, 1999.

Dallas, Jerry W. "The Delta and Providence Farms: A Mississippi Experiment in Cooperative Farming and Racial Cooperation, 1936–1956." *Mississippi Quarterly* 40 (Summer 1987): 283–308.

Daniel, Pete. *Deep'n as It Come : The 1927 Mississippi River Flood*. Fayetteville: University of Arkansas Press, 1977.

———. "The Crossroads of Change: Cotton, Tobacco, and Rice Cultures in the Twentieth-Century South." *The Journal of Southern History* 50(3) (August 1, 1984): 429–456.

———. *The Shadow of Slavery: Peonage in the South, 1901–1969*. Champaign: University of Illinois Press, 1972.

Darden, Robert. *People Get Ready! A New History of Black Gospel Music*. New York: Continuum, 2004.

Delvecchio, Rick. "Last of the Legendary Labor Poets." *San Francisco Chronicle*, February 5, 1988.

Denisoff, Serge R. *Great Day Coming: Folk Music and the American Left*. Urbana: University of Illinois Press, 1971.

———. *Sing A Song of Social Significance*. Bowling Green University: Popular Press, 1972.

Dett, R. Nathaniel. *Religious Folk-Songs of the Negro, As Sung at Hampton Institute*. Hampton: Hampton Institute Press, 1927.

Douglass, Frederick. *The Narrative of the Life of Frederick Douglass, An American Slave*. Boston: the Anti-Slavery Office, 1845.

Du Bois, W. E. B. *Black Reconstruction in America: An Essay Toward a History of the Part Which Black Folk Played in the Attempt to Reconstruct Democracy in America, 1860–1880*. New York: Atheneum, 1983; first published, 1935.

———. *The Souls of Black Folk*. New York: Bantam Books, 1989, originally published in 1904.

Dunaway, David. *How Can I Keep from Singing: The Ballad of Pete Seeger*. New York: Villard, 2008.

Dunaway, David King and Molly Beer. *Singing Out: An Oral History of America's Folk Music Revivals.* New York: Oxford University Press, 2010.

Dunbar, Anthony. *Against the Grain: Southern Radicals and Prophets, 1929–1959.* Charlottesville: University Press of Virginia, 1981.

Dunbar, Paul Laurence. *The Collected Poetry of Paul Laurence Dunbar,* ed. Joanne M. Braxton. Charlottesville: University Press of Virginia, 1993.

———. *Selected Poems,* ed. Herbert Woodward Martin. New York: Penguin Books, 2004.

Dunson, Josh. *Freedom in the Air: Song Movements of the Sixties.* Westport: Greenwood Press, 1965.

Dyson, Lowell K. "The Southern Tenant Farmers' Union and Depression Politics." *Political Science Quarterly* 88 (June 1973): 230–251.

Egerton, John. *Speak Now Against the Day: The Generation Before the Civil Rights Movement in the South.* New York: Alfred A. Knopf, 1994.

Fannin, Mark. *Labor's Promised Land : Radical Visions of Gender, Race, and Religion in the South.* Knoxville: University of Tennessee Press, 2003.

Robert Hunt Ferguson, "The Land, the Lord, and the Union: Earthly and Spiritual Salvation in the Protest Songs of John L. Handcox," *Arkansas Review* 43(2) (Summer/August 2012): 75–82.,

Ferris, William. *Blues from the Delta.* New York: Anchor Press/Doubleday, 1978.

Finnegan, Ruth. *Oral Poetry: Its Nature, Significance and Social Context.* Cambridge: Cambridge University Press, 1977.

Fisher, Miles Mark. *Negro Slave Songs in the United States.* Cornell: Cornell University Press, 1953, and Citadel Press, third printing, 1978.

Fisher, William Arms. *Seventy Negro Spirituals.* Boston: Oliver Ditson, 1926.

Floyd, Samuel A. *The Power of Black Music: Interpreting History from Africa to the United States.* New York: Oxford University Press, 1995.

Foner, Moe. *Not for Bread Alone: A Memoir.* With Dan North. Ithaca: Cornell University Press, 2002.

Foner, Philip, and Ronald L. Lewis, eds. *The Black Worker : From the Founding of the CIO to the AFL-CIO Merger, 1936–1955.* vol. 7 of *The Black Worker: A Documentary History from Colonial Times to the Present.* Philadelphia: Temple University Press, 1983.

Fowke, Edith, and Joe Glazer. *Songs of Work and Protest.* New York: Dover, 1960 1973.

Frisch, Michael H. *A Shared Authority: Essays on the Craft and Meaning of Oral and Public History.* Albany: State University of New York Press, 1990.

Fuld, James J. *The Book of World-Famous Music: Classical, Popular and Folk.* New York: Crown Publishers, 1966.

Garland, Jim. *Welcome the Traveler Home: Jim Garland's Story of the Kentucky Mountains,* ed. Julia Ardery. Lexington: University Press of Kentucky, 1983.

Gellman, Erik S. *Death Blow to Jim Crow: The National Negro Congress and the Rise of Militant Civil Rights.* Chapel Hill: University of North Carolina Press, 2012.

Gellman, Erik S. and Jarod Roll, "Owen Whitfield and the Gospel of the Working Class in New Deal America, 1936–1946." *The Journal of Southern History* 72(2) (May 1, 2006): 303–348.

———. *The Gospel of the Working Class: Labor's Southern Prophets in New Deal America.* Urbana: University of Illinois Press, 2011.

Gilmore, Glenda Elizabeth. *Defying Dixie: The Radical Roots of Civil Rights, 1919–1950.* New York: W.W. Norton & Co., 2008.

Glazer, Joe. *Labor's Troubadour.* Urbana: University of Illinois Press, 2001.

Glazer, Tom. *Songs of Peace, Freedom, and Protest.* New York: David McKay, 1970.

Green, Archie, ed. *Songs About Work: Essays in Occupational Culture for Richard A. Reuss.* Bloomington: Folklore Institute, Indiana University, 1993.

————. David Roediger, Franklin Rosemont, and Salvatore Salerno, eds. *The Big Red Songbook.* Chicago: Charles H. Kerr, 2007.

Green, James. *Grass-roots Socialism: Radical Movements in the Southwest, 1895–1943.* Baton Rouge: Louisiana State University Press, 1978.

————. *The World of the Worker: Labor in Twentieth-century America.* New York: Hill and Wang, 1980.

Green, Laurie B. *Battling the Plantation Mentality: Memphis and the Black Freedom Struggle.* Chapel Hill: University of North Carolina Press, 2007.

Greenberg, Cheryl, ed. *A Circle of Trust: Remembering SNCC.* New Brunswick: Rutgers University Press, 1998.

Greenway, John. *American Folksongs of Protest.* New York: A. S. Barnes, 1960.

Grubbs, Donald H. *Cry From the Cotton: The Southern Tenant Farmers' Union and the New Deal.* Chapel Hill, University of North Carolina Press, 1971.

Hahn, Steven. *A Nation Under Our Feet: Black Political Struggles in the Rural South, from Slavery to the Great Migration.* Cambridge: Harvard University Press, 2003.

Hayes, John Herbert. "Hard, Hard Religion: Faith and Crisis in the New South." PhD diss., University of Georgia, 2007.

Hays, Lee. *"Sing Out, Warning! Sing Out, Love!": The Writings of Lee Hays,* ed. Robert Koppelman. Amherst: University of Massachusetts Press, 2003.

Honey, Michael K. *Black Workers Remember: An Oral History of Segregation, Unionism, and the Freedom Struggle.* Berkeley: University of California Press, 1999.

————. *Southern Labor and Black Civil Rights Civil Rights: Organizing Memphis Workers.* Urbana: University of Illinois Press, 1993.

————. *Going Down Jericho Road: The Memphis Strike, Martin Luther King's Last Campaign.* New York: W. W. Norton, 2007.

Honey, Michael K. and Pat Krueger. "John Handcox, Union Song Writer." *Sing Out! The Folk Song Magazine.* 35(3) (Fall 1990), 14–18.

Horton, Zilphia. *Labor Songs.* Atlanta: Southeastern Regional Office Textile Workers Union of America, 1939.

Hudson, Hosea. *The Narrative of Hosea Hudson: His Life as a Negro Communist in the South,* ed. Nell Irvin Painter. Cambridge: Harvard University Press, 1979.

Hurt, R. Douglas, ed. *African American life in the Rural South, 1900–1950.* Columbia: University of Missouri Press, 2003.

Jackson, Mark Allan. *John L. Handcox Songs, Poems, and Stories of the Southern Tenant Farmers' Union.* Morgantown: West Virginia University Press, 2004.

Johnson, James Weldon. *The Book of American Negro Spirituals.* New York: Viking Press, 1925.

Jones, Arthur. *Wade in the Water: The Wisdom of the Spirituals.* Maryknoll: Orbis Books, 1993.

Jones, Jacquelyn. *Labor of Love, Labor of Sorrow: Black Women, Work, and the Family from Slavery to the Present.* New York: Basic Books, 1986.

Jones, William P. "Nothing Special to Offer the Negro': Revisiting the 'Debsian View' of the Negro Question." *International Labor and Working-Class History.* 74 (October 1, 2008): 212–224.

Kelley, Robin D. G. *Hammer and Hoe: Alabama Communists During the Great Depression.* Chapel Hill: University of North Carolina Press, 1990.

Kester, Howard. *Revolt Among the Sharecroppers.* Intro, Alex Lichtenstein. Knoxville: University of Tennessee Press, 1997.

The Killing Floor. Directed by Bill Duke. 1984. (Film).

Klehr, Harvey. *The Heyday of American Communism: The Depression Decade.* New York: Basic Books, 1984.

Korstad, Robert. *Civil Rights Unionism : Tobacco Workers and the Struggle for Democracy in the Mid-twentieth-century South.* Chapel Hill: University of North Carolina Press, 2003.

Lane, Charles. *The Day Freedom Died: The Colfax Massacre, the Supreme Court, and the Betrayal of Reconstruction.* New York: Henry Holt and Company, 2009.

Letwin, Daniel. *The Challenge of Interracial Unionism: Alabama Coal Miners, 1878–1921.* Chapel Hill: University of North Carolina Press, 1998.

Levine, Lawrence. *Black Culture and Black Consciousness: Afro-American Folk Thought From Slavery to Freedom.* Readings in Black American, 1977.

Lieberman, Robbie. *"My Song is My Weapon": People's Songs, American Communism, and the Politics of Culture, 1930–1950.* Urbana: University of Illinois Press, 1989.

Lock, Alaine. *The Negro and His Music. Negro Art: Past and Present.* North Stratford,: Ayer Company, 1998.

Lomax, Alan. *The Folk Songs of North America, in the English Language.* New York: Doubleday, 1960.

———. *The Land Where the Blues Began.* New York: New Press, 2002.

———. *The Penguin Book of American Folk Songs.* Baltimore: Penguin, 1964.

———. *Hard Hitting Songs for Hard-Hit People.* Pete Seeger, ed. Notes,Woody Guthrie. New York: Oak Publications, 1967.

Luff, Jennifer. *Commonsense Anticommunism: Labor and Civil Liberties Between the World Wars.* Chapel Hill: University of North Carolina Press, 2012.

Manchester, William. "The Cruelest Year." In From *Reconstruction to the Present.* vol. 2 of *Portrait of America,* ed. Stephen Oates. New York: Houghton Mifflin, 1983.

Manthorne, Jason. "The View From the Cotton: Reconsidering the Southern Tenant Farmers' Union." *Agricultural History* 84 (2010): 20–45.

Martin, Robert Francis. *Howard Kester and the Struggle for Social Justice in the South, 1904–77.* Charlottesville: University Press of Virginia, 1991.

McGill, Ralph. *The South and the Southerner.* Boston: Little Brown, 1963.

McLaren, John. "Labor troubadour still inspires," *San Diego Tribune,* January 2, 1989.

Miller, Marc S., ed. *Working lives: The Southern Exposure History of Labor in the South.* New York: Pantheon Books, 1980.

Miller, Marjorie. "Socialist Gains Belated Recognition: Efforts to Organize Poor Farmers Led to Inspirational Music." *Los Angeles Times,* April 14, 1985.

———. "Footprints: John Handcox—Songwriter." With an introduction by Pete Seeger. *Southern Exposure* (January–February 1986).

Mitchell, Broadus. *Depression Decade: From New Era Through New Deal, 1929–1941.* New York: Rinehart, 1947.

Mitchell, H. L. *Mean Things Happening in This Land : The Life and Times of H. L. Mitchell, Cofounder of the Southern Tenant Farmers' Union.* Montclair: Allanheld, Osmun, 1979.

———. *Roll the Union On.* Chicago: C.H. Kerr Pub. Co., 1987.

Mitchell, Samuel Howard, *A Leader Among Sharecroppers, Migrants, and Farm Workers: H.L. Mitchell and Friends.* Canada: self published, 2007.

Naison, Mark. "Black Agrarian Radicalism in the Great Depression: The Threads of a Lost Tradition." *Journal of Ethnic Studies* 1(3) (Fall, 1973): 47–66.

Nelson, Scott. *Steel Drivin' Man: John Henry, the Untold Story of an American Legend.* London: Oxford University Press, 2006.

Our Land Too: The Legacy of the Southern Tenant Famers' Union. Produced by Landon McCray, Kudzu Productions. (Film)

Payne, Elizabeth Anne, and Louise Boyle. "The Lady Was a Sharecropper: Myrtle Lawrence and the Southern Tenant Farmers' Union." *Southern Cultures* 4(2) (1998): 5–27.

Peretti, Burton W. *Lift Every Voice: The History of African American Music.* Lanham: Rowman and Littlefield, 2009.

Polk's San Diego City Directory. R. L. Polk and Co. Publishers: Los Angeles, 1959.

Portelli, Alessandro. *The Death of Luigi Trastulli, and Other Stories: Form and Meaning in Oral History.* Albany: State University of New York Press, 1991.

———. *They Say in Harlan County, An Oral History.* New York: Oxford University Press, 2011.

Ransom, Roger, and Richard Sutch. *One Kind of Freedom: The Economic Consequences of Emancipation.* London: Cambridge University Press, 1977.

Reagon, Bernice Johnson. *If You Don't Go, Don't Hinder Me: The African American Sacred Song Tradition.* Lincoln: University of Nebraska Press, 2001.

———. *Songs of the Civil Rights Movement 1955-1965: A Study in Culture History.* Howard University: Ph.D. dissertation, 1975.

Riesman, Bob. *I Feel So Good: The Life and Times of Big Bill Broonzy.* Chicago: University of Chicago Press, 2011.

Recent History of the Labor Movement in the United States, vol. 1. Moscow: Progress Publishers, 1977.

Robinson, Lisa Clayton. "Dunbar, Paul Laurence." In *Africana: The Encyclopedia of the African and African American Experience,* eds Anthony Appiah and Henry Louis Gates. New York: Basic Civitas Books, 1999, 639–640.

Rolinson, Mary. *Grassroots Garveyism: The Universal Negro Improvement Association in the Rural South, 1920–1927.* Chapel Hill: University of North Carolina Press, 2007.

Roll, Jarod. *Spirit of Rebellion: Labor and Religion in the New Cotton South.* Urbana: University of Illinois Press, 2010.

Rosenthal, Rob and Richard Flacks. *Playing for Change: Music and Musicians in the Service of Social Movement.* Boulder: Paradigm Publishers, 2011.

Ross, James D., Jr. "'I ain't got no home in this world': The Rise and Fall of the Southern Tenant Farmers' Union in Arkansas." PhD diss., Auburn University, 2004.

Roy, William G. *Reds, Whites, and Blues: Social Movements, Folk Music, and Race in the United States.* Princeton: Princeton University Press, 2010.

Rudd, Dan, and Theo Bond. *From Slavery to Wealth [electronic Resource] : the Life of Scott Bond : The Rewards of Honesty, Industry, Economy and Perseverance,* ed.

Electronic. Chapel Hill: Academic Affairs Library, University of North Carolina at Chapel Hill, 2000.

Salmond, John A. *Gastonia, 1929: The Story of the Loray Mill Strike.* Chapel Hill: University of North Carolina Press, 1995.

Sandburg, Carl. *The American Songbag.* Intro. Garrison Keiler. New York: Harcourt Brace Jovanovich, 1990.

Sanger, Kerran L. *"When the Spirit Says Sing!" The Role of Freedom Songs in the Civil Rights Movement.* New York: Garland, 1995.

Schroeder, Rebecca B., and Lance, Donald M. "John L. Handcox: 'There Is Still Mean Things Happening,'" In *Songs About Work: Essas in Occupational Culture for Richard A. Reuss,* ed. Archie Green., Bloomington: Folklore Institute, Indiana University, 1993, 184–207.

Seeger, Charles, and Margaret Valiant. "Journal of a Field Representative." *Ethnomusicology* 24(2) (May 1, 1980): 169–210.

Seeger, Pete. *Pete Seeger: In His Own Words,* eds Rob Rosenthal and Sam Rosenthal. Boulder: Paradigm Publishers, 2012.

———. *Where Have All the Flowers Gone: A Singer's Stories, Songs, Seeds, Robberies,* ed. Peter Blood. Bethlehem: Sing Out, 1993.

Seeger, Ruth Crawford. *American Folk Songs for Children, in Home, School and Nursery School.* New York: Doubleday, 1948.

Shaw, Nate. *All God's Dangers: The Life of Nate Shaw.* Compiled by Theodore Rosengarten. New York, Knopf, 1974.

Shopes, Linda. "Editing Oral History for Publication." *Oral History Forum d'histoire orale* (2011), 1–24.

Siegester, Elie, and Olin Downes. *A Treasury of American Song.* New York: Alfred A. Knopf, 1943.

Sitkoff, Harvard. *A New Deal for Blacks: The Emergence of Civil Rights as a National Issue.* New York: Oxford University Press, 1978.

Snow, Thad. *From Missouri: An American Farmer Looks Back,* ed. Bonnie Stepenoff. Columbia : University of Missouri Press, 2012.

Southern, Eileen. *The Music of Black Americans: A History.* New York, W. W. Norton, 1971.

Southern, Eileen, ed. *Readings in Black American Music.* New York, W. W. Norton, 1972.

———. ed. *Biographical Dictionary of Afro-American and African Musicians.* Westport: Greenwood Press, 1982.

Stepenoff, Bonnie. *Thad Snow: A Life of Social Reform in the Missouri Bootheel.* Columbia: University of Missouri Press, 2003.

Stockley, Grif. *Blood In Their Eyes: The Elaine Race Massacres of 1919.* Fayetteville: University of Arkansas Press, 2001.

———. *Ruled by Race: Black/White Relations in Arkansas from Slavery to the Present.* Fayetteville: University of Arkansas Press, 2009.

Streissguth, Michael. *Johnny Cash: The Biography.* Cambridge: Da Capo Press, 2006.

Taylor, Kieran. "'We Have Just Begun': Black Organizing and White Response in the Arkansas Delta, 1919." *The Arkansas Historical Quarterly* 58(3) (Autumn, 1999), 264–284.

Thomas, Norman, and William Ruthrauff Amberson. *The Plight of the Share-cropper.* New York: League for Industrial Democracy, 1934.

Thompson, Robert F. III. "The Strange Case of Paul D. Peacher, Twentieth-Century Slaveholder." *Arkansas Historical Quarterly* 52(4) (December 1, 1993): 426–451.

Tindall, George. *The Emergence of the New South, 1913–1945.* Baton Rouge: Louisiana State University Press, 1967.

Trotter, Joe William. *Coal, Class, and Color: Blacks in southern West Virginia, 1915–32.* Urbana: University of Illinois Press, 1990.

————. *The Great Migration in Historical Perspective: New Dimensions of Race, Class, and Gender.* Bloomington: Indiana University Press, 1991.

Weissman, Dick. *Which Side Are You On? An Inside History of the Folk Music Revival in America.* New York: Continuum, 2005.

Whayne, Jeannie. *Delta Empire : Lee Wilson and the Transformation of Agriculture in the New South.* Baton Rouge: Louisiana State University Press, 2011.

————. *A New Plantation South : Land, Labor, and Federal Favor in Twentieth-century Arkansas.* Charlottesville: University Press of Virginia, 1996.

Wiener, Jonathan. *Social Origins of the New South: Alabama, 1860–1885.* Baton Rouge: Louisiana State University Press, 1978.

Winkler, Allan M. *"To Everything There is a Season": Pete Seeger and the Power of Song.* London: Oxford University Press, 2009.

Wise, Leah. "The Elaine Massacre," in *Southern Exposure* (1974), 9–10.

Whitaker, Robert. *On the Laps of Gods: The Red Summer of 1919 and the Struggle for Justice That Remade a Nation.* New York: Three Rivers Press, 2009.

Whitman, Wanda Willson, ed. *Songs That Changed the World.* New York: Crown Publishers, 1969.

Wood, Robert. *To Live and Die in Dixie.* New York: Southern Workers Defense Committee, 1936. Library of Congress.

Woods, Clye. *Development Arrested: Race, Power, and the Blues in the Mississippi Delta.* New York: Verso, 1998.

Woodruff, Nan. *American Congo: The African American Freedom Struggle in the Delta.* Cambridge: Harvard University Press, 2003.

Work, John W. *American Negro Songs: 230 Folk Songs and Spirituals, Religious and Secular.* Mineola: Dover, 1998.

————. *American Negro Songs and Spirituals: A Comprehensive Collection of 230 Folk Songs, Religious and Secular.* New York: Bonanza Books, 1940.

————. *Folk Song of the American Negro.* Nashville: Fisk University Press, 1915.

Wright, Gavin. *Old South, New South : Revolutions in the Southern Economy Since the Civil War.* Baton Rouge: Louisiana State University Press, 1996.

Wright, Richard. *American Hunger.* New York: Harper & Row, 1977.

————. *12 Million Black Voices: A Folk History of the Negro in the United States.* Photos by Edwin Rosskam. New York: Viking Press, 1941.

Yard, Alexander. "'They Dont Regard My Rights at All': Arkansas Farm Workers, Economic Modernization, and the Southern Tenant Farmers Union." *Arkansas Historical Quarterly* 47(3) (October 1, 1988): 201–229.

Zieger, Robert H. *The CIO, 1935–1955.* Chapel Hill: University of North Carolina Press, 1995.

Index

"Ain'tGonna Study War No More," 113
African-American
  church, 4, 24–6, 59
  migration, 14–5, 34, 130, 138
  song tradition, 55–56, 69, 87, 91–2, 96,
    153, 157–8 fns 1–7, 176 fn. 67
  soldiers, 16, 34, 37, 38, 92
  women, 20, and *see* STFU, women
  see black press
Agricultural Adjustment Act (AAA), 48,
  50, 51, 52, 53, 73, 98, 103, 123, 124
Alabama, 14, 15, 16, 18, 53, 54, 108, 142,
  158; Sharecroppers' Union, 6, 49, 62,
  67, 76, 128, 134
Allen, John, 60, 113,
Almanac Singers, 111, 140
Amberson, Prof. William, 50, 64
American Civil Liberties Union (ACLU),
  84, 105
American Federation of Labor (AFL), 58,
  64, 77, 107, 138
  and AFL-CIO, 142, 146
American Songs of Protest, 142
Amsterdam News, see black press
Anderson, Winfield, 80
Army Corps of Engineers, 122,
Arkansas, history of, 16–20, 36, and *see also*
  chs. 1–6, and place names

Ball, Jim, 72
Beckley, W.V., 53
Beecher, John, quote, 53
Benson, David, 79, 82, 107
Bennett, Sam, 83
Betton, F.R., 135
Birdsong, Ark., 61
Black press, 88, 124, 125

Black Reconstruction, 14
Black Workers Remember, 7
Blagden, Willie Sue, kidnapping, 84
Bolivar County, Ms, 90
Boll weevil, 34
Bond, Scott, 27–8
Bridges, Harry, 133
Brinkley, Arkansas, 4, 11, 15, 18, 27, 29,
  33, 40
Brookins, A.B., 55, 60, 92, 95, 111, 113
Broonzy, Big Bill, 2, 23, 29
Brown V. Board of Education, 91
Brotherhood of Sleeping Car Porters, 129,
  and *see* Randolph, A. Philip
Burgess, David, 138
Butler, J.R., 54, 62, 63, 108, 120–1, 134

Cairo, Il., 119, 120
Caldwell, Erskine, 36, 51,
Carawan, Guy, 146
Carawan, Candy, 146
Carpenter, C.T., 55
Camp Hill and Reeltown, Ala., 49
Carpentry and carpenter's Union, 143
Cash, Johnny, 32, 88, 92, 97, 136–7
Chicago, Il., 83, 97, 129, 130
Chicago Defender, see black press
Census, U.S., of 1920, 33
Civil rights movement, parallels to labor,
  61, 74, 84, 88, 96, 140, 142, 154
"Climbing Jacob's Ladder," 55
Cobb, Ned, 6, 49, 50
Commissary store, 42
Commonwealth College (Mena, Ark.), 53,
  60, 111, 114, 115, 131, 133, 134, 137,
  140
Company unions, 77–8

Communistsand anti-communism, 35, 49, 50, 53, 54, 62, 86, 91, 92, 107–8, 114–15, 116, 133, 134–6
Cone, James C., 12
Congress (or Committee) for Industrial Organization (CIO), 64, 77, 112, 114, 119, 132–4, 137–40, 141, 145–6
Convict lease, 61
Cook, Camelia, 156
Cook, Joe, 123
Cooperative farms, 64, 90–1
Copyright, discussion of, 10, 145–6
Cotton, and capitalism, 19, 27, 51
Cotton Council, 51
Cotton, harvesting of, 41
Cotton, prices, 33, 34, 35, 36
Cotton Plant, Ark., 15, 29, 59, 92, 134
Cottonseed oil, 39
Cotton, as King, 42, 46, 91
Crittenden County, Ark., 51, 55, 64, 72, 73, 76, 82, 83
Cropperville, Mo., 137
Crosno, Mo., 120
Cross County, Ark., 82
Crump, E.H., 95
Cunningham, Sis, 140
Curtis, John, 80

Dane, Barbara, 2
Daniel, Pete, 37
Davis, Governor Jeff, 17
Davis and Elkins College, 149
Day laborers, 79, 82, 87
Debs, Eugene, 107, 130
Debt and debt peonage, 37, 40, 41
Delta Cooperative Farm, 90–1
Detroit, 130, 131
Deventer, Mo., 100, 122
Dibble, C.H., plantation, 72, 90
Dilling, Elizabeth, 60
Dilworth, Carrie, 63
Douglass, Frederick, 12
DuBois, W.E.B., 12, 14,
Duck Hill, Miss., atrocity, 123
Dunbar, Anthony, 87
Dunbar, Paul Lawrence, 3, 22, 23, 29, 119
Dyess, Ark., 88
Dylan, Bob, 97

Earle, Ark., 10, 73, 75, 80–1, 88
East, Clay, 51–2, 59, 61, 80, 81, 89
East, Maxine, 80
Eddy, Rev. Sherwood, 80, 90
Elaine, Ark., race riot and memory of, 9, 34–6, 52, 55, 61, 63, 72, 74, 75, 113, 131, 134

Farm Security Administration (FSA), 88, 136
Fascism, 74, 85, 107
Federal Bureau of Investigation (FBI), 73, 79, 106, 144
Federal Emergency Relief Administration (FERA), 88
First Amendment, 61, 114
Ferguson, Robert, quote, 102
Ferris, William, 6, 141, 151, 163
Flint, Mi., sit-down strikes, 112
Floods, 5, 43–4, 119–22
Floyd, Samuel, 142
Food, Tobacco, and Allied Workers Union (FTA), 137
Fowler, Newell, 80
Forrest City, Ark., 17, 37, 39, 82, 104, 123
Forrest, Nathan Bedford, 16
Fowler, David, 114
Friends of the Sharecroppers, 124
Frisch, Michael, 8
Futrell, Ark. Governor, 81, 101

Garland, Jim, 86
Garvey, Marcus, influence of, 54, 58, 98, 109
Gastonia, NC, 49
Gennis company, 39, 40, 89
George Meany Center for Labor Studies, 146
Gilmartin, Aaron, 80
Glazer, Joe, xviii, 6, 126, 152, 160
Goldberger, Herman, union attorney, 73
"Gospel Train," 140
Great Depression, 48–51, *and see* chs. 1–5
Great Labor Arts Exchange, 6, 146, 148, 155
Green, Archie, 150
Greenway, John, 76, 83, 142
Grubbs, Donald, quote, 58, 135
Gunning, Sarah Ogan, 2, 86

Guthrie, Woody, xviii, 3
  quote, 45, 49, 140

Haffer, Charles, 92
Handcox, George, Sr., 18–19, 20, 28–9, 33
  death of, 37
Handcox, George, Jr., 20, 33, 75, 154, 155
Handcox, John L.,
  family history, 4–5, 11, 13–16, 18–20,
    21–8, 29, 33, 142–5, 160–1 fns. 8–14,
    and passim
  as entrepreneur, 44, 138–9, 143
  and literacy importance of, 29, 42, 59,
    65, 115
  marriages, 145
  Missouri organizing, 95–117
  Northern travels, 125
  observations on race, 26–7
  poems and songs, see list of first lines
  religion, 24–6, 109, 110
  socialism and communism, 108, 116
  spelling of name, 14
  threats against, 65–6, 89, 93
  writing, purpose, 69–70, 96–7
  See also chs. 1–7
Handcox, Ruth, 43, 45, 93, 104, 105, 127,
  131, 138, 144, 145
Handcox, Vina (Vinia), 18–19, 20; 21, 24,
  29, 143, 150–1
Handcox, Willis (Bill), 89, 93, 143, 145
Hanrahan Bridge (Memphis) 79, 95
Harlan County, Ky., 61, 74
Hard-Hitting Songs, xviii, 1, 2, 92, 126, 142
Hays, Lee, 33, 96, 111–12, 139, 140, 141,
  142
Hays, President Rutherford B., 17
Helena, Ark., 36
Henderson, Donald, 67, 115, 133
Henry, John, 1, 2, 46, 67, 128
Henson, Mo., 101, 102
Herndon, Angelo, 50
"Hero of the STFU," 123
Hertzberg, Sidney, 127
Highlander School, 111, 114
Highway 61, 97, 136
Hill, Joe, 3
Hill House, Ms., 90–1,
Hitler-Stalin non-aggression pact, 135
Holliday, Billie, 141

Honey, Michael, 1, 6, 7, 8, 10, 159, 160, 167
Hood, Everrett, 72, 73
Hoover, President Herbert, 49
Horton, Myles, 111
House Committee on Un-American
  Activities, 135
"How Beautiful Heaven Would Be," 32
Hunger, 20, 29, 32, 39, 42, 49, 50, 74–6,
  82, 83, 87
"Hungry, Hungry Are We," 32, 113
Hurst, Willie, murder of, 73

"I'm So Happy That I Can't Sit Down," 113
"It's Hard to Say Good-bye," 155
Industrial Workers of the World (IWW),
  3, 35, 95
Inland Boatmen's Union hall, 139

Jackson, Aunt Molly, 86
Jackson, Gardner, 61, 114
Jackson, Mark Alan, 7,
"Jesus is My Captain," 55,
Jesus as revolutionary, 106
"Jobless in the USA," 148
"Join the Union Tonight," 102–4
John, President Andrew, 14
Johnson, Amos, 152
Johnson, Leroy, 130
Jones, Arthur, 92
Jones, Scipio, 36
Jordan, Louis, 29, 141

Kahn, Si, 146
Kelley, Robin D.G., 6
Kester, Alice, 73
Kester, Howard, 6, 53, 59, 61, 62, 63, 64,
  67, 74
  kidnapping of, 72–3, 107 and see fn; 114,
    134,
King, B.B., 23
King, Ed, 154
King, Martin Luther, Jr., 92
"King Cotton," 91
Kinton, Ark., 75
Kirkpatrick, J. C., 100, 104, 121
Kobler, Don, 131
Koch, Lucien, 60
Krueger, Patti (Pat), 6, 166
Ku Klux Klan, 5, 16, 36, 37, 56, 61

LaFollette, Sen. Robert, 74
Lakeside plantation, 39, 40, 88
Lambert, Gerald, 35
"Landlord... what is the matter with you?,"
    47–8, 91, 147
Lance, Donald, 6,
Lawrence, Myrtle, 60,
League for Southern Labor, 124
Ledbetter, Hudie (Leadbelly), 2, 141
Lenin, V.I., 116
"Let's Get Old Reagan Out," 148
Levine, Lawrence, 4, 12 fn 4
Lee, Memphis Police Chief Will, 79, 81
Lewis, John L., 132
Library of Congress, 1, 7, 92, 126
Lincoln, President Abraham, 14
Literacy, importance of, 42, 59, 115
Little Rock, 37, 64, 80, 84, 111–12
Logan Heights community, 144
"Lord, I Want to be a Christian in my
    Heart," 101
Lomax, Alan, xviii; quotes of, 18, 19, 92,
    105
Los Angeles Times, 145
Lowndes County, Ala., 62
Lowry, Henry, lynching, 36, 97
Lynching, and vigilante violence, 19, 34,
    36, 123

Manthorne, Jason, 135
"March of Time" film, 84
Marked Tree, Ark., 55, 60, 113
Mason, Rose, 82
Masons, 20, 56
McCarthy, Rep. Joseph, 144
McCray, Ernie, 152
McGee, Henrietta, 75, 111
McGee, Sonny, 142
McGill, Ralph, quote, 51
McKinney, Rev. E.B., 54, 61, 62, 63, 82,
    106, 108, 110, 114, 115, 133–4
"Mean Things (Strange Things) Happening
    in This Land," 71, 91–2, 113, 138,
    146, 152, 176–7 fn. 70
mechanization, 96, 138, 148
Media, means of communication, 2, 5, 6,
    19, 35, 46, 47, 49, 51, 58, 61, 67, 69,
    78, 84, 88, 90, 114, 128, 154
Melon, Andrew, 49

Memphis, Tn., 19, 37, 39
    as refuge, 60, 73, 80, 81, 82, 89
    source of day laborers, 64
Memphis Cotton Carnival, and Cotton
    Council, 51, 78, 91
Mexicans, 113,
Miller, Marjorie, 144, 146
Missouri, organizing in, chapter 5
Missouri Roadside Demonstration, 135–6
Mississippi County, Ark., 99, 102, 120, 123
Mississippi River, *see* floods
Mitchell, Broadus, 50
Mitchell, H.L., xviii, 6, 8, 51–2, 54, 55, 58,
    61, 62, 64
    as Handcox editor, 66–7, 72, 76, 77, 80,
    84, 89; 95, 104, 105, 107, 108, 114,
    115, 125, 126, 127, 137, 138
Mitchell, Samuel, 88
Montgomery, Ala., bus boycott, 140
Monroe County, Arkansas, 11
Moonshine, 44, 100
Moskop, Walter, 115
Music, and African American traditions,
    2, 3, 4, 12, 18, 24–32, 47, 98, 108,
    109, 110
Music, and memory, 3–4, 6–7
Music, freedom and social movement, 2–4,
    8, 9, 10, 57, 68–9, 93, 124, 126, 137,
    140, 146, 153, 154, 187 fn. 75, and
    Marxists, 184 fn. 41
    rap, 3; *see also* singing, congregational;
    see also spirituals
Muskogee, Ok., 87, 112–6

National Association of Manufacturers, 49
Native American, 15, 27
National Association for the Advancement
    of Colored People (NAACP), 28, 36,
    112, 130, 131
National Farm Labor Union (AFL), 137–8
National Guard, and repression, 43, 87
National Industrial Recovery Act (NIRA),
    53
National Labor Relations (Wagner)
    Act, 62, 74, 118,143
    domestic and agricultural exclusion from
    coverage, 62, 77, 137
National Negro Congress, 112, 134
National Sharecroppers Week, 124

National Textile Workers Union (NTWU), 86
National Youth Administration (NYA), 137
Native American heritage, 2, 4, 16, 27, 64, 108, 114
Neal, Claude, 60
New Creation Church, 145, 152
New Deal, 50, 53, 54, 112
New Era School, 110–2,
New York City, and the STFU, 80
"No More Mourning," 86
Nodena, Ark., lynching, 36
Nolden, Eliza, 84, 95, 124
Norcross, Hiram, evictions, 52, 62
Norman Baynard Photo Collection, 144
Nunally, Avin, 52
Nunn, Vina (Vinia), 155

Official Council of STFU Refugees, 121–2
"Oh, Freedom," 111,
Oklahoma, 131, 138–9
"Old Ship of Zion," 131, 140
Orange, James, 146
Oral history, 6–10, 159 fn.11
Oral poetry, 56, 69
"Out on Mr. Snow's Farm," 99

Painter, Nell Irvin, 6
Parchman, Lula, 76
Parkin, Ark., 87
Patton, Charley, quote, 43, 44
Peacher, Paul, 72, 73, 80, 81, 88, 101
Peonage, 80–1, 85, 88
Pine Bluff, Ark., lynching
Pinhook, Mo., 100, 104
Plantation owners (landlords), 32–3, 39
"Planter and the Sharecropper," 67–8, 91
Planters Union Lodge, 77–8,
Poetry, oral, and Handcox, 2–4
    poetry and memory, 6, 22, 24, 27, 67, 97–9, 108, 130, 159
Police, see STFU, repression of
Poll tax, 17, 19, 50
Poor whites, 19, 20, 28, 34, 58, 62, 100, 134,
Portelli, Allesandro, 7,
Post oak land, 38
President's Committee on Farm Tenancy, 88

Race, and racial division, 9, 16, 17, 35, 36, 55, 57, 58, 83, 91, 97–8, 104, 106, 110, 113
Radio, lack of, 41
"Raggedy, raggedy are we," 31–33, 139, 147, 152
Randolph, A.P., 64, 129, 130
Reconstruction, 14, 16–7
Reagan, Pres. Ronald, 146–9
Reagon, Bernice Johnson, 92, 153
"Red" summer, 1919, 34
    and see Elaine Race riot
Reece, Florence, 2, 86
Reese, Jim, 83, 89, 124, 125
Reid, Robert, 60
Religion, role of, 18, 25, 57, 59, 98, 101, 106, 122, 163
Resettlement Administration (RA), 120, 122
    Special Skills Division, 126
Riding boss, 41
Riley, Frank, 121
Rinzler, Ralph, xviii, 6,
Robertson, Sydney, 1,126
Robinson, Senator Joseph, 50, 62, 74, 85, 123, 112
Robinson, Earl, 123
Robeson, Paul, 141
Roediger, David, 150
Rogers, Rev. Ward, 52, 55, 59, 60, 61,
Romaine, Anne, 146
Roll, Jarod, quote, 19, 53, 98, 101, 122
"Roll the Chariot," 96, 146
"Roll the Union On," 96–7, 111–2, 113, 139, 140, 141, 146, 152, 177–8 fns. 4–8, 183 fn. 31
Roosevelt, president Franklin D., 50, 74, 77, 85, 88, 112
Rucker, Sparky, 146
Rust Brothers, John and Mack, 138

Salinas, Kansas, 138
San Diego, Ca., 4, 139, 142, 132,
San Diego *Tribune,* 143
San Francisco Chronicle, 150
Schroeder, Rebecca, 6, 141, 149, bib.
Scottsboro Nine, Ala., 53
Seeger, Charles, xvii, 1, 126

Seeger, Pete, preface, 1, 3, 126, 140, 141, 142, 146, 152

Segregation, 5, 10, 17–19, 54, 56, 58, 59, 97, 98, 104, 108, 112–14, 117, 121, 122, 128, 141

shape-note singing, 4, 24

Sharecropper's Voice, 8, 58, 67, 68, 73, 78, 87, 112, 121, 125, 133

Sharecropper's Week, 124, 125, 127

Sharecropping and tenancy, origins of, 20
and family incomes, 50
terms of, 36, 39, 41, 42

Shaw, Isaac, 51, 52, 75, 169 fn. 15

Shopes, Linda, 6, 8,

Sims, Ballad of Harry, 86

Singing, congregational, 4, 12–13, 56, 110,

Smith, C.H., 52,

Smith, Evelyn, 73, 80, 81

Smith, Viola, 87

Smith, Ruth (Handcox), 43

Smithsonian Institution, xviii

Snitches, 64

Slavery, and skin color, 13–14; *see also* spirituals

Socialism, socialists, 28, 49, 51, 53, 54, 59, 73, 74, 75, 80, 88, 90–1, 107, 129, 130

Socialist Call, 129

Snow, Thad, 98, 99, 105, 120, 136

"Solidarity Forever," 150

Souls of Black Folk, 11

Southern California Library for Social Studies, 150

Southern Liberator, 78

Southern Negro Youth Congress (SNYC), 112

Southern Tenant Farmers' Union (STFU), 1, 5, 9,
and CIO, 137
Churches as meeting places, 59, 72,
Conflicts within, xvii, 5, 132–5, 133–5
Conventions, 64, 112–18, 133–4, 135
Cooperative farming, 114, 138, 154
Dues, 62, 66, 122
membership in, 52, 54, 55, 57, 58, 60, 63, 64, 72, 77, 120, 122
Memphis headquarters (2527 Broad St.), 55, 134
and Missouri Roadside Demonstration, 135–7

in Missouri, chapter five and 119–22

Origins of, 51–62

and preachers, 58, 59, 72; *see also* Williams, Claude, McKinney, E.B., Kester, Howard, Brookins, Shaw, Isaac, Betton, F.R., McGee, Henrietta, Eddy, Sherwood, Smith, C.H.

racial etiquette, 58

and religion, 55, 59

repression of, 55–62, 60–2, 71–5, 77–89

resources, lack of, 104, 105

Reunion, 31, 152

Salaries, 126–7

Self defense v. nonviolence, 55, 61, 73–4

Signs and rituals, 57

strikes, 5, chs. 3–4, 134

union locals, and racial composition, 54, 56, 57, 58, 77, 122

And women, 59–60, 72, 82, 98, 109, 113–14, 122, 172 fn. 1, *see also* Nolden, Eliza, Parsons, Lula, McGee, Henrietta, Smith, Evelyn, **, Williams, Joyce, Kester, Alice, Blagden, Willie Sue,

See also Socialism and socialists

"Solidarity Forever," 140

Southern Conference Educational Fund (SCEF), 2

Southern Farm Leader, 128

spirituals, 2, 11–3, 56, 160 fns. 3–4, 179 fn. 24

St. Francis County, Ark., 17, 50, 72,76, 82, 83

St. Louis, 129, 132, 136

Stith, George, 54, 55, 57, 59, 62, 135

Strickland, Arvarh, 150 (and bib?)

"Strike in Arkansas," *, 91

Strikes, 5, 17; in 1934, 53; 1935, 62–5, 1936, 76–8; 124
general strikes, 113

Student Nonviolent Coordinating Committee (SNCC), 4, 63, 154

Stultz, W.H., 62, 115

Sunnyside, Ark., 52

Taylor, Braxton, 98

Tharpe, Sister Rosetta, 29, 92, 141

"Ten Little Farmer Men," 128

Terry, Brownie, 142

"This Land is Your Land," 45
Thomas, Norman, 50, 51, 61, 64, 74, 85, 115, 124, 135, 137
Thurmond, Rev. Howard, 92
Turner, Leon, 133
Tyronza, Ark., 51

"Union Train," 140, 142
unions, attacks on in 1980s, 147
  industrial, 34
  and right to organize, 53, 123
  company unions, 61
  exclusion of agricultural and domestic workers, 53, 112
  anti-union laws, 100
  sit-down strikes, 112, 119, 134
  and see race and racial division, 36, 58, passim
United Cannery, Agricultural, Packing, and Allied Workers of America (UCAPAWA), 133, 135
United Mineworkers of America (UMWA), 54, 77, 100
United Packinghouse Workers of America (UPWA), 129
United Steelworkers of America (USWA), 129
United States, Justice Department, 62, 74
  Public Health Service, 122
  U.S. Supreme Court, 17, 91
Universal Negro Improvement Association (UNIA), see Garvey, Marcus
University of North Carolina, 9,
University of Missouri-Columbia, 149–50

Vancouver Folk Festival, 149

Walls, Hattie, 140
Waters, Muddy, 23, 97
Weavers, the, 111, 142
Western Worker's Heritage Festival, 149
"We Shall Not Be Moved," 55, 64, 113, 136, 140, 142
"We Shall Overcome," 140, 142, 146
"What a Wonderful World it Could Be," 152
"Which Side Are You On?," 142
White Citizens Council, 91
White, Walter, 113

Wells-Barnett, Ida B., 36
Weems, Frank, 83–6, 125
Weems, Mrs. Frank, 90, 95, 125
Wesley, John, 125
Whayne, Jeannie, 19
White, Josh, 141
White, Walter, 36, 130
Whitfield, Owen, 108–9, 115, 121–2, 126, 127, 128, 134, 135–7
Whitfield, Zella, 108–9
Wiggins, Ella Mae, 49, 86
Williams, Joyce, 84, 131
Williams, Claude, 13, 52, 59
  kidnapping, 84; 104, 105, 106–8, 111, 112, 114, 115, 121, 131
  expulsion of, 132–5
Williams, James, 73
Wilson, Lee, 34, 123,
Williams, Willie, 143
Women, See Southern Tenant Farmers' Union
Woodruff, Nan, quotes, 19, 35
World War II, 143
Work, John Wesley, 101
Workers' Alliance, 79, 107
Worker's Defense League, 75, 80, 124, 125
Works Progress Administration (WPA), 123
World War I, and soldiers, 34, 49
Wright, Richard, quote, 34, 115
Wynne, Ark., 83
Songs and poems, first words of lyrics:
  Early the second Monday in June, 99
  Have you ever woke up in the morning, vii
  I was taking with a group of people, 148
  I started out as a sharecropper's son, 154
  If there is any word that I really hate, 150
  If we all loved each other," 152–3
  In 1933 we plowed up our crops, 103
  It's Hard to say good-bye, 155
  He was a poor sharecropper, 85–6
  In nineteen thirty-three when we plowed up cotton, 47–8
  Jobless, jobless in the USA, 148
  "Let's all join our hands and sing," 149
  Oh Freedom, xvii, 12–14
  Oh, no, we don't want Reagan, 147
  On the 18th day of May, 79

Wynne, Ark—*Continued*
Planter rides 'round cursing, 80–1
Raggedy, raggedy are we, 31–3
Reagan Psalms, 147
Some planters forced laborers into the
fields with guns, 79–80
Stomp your feet, sing and shout, 147
Ten Little Farmer Men, 128

The planters celebrated King Cotton, 46
The planter lives off the sweat of the
sharecropper brow, 67–8
The Southern Tenant farmers union,
131–2
The STFU cannot help but grieve, 123
You landlords get together, 78
Workers starving all over this land, 147

Printed and bound in the United States of America